Copyright © 2026 by Carolyn Oliver
To contact the author email her at carolynoliver26@gmail.com

This memoir is based on the author's personal experiences. Some names and identifying details have been changed to protect privacy. The events are described to the best of the author's recollection, and any errors arise from the nature of human memory.

ISBN:
979-8-218-90807-2

Cover and Interior Book Design by
Richard Oliver

Cover and Interior images supplied
by www.vecteezy.com.

Edited by
Melissa Woods and Zora Knauf

Printed in the United States of America

Contents

Chapter 1 | A New Friend 7

Chapter 2 | The Call 13

Chapter 3 | Leaving Home 37

Chapter 4 | On with the Tour.. 41

Chapter 5 | Bell Economic School................................... 53

Chapter 6 | Wuxi, China 59

Chapter 7 | On My Own 61

Chapter 8 | Letters Back & Forth.. 71

Chapter 9 | The Little Emperor 93

Chapter 10 | New Friends 101

Chapter 11 | Onto Hangzhou.. 125

Chapter 12 | Upcoming Halloween.................................... 143

Chapter 13 | Letters to Friends 153

Chapter 14 | Celebrity Status 171

Chapter 15 | Nanjing & Yangzhou..................................... 185

Chapter 16 | The Commune.. 199

Chapter 17 | Money Sent 211

Chapter 18 | My Days are Limited 221

Chapter 19 | Home 227

Chapter 20 | Continuing Friendships 237

Chapter 21 | Return to China 253

Chapter 22 | Jiangyin.. 289

Chapter 23 | Our Former Students..................................... 297

Chapter 24 | Correspondence Continues........................... 303

Chapter 25 | Australia 317

Chapter 26 | Leo... 325

Chapter 27 | Married... 339

Chapter 28 | WeChat, Emails, & Calls 355

Chapter 29 | Can't Find Her 365

Chapter 30 | Connected Again 369

A New Friend

Chapter 1

Pleasant Hill, California

Late August 1993

"Sixty percent of all Chinese women get car sick riding in cars," she said.

"Not in my car, they don't."

Xi-fen was quiet as I drove down Pleasant Hill Road, having just picked her up from her host's family home.

"Look out the front window and watch things along the road. It won't happen." And it didn't.

Xi-fen's host family was leaving for the weekend and didn't want to take her.

She had arrived from China just three days ago as an exchange teacher from Wuxi, China. She was here for a year to learn our Western teaching methods in a junior high school. I was a volunteer at the high school, helping new American Field Service (AFS) students from other countries staying in the area. I was asked to be a liaison for our visiting teacher, helping her get settled with her life here and her new family.

Xi-fen told me that two weeks ago, in mid-August, she was

summoned to the principal's office in her school in Wuxi and informed that she was selected to come to the United States. She was told she would leave for the United States in two weeks and be gone for a year. There was no time to see her parents since she had to finish teaching her classes, pack, say goodbye to her husband and child, and leave.

"They chose me to come for a year because they know I will return. I have a two-year old son and a husband. They don't let people out of China since they might defect."

"Who will take care of your son?" I asked.

"My mother-in-law. This is the custom in China. The mother-in-law is in charge of the grandchild. He lives with her most of the time. I'm too busy working."

Xi-fen spoke perfect English, but I soon realized that she knew nothing about us. She told me she had been afraid to come to America because she had seen some of our movies. She thought we were a violent and immoral society and all husbands ran around on their wives. I thought of some movies, and I knew she would be surprised to find out we are not what our movies portray.

We had a great time together that weekend. My husband, Mike, liked her, too. She was charming, fun, upbeat, and open telling us about her life and family in China.

She described her husband as a businessman.

"What kind of business?" I asked.

I never got an explanation, only things like, "He does business."

I heard the same job description many times from other people I was to meet later in China. I guess it was too hard to explain.

When we got to my house, I asked her what she liked to eat. I opened the refrigerator. I had some leftovers, and Xi-fen spotted three green onions.

"Would you like me to cook?" she said. "I can use these and give them a Chinese taste."

"Sure, that sounds great," I said.

Dinner was delicious. Xi-fen loved to cook and talk about food.

"We eat this for our health," she repeated many times.

I told her we, too, had foods we ate for our health, but I'm not sure she ever believed me.

A few days later, we had our first AFS meeting at my house. Parent volunteers from the high school came and met Xi-fen. She was shy, sitting demurely with her hands folded, head down, and not speaking. She wore a lovely peach chiffon dress. We all talked about ways to help the AFS International students at the high school this year and Xi-fen's assignment at the junior high school.

School started, and two weeks later, Xi-fen called me. She wasn't happy in her host family. She felt she was treated like a high school student and not the professional teacher she was. She was thirty-two years old and had been teaching for nine years.

I spoke to her host mother and another supervising teacher at her school. Xi-fen's unhappiness grew. It seemed to me to be a conflict in personalities and some cultural differences. Xi-fen didn't fit well into her host family. They were a busy family with two children. Her unhappiness continued. My husband and I discussed having her come live with us. We had adult daughters living away from home, and our youngest was an AFS high school exchange student in Northern Sweden for the year.

Xi-fen would become a part of our family, staying in our daughter's empty room. My "carpooling" days would return. I would be driving her to her school every day and picking her up in the afternoons. This schedule wouldn't interfere with the English as a Second Language classes I was teaching. Mike loved the idea, as we had her over a few times on the weekends and had gotten to know her.

Now my liaison job took over. I had to make sure everyone could "save face" and feel OK with a proposed change in the situation.

It was a rainy Saturday afternoon at the host family's house. On the phone before this meeting, I told Xi-fen not to worry. Whatever was said at this meeting still meant that she was coming home with me. The host mother was also her co-teacher at school—the teaching supervisor from the junior high school. Xi-fen and I sat together in the living room.

The meeting went on for two hours as everyone discussed what to do. What were the problems? What was the solution? Everyone had their say. Xi-fen cried, not really knowing what to do. I remained calm and tried to be casual.

Finally, I said, "Why don't we have Xi-fen move to my house and just see how that goes—on a trial basis." I acted as if it could be temporary, knowing that it wouldn't be.

Everyone seemed relieved and accepted this idea, and there seemed to be no hard feelings. I think the host family was happy to get out of this situation.

Xi-fen packed things from her room. I told them I would call later and pick up the rest of her belongings. A few days later, I called, and Xi-fen and I went over to get them when the family was away. The unhappiness ended.

Our school year of 1993–1994 with Xi-fen was full of fun adventures. Mike and I were used to being involved with AFS activities since we had had Germán, my "Spanish Son," live with us in 1991–1992. Germán was a senior, and our youngest daughter, Lynessa, now graduated from high school, was an AFS student in Sweden.

We had so much fun with Xi-fen. She told us about her apartment in the large city of Wuxi, about an hour west of Shanghai. She had no hot water and had to boil all water used. She did not have a 'western toilet,' only a hole in the floor in the bathroom. A hot water heating unit could be put in her kitchen, and bathroom fixtures could be added. These situations could be helped with money.

Xi-fen was comfortable speaking to people and groups. We set up speaking engagements with the Rotary and other local groups. People were interested in hearing and learning about China. China had been closed. It finally opened in the eighties, and people were curious. She was an expert in describing the educational system and her government. Groups paid her honorariums. I was her new "agent." We set up cooking luncheons for groups, where she would also be paid. She was saving money to take home and improve her housing situation.

We went to Lake Tahoe in the snow. "I can now ride in the back seat and even eat," she announced, proudly remembering her comment about car sickness. Most of her life, she had ridden a bicycle, taken a bus, and hailed short taxi rides.

We went to Monterey. While at a restaurant, she announced that she was hot.

"What's wrong?" I asked. It was a cool day.

"I have five layers on because I thought it would be cold," she said. "We always wear five layers to keep warm." She removed three in the ladies' room and felt better. She ordered her usual hot water instead of tea.

I drove us to Disneyland with my young neighbor, Emily. I had fun, enjoying all the attractions through Emily and Xi-fen's eyes.

She loved to cook, so we went into Oakland Chinatown every other week to get the food and supplies she wanted. We laughed and giggled when she taught me how to make delicious Chinese dumplings. One day in Chinatown, she decided that she wanted to buy a fish. "It must be a live fish," she said.

We searched and could only find whole fish on ice. "Well, I can look at the fish's eye and tell if it is fresh." She examined each fish eye and found a fresh one. She would give it that delicious Chinese taste. We were used to many Chinese dishes on a table. I asked, "What do you do if you have a dinner party?"

"One person decides he or she will do all the cooking, and then they stay in the kitchen just cooking," she explained.

"Here, we like to be able to sit with our guests." We had been planning a dinner party for Chinese New Year.

"Can we figure out a way to make things ahead so you can sit with the guests?" She and I worked on this idea and the food. Our Chinese New Year dinner was a gastronomic success. We had dumplings for luck and many dishes and foods for "our health." We still spent a lot of time in the kitchen.

During the year, Xi-fen occasionally called her husband in China, which was difficult because of the time difference. She wasn't happy with these phone calls. She was frustrated that she wasn't getting a good picture of what was going on. She missed her son and could not talk to him because he was with her mother-in-law.

Xi-fen made many friends during the year. We became close friends. She explained our relationship like, "There is a string attached to each of our hearts. Fate pulled the string and brought us together."

A few months before being sent to America, she visited a fortune teller. He was a blind, old man on the street in Wuxi. He felt Xi-fen's palms and told her she would be traveling overseas. She didn't believe him. No one she had known had gone overseas. It could never happen until it happened to her. When she got home from the U.S., she searched Wuxi to try to find him again. She never did.

After she returned to China, we corresponded by letter and an occasional phone call. Xi-fen's life took a bad turn. Her husband had gotten a girlfriend while she was gone. He also collected her teacher's salary, which she had continued to receive in China while she was here. He had gambled it all away. I asked how that could happen. She explained that people told him he was very smart and should do this or that investment with the money and get richer. He fell for these lines. Xi-fen was angry. They ended up getting a divorce. The mother-in-law was still in charge of the grandson. Xi-fen had her apartment in Wuxi and was able to get a hot water heater installed and update her bathroom with "Western fixtures." She saw her family in Wuxi and returned to teaching in her school.

We stayed in contact with letters, and I would call her occasionally.

The Call

Chapter 2

Lafayette, California

February 2, 1998

Our phone rang at 2:00 a.m. Mike picked it up, listened, and reached across the bed, saying, "It's Xi-fen for you."

"Hi, Xi-fen, how are you?" I said, trying to sound awake.

"Carolyn, can you come and teach here at my school? You will have room and board, a salary, and we'll reimburse your plane ticket. We have everything you need—everything but a car."

I heard a muffled male voice coaching her in the background.

I was immediately awake and trying to decide what to say.

"Well, what's the minimum amount of time I would have to stay?" I asked.

There was mumbling in the background.

"Three months," Xi-fen said.

"When do you want me to come?"

"Can you come now?" she asked.

"Xi-fen, I can't come now. My daughter is graduating from college soon, and I have a job."

"When can you come?" she said

I paused and was trying to decide what to say. "Well, maybe September?" I replied. Could I really do this? I wasn't sure.

"Good. I'll send you a fax." She hung up.

A few months later, when we arrived in China, I said, "You sent for me."

"Yes," she said, "I did."

When Xi-fen spent 1993–1994 living with us, we talked about me going to China to teach. She had been teaching in a school in Wuxi but was now helping set up a new private school in Jiangyin, about one hour away, on the Yangtze River. The faxes from Xi-fen following that late night call explained that this new private school would have all new accommodations. I understood that we would be working together, with me teaching and her in charge of the English department. We would be able to travel together. I knew if I went, Xi-fen would take good care of me, since I had done the same for her. I trusted her completely.

Xi-fen's faxes told me that Bell Economic School would pay my economy flight round trip, and I would be paid half my salary in Chinese yuan and half in American money. The salary would be $1,000 monthly. I would be going for the cultural experience and to spend time and travel with my dear friend. This salary was ten times what the teachers at her school were paid.

Mike and I talked over this proposed trip. My first reaction was that it was a crazy idea. My husband and I had never been apart that long in our thirty-seven years of marriage. I decided that I would go if he came, and we traveled with Xi-fen before school started in September. He would return home, and I would stay to teach for three months. Mike thought it was a great idea and encouraged me to go. Our youngest daughter, Lynessa, would be here to stay with him while she found a new job after her recent graduation from the University of Oregon. Mike would have our precious miniature poodle, Muppet, with him for company.

After that initial call, the faxes started coming, explaining more about what my experience in China would be like and what I had gotten myself into.

Jiangyin, China
February 9, 1998
Fax from Xi-fen, handwritten
Dear Carolyn and Mike,

. . . After I got your letter, I talked to Mr. Chang, one of the headmasters from Taiwan in charge of inviting the foreign teachers. He was very glad to know that you intend to teach at our school and hopes that you will teach here for at least three months. If you would like to teach for more than three months, that's even better. The teaching credential is not important, as you have experience teaching. I told him about you. You are so capable and have a wonderful personality. That's no problem at all, especially since you are willing to come next semester. We need foreign teachers to teach spoken English and to apply the western teaching style, customs, and culture.

The situation at this school is this: The school is newly built, located south of Jiangyin City, which is about a two-hour ride from Shanghai. The campus covers about 122,000 square meters. It opened last semester, on September 1, 1997. At present, there are three levels in the school: the kindergarten level, the elementary level, and the technical school level. The school puts special emphasis on English study and wants to apply advanced methods in English teaching. When you come to teach, you'll teach spoken English and are expected to teach about eighteen lessons a week . . .

You will teach the first-year students in the technical school level, ranging in age from sixteen to seventeen years old. You will also teach English conversations for the students in elementary school level, ranging in age from seven to ten years. You can also choose to teach kindergarten or preschool, aged four to seven years. Technical school classes have thirty-five to forty students. The elementary level has twenty-five to thirty in each, and the kindergarten and preschool are much smaller classes.

The school will provide you one bachelor flat with a bathroom and all the daily necessities, free of charge. The school will be responsible for your round-trip international airfare. However, it should be economy class airline ticket, and you'll be reimbursed once you arrive at our school. You can have meals at special prices in the school dining hall, or you can do your own cooking in the public kitchen in the foreign teacher's building. . .

There is a medical clinic on campus. You can be taken care of by the clinic when you become ill. However, you are responsible for your medical insurance and bills when you have to go to the hospital. You will also pay for your telephone and fax expenses. Water and electricity expenses are free. There is hot water, heating, and air conditioning in your flat.

Carolyn, this will be a chance for you to come to China. Of course, the living conditions and environment can't compare with that of your home in America, especially not having a car. But we have many kinds of public traffic (transportation), and there are taxis everywhere. . .

Also, when you come in this kind of way, it will be easy to get your passport and visa. You don't have to apply. Well, the Provincial Education Commission in Charge of Foreign Affairs will send a certified letter as cultural exchange. Carolyn, please send a letter and your resume to the school if you have decided to come.

Love,

Xi-fen

June 6, 1998

I received a fax from Xi-fen with five pages to fill out with my information: name, education, health status, family, and my attitude toward China. Xi-fen translated the Chinese for me.

Lafayette, California
June 9, 1998
My fax to Xi-fen
Dear Xi-fen,
Thank you so much for sending the fax and answering my questions. I got five pages, but I don't think the last one came through. Were there more? My student Juin sent my fax for me, and I can also send my faxes through Mike's office.

I'm excited about coming to see you and teaching in China. I have questions about when school starts. Shall we come in August and plan to travel together? Where would you like to travel? Guilin? Xian? Beijing, too? Would we take the train? Should I look for a ground tour? Mike and I will pay your way because you will be helping us.

Mike fell off a ladder last Saturday. He broke his wrist and is going to have surgery on Thursday. It's a problem because we are driving to Oregon for my daughter Lynessa's graduation. We will still go, but I'll be driving his sleepy body the ten hours it takes to get there. We can't miss this graduation.

Is there any way I can call any of the American teachers who have taught at your school?

I'm trying to plan our airline tickets. A short fax with the dates is

OK. Fax soon.
    Love,
    Carolyn

Lafayette, California
June 20, 1998
My fax to Xi-fen
Dear Xi-fen,
I am so excited about seeing you and coming to China. It will be like a dream.

Mike has to have surgery again on his wrist this Wednesday. He will have a smaller cast.

Lynessa's graduation in Oregon was wonderful. She came home two days ago, and then two of her Swedish friends arrived, so it's been busy here.

I'm sorry to be slow with these papers. I had to renew my passport, and because they are slow, I expedited it. It arrived yesterday. I can now send you a copy.

I would like to get some idea of what materials I might need. I would like to teach the high school level students.

Your first fax came with five pages, then another fax arrived at Mike's office, and I didn't know about it. Meanwhile, I had my student Juin fax you. Then you sent the ten pages again. The fax does work.

I'm working with a travel agent here on the dates for our tickets. I'm waiting to confirm the dates.

I will call you. When and where is a good time to reach you?
Love,
Carolyn

Lafayette, California

July 4, 1998

My fax to Xi-fen

Dear Xi-fen,

I was hoping to get a fax from you this week. I bought our tickets, and now we are coming for sure. We are on United Airlines, leaving San Francisco on August 11 and arriving in Shanghai on August 12. Mike is scheduled to return August 28, and my return is December 6.

I think we should get a hotel in Shanghai the first night. Will you be able to make travel plans for us? We would like to go to Beijing, Xian, and Guilin. I don't think we have time for the Three Gorges. Can you come with us? In Guilin we would like to stay at the Sheraton on the river and maybe the Xian Sheraton as well. Can you arrange them, and how do we go about paying you in advance for these tours?

Today is the Fourth of July. We had a big party for Lynessa's graduation last week, so we are having a quiet holiday weekend.

We bought clothes for Mike for China since we know it will be hot. He is very excited to come.

Are you on vacation? I hope you are getting a little time off. You work so hard. How are things with your son? You probably don't have time to tell me now, but I'm hoping to meet him.

Mike had the surgery on his wrist and will do physical therapy soon.

Please write or fax soon!

Love,

Carolyn

Jiangyin, China
July 4, 1998
Fax from Xi-fen to me
Dear Carolyn,

I'm sorry I didn't give you an answer right after I got your fax, including the filled-out papers and a copy of your passport. Your paperwork is fine. I have all of the materials to proceed with the visa you will need. If you come after August 10, it will be a little cooler.

I talked to Peter, the American teacher who has been teaching here for one month. You can call him after July 14, when he will be back in the U.S.

I will arrange for you to teach the high school students. I don't think you should try to ship a package with materials here. When I left for China four years ago, you helped me ship several packages. They took more than two months to get here.

Carolyn, the problem is that I have no home phone in Wuxi since my divorce four years ago. I'm seldom home during the semester and only on every other weekend. You can call the school, but I'm so busy I never know when I'm going to be here. So, it's better to fax and tell me when you are going to call. Then I can wait for your call.

Before I leave for Wuxi, I'll send a fax and figure out how you can call me. We need to keep closely in touch. Is that OK? I'll get everything arranged for you.

I'm sending with this fax a contract the principal of our school has signed. It's a three-page contract. When you get the contract, please sign it and fax it back as soon as possible. This will start your visa application procedure.

Please let me know if you have any questions. Fax me soon.
Love,
Xi-fen

Lafayette, California

July 6, 1998

Fax sent to Xi-fen

Dear Xi-fen,

I got your seven-page fax yesterday. Thank you. I'm sending you four pages with the signed contract and this letter.

Yesterday on the internet, I found the name of a travel agency in Shanghai. They say they are a large company with a large staff. I hope they will email me back. I am sending their information.

I will leave it up to you to decide. I hope this is not too much to ask. I know you have much better access to information than I do. I can find a list of hotels in travel books here and could fax you those lists if you think that would be helpful.

We are so excited to see you. Mike said he has wanted to go to China since he was a little boy, and he wants to spend time with you.

I understand about not being able to reach you in Wuxi. It shouldn't be a problem because we will have arrangements made by then. I will call Peter later in the month when he returns from China.

I think I should go ahead and get my travel visa at the same time you are working on the Cultural Exchange one. I think I must have one to travel. Do you know about this? Sorry to have so many questions.

If I call you on those July dates, I will tell you in advance by fax. Will I be able to get through Bell School's switchboard by just repeating your name? I have tried this and couldn't get through; that is why I had my student Juin help me. Thank you for answering all my questions and sending me all the information.

Love,

Carolyn

Jiangyin, China
July 13, 1998
Fax from Xi-fen to me
Dear Carolyn,

I'm very happy about you both coming to China. We will travel from south China to north China. We will travel to the places you want to see. When I told my brother about this, he joked with me, saying, "You are going on Clinton's trip!" It's a long travel line and will take at least twelve days. I have to be back to the school before August 26. The time for our journey will be kind of limited. Maybe we should only travel by plane. Anyway, we'll do it. I'll arrange the travel details, even though I haven't been to any of these places. Don't worry, Carolyn. I can arrange this long travel. I'm inquiring about the best travel line both for money and time. The travel line will be approximately this: from Shanghai to Guilin, from Guilin to Xian, from Xian to Beijing, and from Beijing to Shanghai. We'll take five days in each place and then come back to school. We will still have some time before Mike leaves, so we can see cities around here.

How much luggage do you have? I'll come to the airport and pick you up with a school car. Then the school car will take your luggage and put it in your room here at Bell School. I'll stay with you for the night, and the next day, we will leave directly for Guilin.

I'm waiting to get the signed contract back. I have all the materials ready.

Love,

Xi-fen

July 13, 1998

Fax sent to Xi-fen

Dear Xi-fen,

I got your fax today, saying you did not receive the signed contract and my last letter. I sent it right away on July 6. I'll wait a couple of days to see if you get it. Then I will resend it.

Your proposed travel plans sound great. All by plane is fine. The school car is great. I know the time is short.

Yes, it is President Clinton's trip, but I had it in mind first! Unfortunately, we don't have Air Force One to take us from place to place.

I can give you an American Express card number to pay for the plane reservations. Let me know.

I'm busy trying to finish both my jobs and get ready. I'm so excited about this great adventure. I will go to the Chinese Consulate in San Francisco this week to get our tourist visas.

Love,

Carolyn

Jiangyin, China

July 16, 1998

Fax from Xi-fen

Dear Carolyn and Mike,

Just when I went to send you another fax yesterday afternoon, I got your six-page fax, which included the signed contract. I need to give you more visa information.

You told me you want to go ahead and get your travel visa and L visa while I'm working on your cultural exchange one. Carolyn, that doesn't work out for your three-month stay. The travel visa is only valid for one month. Then you would have to go out of China to get the cultural exchange visa (F visa), which is valid for three months.

Even if you want to stay a little bit longer, I can help extend your F visa in the Police Service Bureau in Jiangyin City. It's much easier and saves time and money. Carolyn, don't worry. I'll get everything arranged for you to come to China.

You'll get a certified letter from our Provincial Authority in the beginning of August, and you can obtain your F visa with this letter. I'm applying for this certified letter for you. I'm trying to apply for Mike, too, but I'm not sure if I can get his.

Which Chinese Consulate General will you apply to for your visa? Is it San Francisco? I need to know exactly, as the letter requires the exact name of the Chinese Consulate General.

I have more information about the travel details now. I got in contact with a classmate of mine who is working at the travel agency in Wuxi. I told him about our travel plans. He said there isn't an established group tour for just these places. He will contact the chain travel agency English that for those big cities. I'll see if he can help us when you arrive. My brother has a friend who works in another travel agency, and he is going to inquire about the travel details and the cost for the whole trip. I'll go back to Wuxi next Monday, July 20, and figure out the arrangement and the cost. I'll compare the two travel agencies and make a final decision. What do you think of this, Carolyn? Let me know if you have a better travel plan.

Carolyn, I don't know what an American Express Card is. Don't worry about paying for the plane reservations. I will have those done.

I'll go back to Wuxi next Monday, but I'll be back a few days later to do the application procedure for the other American teachers. They will stay in our school for one year, and we'll try to get work visas for them. That's part of my job, so I still have to work during summer vacation.

Carolyn, our travel plan is fine; the time is limited. Do you want to switch your time a few days earlier? Can you switch the arriving time to a few hours earlier than 8:05 p.m.? It takes more than two hours for our school driver to drive back. It's just a suggestion. It's up to you to decide. Please fax me as soon as possible. I need to know the exact time of your arrival at Shanghai airport to arrange things. You told me you want to stay in Shanghai for the night. Do you want to stay in Shanghai for another day or leave for Guilin the next day? Let me know as early as possible.

When I am in Wuxi, you can fax my brother. There is a fax machine in his work office. You'll have to write to Hua Ming-shi. His fax number is [. . .], or you can call me by this number [. . .]. That's my neighbor's telephone number. Usually, I'll be home at night. I'll tell my neighbor that if they hear someone speak English, they should just call me. When I go back to school, I'll fax you. If you tell me the exact time of your call, I'll definitely wait in my office. Fax me back as soon as you can.

Love,

Xi-fen

Lafayette, California

July 18, 1998

Fax to Xi-fen

Dear Xi-fen,

I will try to call you on your Tuesday at 8:00 a.m. your time, July 21. If I don't reach you, I will try again the next day. You said you were doing a summer camp, but I don't know if it is at your school site.

I tried to call Peter today to talk to him about teaching at the school, but the number didn't work. I also tried a second number that didn't work. Can you check his number? I would really like to speak to him. Thank you.

Is there anything you would like me to bring to you from here? I would be happy to bring anything you want. Are there any particular gifts that people I meet might like from here? I am very open to gift ideas. Help!

I'm hoping to talk to you soon. I am so excited about you coming!
Love,
Carolyn

Lafayette, California
July 23, 1998
Fax to Xi-fen, Bell Economic School
Dear Xi-fen,

I tried calling your neighbor this morning, but I guess I missed you in Wuxi. I should have called a couple of days ago. You are probably back at school, so I hope you get this fax.

About the visas, I applied for our one-month tourist visas, so don't worry about Mike's visa. He is all set. When you send the special letter or documents, I will go back to the Chinese Consulate in San Francisco and have mine corrected. I was afraid to not get something started. The consulate takes our passports and holds them for a week before giving them back. Please try to hurry with the Cultural Exchange visa papers. I will need at least a week to get it. I was unable to find the name of the Consulate General in San Francisco. Do you have the address and the information you need? I have the address.

I can't change the air flight. It is just how they schedule San Francisco to Shanghai. We have to do the best we can with the time we have. Would it be better for the school driver to bring you in early the following day, the twelfth? We would find our way to a hotel. We will have to claim our luggage and go through customs, so it could get quite late. Perhaps it is possible to leave for Guilin later the next day.

I don't know how the Chinese flights run, so please make the best decision for you and the school driver. We will adjust happily.

We are happy for you to make the travel plans. Just go ahead with the decisions you think are best, and don't worry about consulting us about price or time. We are getting excited about seeing you.

I will fax you a copy of Mike's passport as soon as I get it back from the Chinese Consulate tomorrow.

Can you check Peter's phone number? It just tells me it is not a good number. Maybe he canceled his phone when he went to China.

Love,

Carolyn

Jiangyin, China

July 23, 1998

Fax from Xi-fen, Bell School

Dear Carolyn and Mike,

I got your fax (four pages, including the signed contract) on July 20. I can see you didn't get my last fax, which was five pages long. In my last fax, I told you I would be in Wuxi for the whole week. Things have changed. I'm at school, and I have something to deal with. I'm in charge of hiring ESL American teachers, and I haven't finished the work.

At the end of June, we contacted two universities in America, where they run ESL programs and train teachers, specifically to teach in China at different levels. Now, one of the universities that promised to help send us two ESL American teachers can't move any of those teachers in their program for this semester, as we contacted them too late. Now we need two more ESL teachers. I am in charge of this.

I really feel worried about it. Can you help, Carolyn? Can you help me find one or two ESL teachers to come teach just for three months, or for this semester only? Even if they aren't ESL teachers, it's fine as long as they can teach spoken English. Does your youngest daughter want to come? You know the details of the school, and it would be the same arrangement that you have.

In my last fax (on July 20), I told you the detailed arrangement of our travel. This weekend, I'm going to bargain the cost of the whole travel service if you like this arrangement. It's about $1,300 for each person. It includes room, board, and everything.

I'm sorry I gave you the wrong numbers for Peter. Try these two numbers [. . .]. See if one works.

Carolyn, don't worry about bringing me anything and the particular people you will meet. If you really want to bring some, maybe American ginseng, pistachios, skin oil, that is five U.S. dollars for one hundred pills. These things are heavy, so you decide.

If you want to call me, please fax me in advance and let me know the approximate time. I'll be at school except for weekends. Please fax me as soon as possible.

Love,

Xi-fen

Lafayette, California
July 27, 1998
Monday
Fax to Xi-fen
Dear Xi-fen,
Thank you so much for making all those travel arrangements. I found another way to pay for the tour reservations. It's called a MoneyGram, and I can send it directly to you at the Civic Industrial Bank in Wuxi. Would this help, or did the American Express card work? If you are interested in this solution, call the bank and ask them about it. Would the money be in the form that the travel agency wants, like American dollars, or Chinese money? I don't know the details, except that I would send it from my local Safeway grocery store. Can you believe that?

I just called the last number you gave me for Peter and got him on the phone. He was very helpful, answering the questions I had. I told him you need teachers now for the following semester and year. He said he would work on it. I will also try putting up a sign at my school and seeing if anyone would like to come to China.

My youngest daughter wants to get a job here. She has been gone for a year and is tired of traveling for a while. It's too bad because she would be a very good teacher. She has been working on finding businesses related to Sweden and the Swedish language.

Would you like me to post the job offer at Bell School on the University of California at Berkeley job board? I can easily do it, and it's free. I would just give some details and tell them to fax you. I can offer to answer questions until August 11. I know how to write up the requirements. Is this a good idea? Let me know.

I hope to hear from you soon. I'm sending a copy of Mike's passport. I was supposed to get my home fax today, but the phone company hasn't shown up yet.

Love,

Carolyn

Jiangyin, China

July 30, 1998

Thursday

Fax from Xi-fen, Bell School

Dear Carolyn and Mike,

I received your fax yesterday, as I stayed in Wuxi for a few days and went to the travel agency with my brother. My brother knows the manager of the travel agency, and he also made some inquiries to another travel agency. We talked about our travel details and the cost. We bargained a little bit, and now it is all settled.

Our travel plan is this: I'll come and meet you with the school car to take your luggage back to school. Then I'll stay with you in Shanghai for the night. The next afternoon, we'll fly to Guilin. We'll stay in Guilin for three days, then fly to Xian and stay there another three days. Then we'll fly to Beijing, stay there for four days, and then fly back to Shanghai. That will be at lunchtime on August 23. We have arranged for a little bit of looking around Shanghai that day. Do you want to do this, or do you want to go back to school right after we get off the plane? Please let me know.

It's a ten-day trip; however, we can see all the places of interest. This travel agent has a chain of travel agencies in these three cities.

They will provide us with a car, a driver, and a tour guide. She will arrange everything for us, including booking the ticket, room, and board. It will be a nice trip, but it's really very expensive for me. It will cost almost half of my yearly salary; anyway, I will go with you. It's rare and precious to travel with you both. I don't know these places. I'm Chinese and can give you some help on the way. Besides, I really need to go out for some time and relax, as I have suffered a lot in life. I have had a lot of pressure at work these years.

Carolyn, every time I think of you and the time we spent together, I feel that my life still has some meaning. Your great concern and help have warmed my heart. You played an important part in my life these years. Sometimes, especially after my son went to Australia at the end of May, I was frustrated and felt that life was meaningless. I felt that I had nothing in the world, only the hope of your coming to see me in China. The thought of traveling with you reminds me that I still have something to fulfill my life and enjoy.

About the details of how my son had to leave, I'll tell you when we are together.

I treasure this travel opportunity. I would like to go with you.

The cost for this whole trip is now $1,300 in U.S. dollars per person after bargaining. We can pay with U.S. dollars or yuan. If it is paid in RMB, it's 10,000. RMB for each. I asked about using the American Express card. They said it should be signed by you or it is invalid. We reached an agreement that we'll pay ¥5,000 cash as a pledge for the trip and pay off the rest of it after the trip. I'll manage to pay the ¥5,000 cash pledge first. Now I have signed the agreement. Is that fine, Carolyn? Let me know.

Now, about the exact time of your arrival in Shanghai. You told me it's August 12 at 8:05 p.m. Is that Chinese time? We checked your airline flight on United #837 leaving San Francisco. There is a ten-minute difference. Can you check to make sure it is August 12 with Chinese time and the same flight?

Carolyn, thank you for helping me hire ESL American teachers. Just go ahead and do what you said. It is kind and helpful. You can write up the requirements. If they want to speak to me, it must be before August 11 and after we return from traveling on August 23.

Please write right after you receive this fax, as I have to go back to Wuxi on August 6. I will be going to the travel agent and getting ready to travel with you. I'll be back here at school on August 11, getting things ready here with the arrangements for your room and the school car.

The time is running short. I'm very excited about seeing you again in China. I have been longing for this since I left you four years ago! Now it has become true. I thought it would only be a dream, so you can imagine how excited I am.

The certified letter for your F visa will be sent to you around the beginning of August. I have contacted the man in charge of this in the Provincial Educational Commission and told him to fax it to you.

If you have any questions let me know as soon as possible.

Love,

Xi-fen

Lafayette, California
Thursday, July 30, 1998
Fax to Xi-fen
Dear Xi-fen,
I received your fax from July 30. All the arrangements sound fine, wonderful, in fact. How nice of your brother to help us. I'm thrilled with three days in Guilin, Xian, and Beijing.

I was wondering about your son and what was happening. I'm anxious to hear the whole story. I am so happy that Mike and I can come and cheer you up! Yes, you do deserve a vacation, but we want to pay your way. You are part of our family. Yes, it's fine that you signed the financial agreement. I think we will bring the money in American Express traveler's checks unless you suggest something better.

About the flight, I'm sure it's the same flight. Sometimes they change the time a little bit. Before you leave for the airport, call United Airlines to confirm the arrival time. Sometimes they lose time. Sometimes they come early.

I'm faxing you copies of our flight schedules. Yes, it's Chinese time.

I will look for the visa letter. It's fine to use Mike's office fax, but now you can fax directly to me.

Remember, we could still do the MoneyGram from my grocery store if needed.

Love,
Carolyn

Lafayette, California

Fax to Xi-fen at Bell School

Dear Xi-fen,

I received your fax and the visa fax. I will go today to the Chinese Consulate in San Francisco. I have just seven days left, and they will take my passport. It makes me nervous!

Our home fax is working well. It's such a luxury to have it here.

All the travel arrangements are great. We are so excited. My daughter Michelle came from Dallas, Texas, so I saw all my daughters this weekend! My friend Kathleen gave a goodbye party for me. There were about forty people there.

Should Mike and I bring American whiskey as gifts? Would anyone in your family like that? Your brother or your father, or the travel agent?

I am having "business" cards made at a printer in Oakland Chinatown. It will have the school address and my California address, all in English. It will also have the Chinese translation on the other side. I can give it out to new friends and students. My Chinese ESL students thought my last name should be O and wrote out "Carolyn" in Chinese characters. We'll see if it is successful. I still have three more days to teach. On Thursday, the class will have a goodbye party for me!

I hope things are going well for you. Thank you for doing all this work.

We'll see you soon,

Love,

Carolyn

Second fax of the day, Lafayette
Monday, August 3, 1998
Dear Xi-fen,

I have just returned from the visa office in the Chinese Consulate in San Francisco. They said I must have two letters. I showed them the letter from the Jiangsu Education Commission. I told him it was for a Cultural Exchange Visa. He said he needed one of the following letters, either one from the Foreign Expert Bureau or one from the Labor Department, to go with the "local letter." There was nothing I could do. Do you know about this? Should I have gotten two letters by fax today? Please advise me as soon as possible. My visa now goes until October 16, so it's more than thirty days. They do have a way to speed up the seven-day hold on my passport. I will just pay more money. It's possible.

I will send another copy of this fax in care of your brother at his office in case you're in Wuxi.

Love,
Carolyn

Jiangyin, China
Tuesday, August 4, 1998
Dear Mike and Carolyn,

I'm sorry that the letter from the Jiangsu Education Commission for your Z visa didn't work out well. I called the person in charge right after I got your fax this morning and told him the problem you had when you presented the letter for your Z Visa. He checked the content of the letter. His assistant wrote it, and there were a few mistakes. He didn't emphasize that you are coming for the Educational and Cultural Exchange instead of teaching and wrote that you were applying for your F visa. Now he has sent you another letter for applying for your Z visa. It should work out well.

When you get the new letter for your Z visa, please go to the Consulate Office again and explain that you have been a volunteer of AFS for many years, and you hosted a Chinese teacher for a year, and now the Chinese teacher's school is inviting you to visit, as you are a teacher. Now you are coming for the purpose of Education and Cultural Exchange for a short term. This should work out.

Please fax me after you get back from the visa office; I will wait here at school to make sure you don't have any problems.

Love,

Xi-fen

Lafayette, California

Tuesday, August 4, 1998

Fax to Xi-fen at Bell School

Dear Xi-fen,

I just returned from the Chinese Consulate's visa office in San Francisco. I went to another window so I didn't get the same man. This time, they took my papers and passport. Everything seemed OK, and I will pick up the visa and the passports on Friday.

We are all set. I am busy getting everything ready to go. I hope things are OK with you.

Love,

Carolyn

Chapter 3
Leaving Home

San Francisco Airport

August 11, 1998, 2:40 p.m.

From my journal

Mike and I are on the plane, sitting on the tarmac at San Francisco International Airport. The flight should've taken off forty minutes ago. It's bizarre that the flight engineer is missing. He had car trouble on the freeway, getting to the airport, and has been in contact with the plane by cell phone. He said he would be late, but now they have lost all contact with him.

He finally showed up, and we were off an hour and a half late. I hope we make the connection in Narita, Japan, to catch our flight to Shanghai. Captain Featherstone is now in charge and seems to be making up time.

We landed in Narita and went directly to board our next plane. The gate was well-marked and easy to find. It was 1:00 a.m. San Francisco time. I changed my watch to 5:00 p.m., August 12. We leave just before 6:00 p.m. their time.

We used frequent flyer miles to upgrade to business class, and it was wonderful. The weather here in Japan looks to be hot and humid. When I looked out the plane window, it reminded me of Heathrow, two stories, people moving in corridors, buses piling up to transfer people—a busy place.

On the flight to Shanghai, we changed our clocks back an hour. China has one time zone, Beijing time, across what would be five natural time zones. In 1949, Chairman Mao decreed a single time to unify the country.

Shanghai, China
Wednesday, August 12, 1998
From my journal
Xi-fen was at the airport with a driver from her school to pick us up and take us to a hotel in the southwest part of Shanghai. The driver took my big luggage back to the school after he dropped us off. The hotel was comfortable. We were on the top floor of the hotel with a view of the new stadium.

Shanghai
Thursday, August 13, 1998
From my journal
We met Xi-fen for breakfast at eight. The hotel buffet was huge. No dry cereal, but they had sweet rolls wrapped in plastic for us.

Before meeting our guide at 9:00 a.m., I called home from the lobby to my Uncle Bud through AT&T. I told him we were in Shanghai and to call our daughter Lynessa and tell her we had arrived safely. My uncle is elderly, living alone in San Mateo, and is concerned about this adventure. Our daughter moved home after graduating from college and will be looking for a job.

Ms. Wong, our guide, met us in the lobby. She took us to the downtown area of Shanghai, where we saw the new shopping complex. We entered the park and garden and admired the new Ming Dynasty-style buildings. Yu Yuan Park was built to honor the builder's parents. It was incredibly hot. We last checked the temperature at the airport last night when it was 96 degrees Fahrenheit at 10:00 p.m. Goodness knows what it is now in the heat of the day.

We went to the Arts & Crafts Section of Shanghai for a Mongolian Barbecue. Hot tourists were picking out their meat and vegetables. Workers cooked it on huge flat "grills" in about thirty seconds. Those poor cooks! The meats were thinly sliced. It was good. You get one small glass of beer, and heaven help you if you want a second. They were too busy to help. We sat across from three German girls who sipped Schnapps so they "wouldn't get sick"—it was funny. Mike thought they were backpackers.

Across the driveway was a jade carving factory. The artisans did intricate work under bad working conditions, with hot stone dust everywhere, but they produced beautiful pieces.

Ms. Wong and her driver picked us up to go to the airport, but just before we went up the departure ramp, Xi-fen spotted a noodle restaurant. She worried we wouldn't get food on the plane and insisted we stop for noodles, so we did.

Ms. Wong got us checked in. We paid the airport tax and found Guilin on the board—Gate 7B. We sat for one and a half hours, close to take-off time. We got in the Guilin line, only to find we were at the wrong airline. We needed Shanghai, not China Air. We started to hurry in the other direction, not knowing where we were going, when Xi-fen heard her name called. We rushed to Gate 3—just making our flight. What a close call. Xi-fen took it in stride.

"Oh well, we made it!" she said. We had a two-hour flight to Guilin. It was crowded, and the food was not good, but we had had lunch and noodles. We arrived at the new Guilin Airport, where President Clinton was just a few weeks before us. The drive to the FuBo Hotel right on the river took forty minutes. I was very excited when I saw that the "night market" was right down the street. After dinner, Xi-fen and I sat down in the hotel lobby. I asked her about her son when we were in Shanghai, and she wouldn't talk about it.

"Something is wrong, Xi-fen. How is your son?" He is eight, and her ex-husband's mother had been taking care of him.

"My husband and his mother have taken him to Australia, and now they told me they are going to immigrate there. My son is not coming home."

"How could that happen?" I didn't know his grandmother had moved to Australia.

"They tricked me into signing the papers for him to leave. They pitted my son against me. He thought I was the one holding him back from a trip to Australia to see his auntie and grandmother. My son begged me to let him go and was mad at me for not letting him. My ex-husband promised me they would be coming back, so I signed the papers. He knew how important my son was to me. When they got there, he announced that they were staying."

"I'm so sorry! No wonder you're so upset. That's terrible news. Is there anything you can do?" We talked through the problem and circumstances a little more. There was nothing that could be done. She would not see her son for several years.

On with the Tour

4

Guilin, China

Friday, August 14, 1998

From my journal

This tour is incredible already. It includes airfare, hotels, English-speaking guides, drivers, and three meals a day. Xi-fen gave us each ¥1,000 so we wouldn't have to go to the bank right away. Mike called her his rich Chinese cousin. It made her giggle.

Guilin, China

Saturday, August 15, 1998, 9:00 a.m.

As I'm writing in my journal, the guide arrives with the driver. It's so hot, about ninety degrees Fahrenheit again, with high humidity. They are having a heat wave. Just our luck! We watched groups of people along the riverside dancing, and another group exercising. It reminded me of when I drive into my school's parking lot and see my early students doing Tai Chi on the blacktop, waiting for class to start. A man had spread out a blanket on the ground for "cupping." He was placing heated cups and creating a suction on the person's back to relieve some ailment. This city has huge old trees and countless bicycles.

We went to see the Cave of 1,000 Buddhas—actually, there were only about twenty-four. We climbed the mountain in the heat, and then rain poured down on us. It's tropical here and reminds me of Hawaii, where rain can come at any time. From the top of the mountain, we could see the Li River and the city, which has a population of about 450,000. Our guide said there are 2,500 rice noodle stands here. This is the hometown of one of my ESL students in the U.S. Hot, hot, hot!

We saw the huge limestone caves in Five Star Park, all lit inside with multi-colored lights. Camel Rock, where President Clinton spoke, was on the grass in front. They are so proud that the President of the United States came to their city. I'm thinking that it looks like we are following in his footsteps; however, I had this planned before he announced his itinerary!

Lunch was at the Palace Hotel. They thought Xi-fen was our tour guide and didn't want to give her food. She was indignant and told them she had paid for this. These conversations are all in Chinese. She had to tell us what was said.

We rested at our hotel and were picked up for dinner. In every hotel, Xi-fen was just a room away. After dinner, Mike decided to rest, and Xi-fen and I went shopping.

The night market was about two hundred stands of "antiques," linens, and souvenirs, all sold by aggressive salespeople. They followed us, yelling, "Teacher, teacher, teacher." It went on and on. I said to Xi-fen, "How does he know we are teachers?" Then it dawned on me that he was calling out, "T-shirt, T-shirt, T-shirt." I am going to have to get used to this kind of pronunciation. We bought a few things, walked a long way, and came home by taxi.

Sunday, August 16, 1998, 8:40 a.m.

From my journal

We were picked up at our hotel for the Li River Cruise. The driver and guide drove us for forty-five minutes, where we boarded our luxurious boat. We had large, comfortable seats with air conditioning, and lunch was served on board. The cruise went past the spectacular "Dragon Tooth" mountains. Ancient, sharp peaks poke up from the flat landscape. It's dramatic scenery with lush green farmland. We saw an old lady in black, fishing from a boat with a cormorant.

Our wild van ride, speeding back to Guilin, went through more extremely beautiful countryside. They were building a cement highway for miles in the ninety-six-degree heat. I wished I could take pictures of the water buffalo, white ducks, and huge pink pigs, but we were going too fast. Dinner was at our hotel.

Monday

From my journal

We headed to Xian today, but before reaching the airport, our tour guide took us to the beautiful Flute Cave. In front, kids were selling flutes. Some wanted one flute for one yuan, two for two yuan, or five for two yuan. They needed help with their numbers.

Off we went to the airport with no picture of a pink pig. It seemed like everyone was on a bicycle with a basket. There were lots of stands selling umbrellas. Our best photos were just outside our van as we whizzed past.

At the airport, we found that our plane to Xian would be at least six hours late, so they bused us to an airport hotel and gave us rooms to rest. The plane took off at 8:00 p.m.

All along, Xi-fen kept close tabs on our itinerary to make sure we were getting all that she had arranged. It was great to have someone looking out for us. Everything was in Chinese. It would be difficult here without a translator. The Guilin guide spoke English well, but he didn't understand us when we talked to him. Xi-fen said he was not patient in Chinese either. The food was generally good.

Late that night, we arrived in Xian. The guide and driver had been waiting for six hours at the airport for us. The airlines gave them no information until we were in the air. The NW China Airlines plane was new and nice. It was a two-hour flight. The airport was way out of town. It took an hour to reach our hotel in the center of the old Xian city.

Our hotel was modern and pleasant. We were on the sixteenth floor. I heard helicopters all night. I kept wondering, why? I had read that eighty-four Chinese helicopters were being used to rescue people in floods, the worst in forty-four years, but I knew the floods were hundreds of miles away on the upper Yangtze River. I decided there must have been construction going on. Looking out from our room in the morning, I could only see fog.

"Xi-fen, what was that loud helicopter noise going on all night?" I asked.

"That noise is the small farmer's trucks. They're only allowed here in the old city at night because they pollute and are so noisy," she said. I thought it was a good example of sound raising up. I hoped I would be used to them by tonight so I could sleep.

Xian

Tuesday, August 18, 1998

From my journal

In the morning, our guide picked us up to see the Terracotta Warriors, but on the way, we stopped by a museum to see the oldest digs and artifacts from the earliest people. There were clay urns for children's burials. I bought a book on pottery. We went to the factory where they made life-sized warrior replicas. They will ship them to the United States for $1,500—a real steal. President Clinton bought two. I wanted to buy one, but I was not sure what my money situation would turn out to be. Maybe I would need cash later.

We bought a lovely nine-tile picture of a vase of flowers. I will have a frame made for it at home. We also purchased an eight-inch-by-thirty-inch tile mural of the famous four horses. Xi-fen bought a small tricolored horse statue to put on her desk at school.

The countryside near the Tang Dynasty Hot Springs was quite poor. The Xian area is polluted, but rain helped us get "cleaner air." It was still hot. The weather is really awful, no blue sky, no clear air.

Out to see the famous Warriors—it was a huge area. There was a large room with a twelve-foot-high circular vision movie in English that surrounded us, giving us a sense of place and time, and showing how the warriors were made.

The magnitude of the site is surprising. It was in three huge separate areas and only partially excavated with much more work to be done. The reassembly process is slow and tedious. Each warrior is a separate individual. The whole idea of building hundreds of individual clay figures with the coil method, with personal details so long ago, is mind boggling.

After seeing a small portion of the many huge warehouses where the statues were exhibited, we went into the gift shop where a man was signing books. He was supposed to be one of the farmers who discovered the site. I'm not sure I believe this story, as there is always someone signing books who was supposed to be the one who discovered the site. This has gone on for years. I bought the book with his signature anyway.

We had lunch at what Xi-fen called a "tourist lunch place." Lunch was included, of course, on this tour. I liked the noodle dishes. Xi-fen said they weren't expensive dishes.

I can't believe this tour. It included four flights, all hotels, three meals a day, guides, drivers everywhere, and all admission costs for three of us. Mike and I haven't paid a dime, and Xi-fen has booked it on trust and a deposit. Xi-fen explained to us that the Chinese do not tip. She is insistent on this idea.

On our long trip back to Xian, we went through fruit orchards and farmland. They burn coal here, and the still air becomes trapped in the valley.

Xian, China
Wednesday, August 19, 1998
From my journal
On our last day, our guide took us to walk on the city walls and then to the Stone Tablet Museum. We saw the famous, original relief of ceramic horses. We bought tiles and "old" jade, but the prices were high.

Our guide overheard Xi-fen telling me not to tip, because the "Chinese do not tip." The guide took me aside and gave me a long explanation about how little she and the driver were paid and told me that they relied on tips. This made Xi-fen angry and upset. She vowed to report it to the travel agency, which she promptly did when we got to Beijing. She called the agency, and they told her, "Tip is tip," whatever you think. Mike and I did tip the guide and the driver.

Xi-fen was not happy when she surmised that the guide was being nice to us just to get a tip! Our guide was knowledgeable and said she was a university professor "moonlighting" as a guide in the summer.

Forever after, Xi-fen refers to this as the "Xian Incident." It makes her so angry, and she has reported and complained about it to the travel agency several times.

A driver dropped us off at the Xian Airport for our two-hour flight on China Air to Beijing that evening.

We went through metal detectors for security, where they found a 8-inch narrow-bladed knife in Xi-fen's purse.

"That's my fruit knife," Xi-fen said.

Xi-fen loved to buy fruit as we went along on this trip. She should have put it in her luggage because they wanted to take it away.

She protested and said she wanted them to find her suitcase that had already been turned in so she could put it inside. Mike waited upstairs while she and I went down into the dark lower levels under the main airport. It was amazing that we found her suitcase in a dark room among so many others. She put it inside. The knife was saved for future fruit.

Beijing

Our new guide met us upon arrival in Beijing. She was twenty-three years old, named Zoe. We liked her. She was knowledgeable and sweet.

She first took us to the Temple of Heaven. It was packed with people. Xi-fen had to have her picture taken in front of every sign and major building. She wanted to prove she was there.

On the way to dinner, we stopped by an old Beijing hutong. These homes and neighborhoods are rapidly being bulldozed and replaced by concrete housing blocks. The old compound was surrounded by a high wall, with a courtyard and separate rooms off the open center area. Several families or family members could have their own separate rooms, yet they all live together. This was an example of the traditional northern Chinese home of the past.

We went to dinner at a restaurant that Deng Xiaoping frequented. We were told we were sitting at his table. Humm. . . not sure. Deng Xiaoping is thought to have said, "To get rich is glorious." Even though it may not be an official quote, it has given the Chinese people "permission" to pursue businesses, enter the market economy, and make money. He is known as the person responsible for modernizing China. He opened universities in 1978 that enabled young people like Xi-fen to get university educations.

Beijing, China
Wednesday, August 19, 1998
From my journal
This morning, we went to the Ming Tombs out near the Ming Reservoir. It's a huge valley with many unexcavated tombs. This area was the burial place of thirteen of the sixteen Ming dynasty emperors from 1368 to 1644 CE. We entered a large, dark, gray stone cavern, known as the "Underground Palace." Inside were stone thrones with melting candles on the floor. In another chamber were two dark red wooden coffins surrounded by many large stone boxes that had been filled with things for the afterlife. It was dark and gloomy inside and a little creepy, with not much to see.

We had lunch at the Friendship Store. This state-owned store sells exclusively to foreigners and tourists. Mike and I remembered shopping at one in Hong Kong in 1973.

The Badaling entrance to the Great Wall is fifty miles from Beijing but still in its municipality. It was built during the Ming dynasty in 1504 CE and is the most visited part of the wall. It was a hot, humid climb. The good views from the top were the walls running up and down over the hills in the distance. We walked on the wide wall and saw the military lookouts along the sides. Its wide top accommodated five horses with riders side by side. It was quite a feat of engineering.

Xi-fen wore a special outfit for her climb today. She calls it her "squirrel outfit." It's shorts with a top that has cute squirrels printed on it, and it goes with her canvas squirrel shoes that have elastic straps to keep the shoes on while climbing.

When we came down from the wall, I saw a "Princess Diana" Beanie Baby. It was purple with a white rose on the Beanies' chest, and I decided I wanted it. Xi-fen bargained with the woman in her souvenir stall for me. It made the woman angry because she knew she could get more money from me than Xi-fen. Xi-fen was a tough bargainer, and I am now the owner of the stuffed bear.

We stopped at a Beijing Park on the way back.

Thursday, August 20, 1998

From my journal

Our Beijing hotel is modern, but there is a woman in the lobby with a dirty mop and water washing the floors. We have seen this before. Are they trying to say, "The place is clean"? The cleaning goes on all day, even when the lobby is busy and people have to walk on wet floors.

Beijing

August 21, 1998

From my journal

Today, in the hot and hazy weather, we went to the Summer Palace by Lake Kunming. The roofed walkways through the landscaped gardens had five thousand hand-printed pictures above our heads. We saw the theater used by the Empress Dowager Cizi, who ruled China from 1861 until her death in 1908. She liked to attend Peking operas in her specially built opera house. She is always depicted in yellow, her royal color. She lived through fascinating times.

Next was the Lama Temple, a Tibetan Temple of the Yellow Order. There were actually six temples, one after another, that we stepped through to get to the next one. Xi-fen bought incense to burn and offer to Buddha. She said prayers in each temple and either burned the incense or left it on the altar.

We were driven to Beijing University to meet with a doctor who could distinguish between twenty-six different pulses to diagnose a person's health problems.

Xi-fen didn't want to go because she said, "They always find something wrong with you and want you to take medicine. The medicine always tastes terrible."

The doctors did not speak English. Mike bought some unknown pills, and Xi-fen got a prescription for Chinese medicine that would have been in tea form if she had filled it. They told me I should not gain weight.

Tiananmen Square was close to our hotel, so we walked there to see Mao Zedong's tomb. Xi-fen didn't want to go. Mike and I waited in line for thirty-five minutes to view Mao's preserved body. He died in 1976 of a heart attack. Mao's wishes to be cremated were ignored by his widow, who wanted him remembered like Lenin, Stalin, and

Ho Chi Minh. He was embalmed and put on display. Many people were buying flowers as they waited to go inside. We saw his body in dim light. He looked sallow and waxy, not really preserved. He would have been right at home in a wax museum. People placed their flowers a few feet from the body. After the people passed by the body, workers picked up the flowers, took them out the back door, and around front to be sold again. No one seemed to notice.

We crossed the square and saw the giant clock showing the countdown until China would take over Macau. At the far end of the square was the large picture of Mao and the entrance to the Forbidden City.

Beijing
August 22, 1998
From my journal
On our last day in Beijing, we went back to Tiananmen Square to see the Forbidden City. We were attracting a lot of attention, two tall Caucasians and a Chinese woman. People were surprised to see us. A family wanted to have pictures taken with us in front of the Forbidden City gate and under Mao's portrait. We smiled, laughed, shook hands, and took the photos, none of us speaking the other's language.

We went in through the center gate. Thank goodness we had a guide. There were so many people, no English was spoken, and the ticket-buying procedure was complicated.

We toured each temple or pavilion and heard about the life here and some of the old national testing done for people to get higher education and government jobs. It was fun to see the grounds and remember that some of the movie *The Last Emperor* was filmed here.

Our lasting impressions of Beijing were of huge traffic congestion and crowds. We were told it has a population of sixteen million with a "floating population" of four million. We saw many people near our hotel arriving from the countryside with their clothes in rice sacks. Xi-fen explained that in China, you are registered as a countryside person or a city person, and you are supposed to stay where you are. You can't just decide that you want to move to the city, although it was obvious that many people were doing just that.

Chapter

Bell Economic School 5

Arrival in Shanghai

Bell Economic School

Saturday, August 22, 1998

Our comfortable flight on China Air to Shanghai was on another new plane. Mike and I were excited to see the new school, where I was going to be teaching for three months.

Xi-fen had arranged for a school car to pick us up, and our driver, Lu Ping, was there at the airport. After getting lost trying to find the airport exit, we were at last on our way to Jiangyin, the city and area where Bell Economic School was located.

It was a two-hour drive through green countryside that looked more productive than where we'd been. It's considered one of the most prosperous areas of China, with rice fields, no water buffalo, fish ponds, some with fresh water, and oyster beds for oysters and fresh water pearls. Houses in the distance were two-story cement structures, some with blue glass on the top story, perhaps for energy conservation, and curved Chinese-style roofs with decorations on the roof ends.

When I pointed them out to Xi-fen, she said she had never paid much attention to the roofs. The first hour going west to Wuxi is an expressway. Honking to pass or overtake went on constantly. It was chaotic, like a fish fighting its way upstream. There were trucks, motorbikes, buses large and small, and bikes, some pulling wagons, all going at each other with no lanes. Yikes! We hadn't seen an accident yet, but they came within a hair's distance when honking and passing, "horning," as Xi-fen calls it.

The last eight miles before reaching the school had been under construction for months. It was approximately four lanes across and a dirt road. It is not really a washboard. It's more like moguls on a ski slope. Imagine a small taxi going up and down this road. This is the main artery going north and south for at least 150 miles.

We arrived at Bell Economic School, an impressive sight. We drove through two bell-domed gatehouses with guards on each side of "Sather Gate." Mr. Chang, the architect from Taiwan and CEO of the school, designed the wrought iron gate after the famous one on the UC Berkeley campus. The school buildings and campus look like a fancy country club, with expansive grass areas in front and between the buildings. Mr. Chang attended several American universities and took his architectural inspiration from American college campuses: Stanford, Berkeley, UCLA, and University of Pennsylvania to name a few.

Bell School does look like it's brochure pictures. The building called "The English Club" is a Chinese version of "English Tudor style" outside. It's three stories, with living quarters on the top floor, classrooms and the English office on the second, and a main floor that will be an English lounge for students. I picked out the largest room on the third floor, where all the foreign teachers will be. We all have individual rooms and a community kitchen. I have two rooms and a bath. It's all new, but the floor tiles were a little crooked, the painting job is not great, and the doors look to be rough, maybe hand hewn.

The view from here may get nicer. It's hazy now. Across the ceiling are four slanted wood beams. Mr. Chang, the developer, thinks this style makes it "Western." There is wood panel wainscoting around the room. I also have an "ante room" for an entry next to the bath. Both rooms are hot as saunas. At least they finished putting in the A/C unit at 2:00 a.m. last night. I checked and did find screens on the windows, but some screens have small holes. With all the water in the area, I'm sure there are mosquitoes. The brand-new double bed was small and very hard.

We went out to eat, with the school car and driver. Xi-fen told us this restaurant served cuisine from a southern area of China. Glowing red lanterns lined the front of the building.

Bell Economic School to Wuxi
Monday, August 24, 1998
Mike and I took a tour of the school and heard more about how and why this school was built. There is a technical school (their name for high school), dorms for those students, a junior high school with dorms, and an elementary school. There are dorms for preschoolers and elementary students. There are some Chinese teachers living on campus as well.

The school is a joint venture between Taiwan and China. There are five Taiwanese partners, including Mr. Chang. There are two Chinese partners, meaning investors, and owners of the company. Presently, the school is partially supported by the Chinese government, but in two years it will be completely owned by the Taiwanese. If Xi-fen stays here, she will lose her teacher's retirement and health benefits because this school is private.

The main office building is four stories with a capitol on top. It will also be the library when they get books. It was unclear where the books would come from. We saw the dorms where the students will live. This is a boarding school, and students will live here for two weeks at a time, go home on Friday, and return on Monday. Xi-fen and I can then travel farther distances on those away weekends.

At 5:00 p.m., we planned to take a bus to Wuxi, a big city about an hour away, halfway back toward Shanghai. We just found out that the other new English teachers are coming tomorrow instead of the 28th. Xi-fen is not happy about this, as it means we have to be back from Wuxi tomorrow by 6:00 p.m.

The bus to Wuxi was the local bus on the dirt road out in front of the school. Xi-fen paid for the bus for all of us. The driver told her, "Ten yuan."

"I always ride this bus, and it's eight yuan, not ten."

Xi-fen argued some more until finally the driver said, "OK, eight."

I think he saw us and thought he could get more money. It was a bumpy, hot, dusty ride, but at least we had seats. I played peek-a-boo with the toddler girl in the seat in front of me. She had turned around to stare. I made her laugh. Peek-a-boo is universal.

People on the bus stared at us when we all spoke English. The child was wearing pants with a split that opened in the crotch. From the bus, I had seen parents hold their child to their side and let them pee in a convenient place, without taking off clothing—so much for needing diapers.

Xi-fen's parents had invited us to dinner in what they called their "very humble home." From the bus station, we went by cab to their apartment. The neighbors knew we were coming and came out to look, smile, and wave at us. It was an event they had never seen. We climbed the three flights of unlit stairs in this large tenement building. We were welcomed into the largest of three tiny rooms, where five people in the family lived. After introductions, smiles, and head bowing, we were invited to sit around the family table with Xi-fen's parents, sister, brother-in-law, and two nieces.

The ceiling fan served as their air conditioner, but it was incredibly hot. Xi-fen said the beer had been iced, maybe sometime in its life, but it wasn't cold now. They had no refrigerator.

We were all curious to meet each other, even though we couldn't speak each other's language. They had heard so much about us, and we them from Xi-fen during her year's stay with us. Xi-fen translated. She is an expert in both languages and quick at translating. Her father had cooked all the dishes in his tiny kitchen.

I was anxious to meet Xi-fen's parents. I knew how Xi-fen's father had tutored her in all subjects in 1976, so she could pass the newly revised test that would enable her to attend a university. During the Cultural Revolution (1960–1977), there was no regular education for children. Children were required to memorize Mao's *Little Red Book* forward and backward. Xi-fen, born in 1960, spent her school years traveling with other children in her countryside village to nearby villages, folk-dancing and singing the praises of Chairman Mao. With her father's tutoring, Xi-fen was able to pass the required test despite not having any formal education, and she went to a university in 1978 in northern China.

The cold dishes were served first on the big, wooden, circular tabletop set over a square mahjong table. This mahjong table had been proudly procured by Xi-fen's mother during the Cultural Revolution. The three-foot square table, now a table base, had been taken away from some capitalist family and resold on the street to her mother for "very cheap."

Tiny bowls were passed to each person, and chopsticks enabled us to reach across the table to take bite-sized amounts of the dishes. Family-style dinner means that everyone spits bones, seeds, and shells from the shrimp, chicken, and anything else that can't be chewed onto the table top.

Her mother noticed that I was having trouble doing this, so they brought me a little dish. I just couldn't do the spitting thing. Xi-fen explained to them that we didn't do this in America. They were so hospitable. Her father liked to cook and made delicious dishes. Her parents were amazed that we would come to their home and eat with them, and that we were proficient with chopsticks as well.

After dinner, we took a cab to Xi-fen's Wuxi neighborhood. She had owned this apartment for many years. Mike and I checked into a brand-new hotel, owned by the Wuhan Air Force, just down the street. The room was only thirty-five dollars. We walked to Xi-fen's apartment, ten minutes away and up six flights of stairs. Moonlight occasionally lit part of the stairs. There are so many hazards here in this country. No one pays attention to or worries about them.

Xi-fen showed us the water heater and western bathroom appliances she was able to buy with the money she earned when she stayed with us. In the bathroom, where there had only been a hole, was a modern western toilet. Everything in the furnished apartment was neatly arranged.

We had a hot walk back to our hotel. We were so thankful to get there, bathe, and drink cold water. Traveling here is tiring.

Chapter 6

Wuxi, China

Tuesday, August 25, 1998

From my journal

After a delicious breakfast buffet at our hotel, we met Xi-fen and went by cab to the travel agency to pay for this trip. Xi-fen said that according to Chinese custom, we must bring gifts to the agency staff. We shopped at the department store on the bottom floor of the building and bought a shirt for Xi-fen's brother's friend, who planned and arranged our trip. She assured us she could guess his size. We purchased a Christian Dior lipstick for the secretary; brand-name was most important.

It was unbelievable to Mike and me that we had not paid anything so far. Xi-fen had made a small deposit—¥5,000, about $600 U.S.—and the rest was on the confidence that we would show up and pay after the trip. Never in America, but in China, it's who you know.

Tea was served, and two-hour negotiations began. Xi-fen, the only one who spoke both English and Chinese, talked to the agent and three occasional helpers. We explored the various combinations of traveler's checks, Visa card, and cash to yuan until the right ratio was found. Every type of money except U.S. cash had its price. This was the first place that would accept cash. Xi-fen continued the translations. Tea again, though it was actually just hot water added to the shredded leaves in the pliable plastic cups. Xi-fen explained to the agency how the exchange rate should be calculated and made sure we understood every yuan. Tea again, and finally, a deal was struck with handshakes and smiles. We decided on a combination of traveler's checks and cash. The total for our grand tour of China for ten days—covering four flights, hotels, English guides, tours, and three meals a day for three of us—was $3,750, a bargain as far as we were concerned. I was exhausted and hadn't done any of the work.

Two days prior, Xi-fen had finally agreed to let us pay her way. She was reluctant but thankful and happy. She then told us of the possibility of her buying her own "house" in Jiangyin. We were thrilled for her. I would get to see where it was being built while I was here.

We all took a taxi to see the famous park in Wuxi, touring the old buildings and lovely grounds with their natural rock formations. We had lunch and then went out to Li Gardens on Lake Taihu. When Xi-fen lived with us, she thought it was so amazing that we had Lake Tahoe, and she had Lake Taihu here. They sound similar, well, almost! Again, hazy and hot, but we got an idea of the general setting and size of the lake.

Chapter

On My Own

7

A taxi took us to pick up the photos I dropped off earlier in the day. It was only twenty dollars for twelve rolls of film. Mike will take the pictures home with him. We did some shopping and bought Mike a carry-on for our many souvenirs. We got a taxi and decided to take it all the way back to Jiangyin and avoid the bumpy bus ride. It was ¥58, a bargain because we got there in half an hour. It was just in time to greet the new teachers.

They were Don and Pamela, also known as "Pam," from the University of Memphis. They were with Dr. De-an from their school. She was anxious to get her elderly sister to teach us Mandarin. Don and Pam seemed pretty mellow and easy to get along with.

We all went by school van for a welcome lunch in a nearby town. The Chief of Police, the hotel manager, and his assistant toasted us with "bottoms up." It's the only English they know. A cousin of Xi-fen's, who is considered a "society woman," treated us all to lunch. She was not there.

I have been introduced to several people who work at this school. Everyone seems to be a Mr. Su or Mr. Lu, with varied pronunciations. The Mandarin language has four tones and many meanings associated with a myriad of variations. I don't know how I will keep them all straight. They stared at each other when they heard me speak. Some giggled and smiled.

"She sounds just like the Voice of America," they told Xi-fen. I will teach spoken English. It's good to know I'm authentic.

Xi-fen said the gardeners have asked for my help. The grass seed used in the expansive lawns was bought in the United States, and they are having trouble with it. It doesn't look very good, and Mr. Chang, the school's designer and the person who insisted on "western grass," is due to arrive in a couple of weeks from Taiwan. They say he will not be happy if his grass doesn't look good. What should we do?

"Xi-fen, your friend is from the west. Ask her what to do. She must know," the gardeners said.

I suggested that they should ask where the grass was purchased. They said that was impossible. Suppose they couldn't do that. I suggested they start pulling up all the plants and weeds now growing randomly in the grass.

The next day, fifteen people were out pulling up all the plants and weeds. It did look much better, but it took several days for the huge piles of dead weeds piled on the grass to be picked up.

Bell School
August 25, 1998
Fax to our daughter from her dad
Hi Lynessa,
We are having a great trip. We arrived at the school on Sunday, and it is all very nice and new.

Your mom and I met the Chinese teachers and staff, and they have been very welcoming. The two U.S. teachers arrived yesterday. I think they will be fine.

Pick the big tomatoes and ripen them in the window. I expect to eat some. You may be in for a very interesting menu on my return. I will expect to meet you and Muppet right out the door at the airport. I will have lots to tell you and photos to show you.

Love, Dad

P.S. from Mom

We are going to Shanghai for Daddy's last two days. I'll call you from there.

Love,

Mom

Later, on August 25, 1998

Bell Economic School

From my journal

Today, arrangements have been made for us to have a mini-school van from Bell School take us into the city of Jiangyin. There were seven of us: Mike and I, Xi-fen, Don and Pam, the other new teachers who will be here a year, their supervisor, Ms. Su, and her sister, who works in some capacity at Bell. Ms. Su will be teaching Chinese language lessons. They were offered to me as well.

We tracked down a newly opened email place advertised in the local paper. Our arrival at the Internet Cafe was a photo event. The Chinese government had just started allowing these kinds of places with computers for rent by the hour. It was about a fifteen-minute drive from school, and I tried to memorize the route. I'm not sure how I will be able to return here. I got a new email address at Yahoo. While there, we met an American engineer for the suspension bridge under construction. I showed him how to get a Yahoo address.

The bus drove us around Jiangyin. There were no foreigners. I was so glad Mike got to see the place where I will be until December. It would be difficult to explain on the phone.

We walked into the downtown supermarket. It's actually just a small section of the bottom floor of the five-story department store. The market has a housewares section, milk, some juice, everything else, fruit, and cereal. The crackers are dry and in packages. There are no eggs, fresh fruit, vegetables, or meat. Those, I'm told, are in local markets somewhere else. So much for the "super" in supermarket.

I bought some "dlied apricots," the spelling on the package substituted "l" for "r," and some peanuts that looked like ones at home. We can buy things here, not knowing Chinese. There is no bargaining in this kind of store, thank goodness. The clerks seem to know some numbers in English. I can say "hello" and "thank you" in Chinese.

We foreigners attracted a lot of attention. People pointed, babies stared at us, and some smiled. All seemed curious.

These people are so small and so very slender. I think they must be related to birds. I told Xi-fen that I felt "conspicuous and gigantic."

Xi-fen said, "Carolyn, you are a crane among chickens." Mike laughed. Xi-fen makes us both laugh.

The Chinese never miss a meal, and Xi-fen makes sure it won't happen to us. In the early morning, 11:30 a.m. or 5:30 p.m., be it in the school cafeteria or a restaurant in town, we have a hot meal, hot soup included, even in this heat. Xi-fen tells me that the Chinese think having something hot will make you cooler. I'm not sure it's true for me.

Xi-fen had talked her cousin into hosting a banquet for us this evening. We were almost to the restaurant. Xi-fen decided Mike should see the Yangtze River.

"Mike, don't you want to see the Yangtze River?" Xi-fen asked.

"Well, yes," Mike said.

"OK. We'll go there," she told Lu Ping, our driver from the airport, the plan in Chinese.

It was getting dark, but with Xi-fen as navigator for Lu Ping, we drove up and down roads and highways. From time to time, Lu Ping hopped out of the minibus, asking people for directions. This went on for forty-five minutes. We couldn't find the river. At last, a woman told us the correct way to the riverside park.

After we drove to the park, we discovered that we had to walk several hundred yards into a narrow cement tunnel through a mountain to get to the river. We emerged from the tunnel to see the dark Yangtze and the new suspension bridge being built across it. The cables on the bridge were lit in the dark sky above. It reminded us of the Golden Gate Bridge at home.

When we got to the restaurant an hour and a half late, her cousin had come and gone. No problem. Xi-fen just took it in stride, and we went on with dinner anyway. She cheerfully ordered all the dishes she thought we should try, including their famous river crabs, which she had told us about. Her cousin came later, toasted us with the traditional "bottoms up," and paid the bill. Xi-fen says his governmental agency will pay for our dinners. She says that in China, he is known as a "society worm," charging personal expenses as business. Our dinner expense could be rationalized because I am here for education.

Bell School to Shanghai
August 26, 1998
From my journal
Mike and I have been staying in my new room. I actually have two rooms and a bath. Not bad. My new bed is a wooden box covered with quilted mattress material. It will probably be good for my back as soon as I get used to it. I was given a quilt, a matching sheet, and a bamboo mat to sleep on to escape the heat. The mat looks hard and scratchy and like something to avoid, although Xi-fen swears by its cooling properties.

We three foreign teachers, Don, Pam, and I, have something no one else at school has. We each have a wall-mounted air conditioner in our rooms. They're brand new and work well. Everywhere else, it is incredibly hot, humid, and hazy day and night. The teachers from Memphis are more at home in this weather than Mike and me, spoiled Californians. Our rooms are all located in the brand-new "English Club." This three-story building has empty rooms, all slated to become classrooms, audio-visual rooms, offices, a library, and a potential student lounge area on the first floor; that makes it a "club." This is really more of an English Center.

Mike packed his bags and the souvenirs for his trip home. We all three went to Suzhou with the mini-school bus and Lu Ping, our driver. Mike and I will take a train to Shanghai and stay two nights at the Sofitel Hyland, recommended by a friend of Xi-fen's.

Lu Ping drove us directly to the train station as we arrived in Suzhou. Nothing on the train schedule was written in English, not even major cities. Lu Ping went to the head of the line, waved our passports at the woman clerk, made some demands, and was instantly given our tickets. There is no way for a non-Chinese speaker to cope with this system. We had our soft seats reserved. Xi-fen said soft seats were important for the hour-and-a-half trip into Shanghai. We also paid extra so we could sit in the air-conditioned waiting room when we came back a few hours later.

Chinese tradition requires goodbye gifts. Xi-fen ran over to some unseen store to get Great Wall wine for Mike to take home and bought me a large flat cracker covered with sesame seeds, famous here.

We got back into the mini-school bus, and Lu Ping found the way across the old part of town to see the renowned "Humble Administrator's Garden." I enjoyed the ponds filled with pink blossoming Lotus plants, surrounded by lovely Chinese Pavilions. The lotus in China symbolizes purity since it rises to the surface from the mud, beautiful and untainted.

Xi-fen talked a tiny restaurant in the neighborhood into serving us lunch on trays instead of individual dishes. She calls this "Chinese fast food," and it's very cheap. We drove on to see Tiger Hill, a challenging feat since both Lu Ping and Xi-fen are unused to using maps.

I guess this Pagoda is remarkable because it is old and several stories, but God, it's so hot and humid you really don't care what you're looking at. Xi-fen and I put our umbrellas up for the sun, but we soon needed them for rain. Mike suggested we drive to see the Silk Museum, indoors, a great idea. We studied the history of silk, worms, looms, and the expensive things in the gift shop. They were prepared for busloads of tourists. Then it was time to catch our train.

At the train station we went into the special soft seat lounge, paying another yuan, .08 U.S., for the non-riders with us so we could all sit together and await our train. On the back of each seat was printed 'Wel Come.' I guess they think the word has two meanings, like two Chinese characters. There was a tour group of French tourists, actual foreigners, who later turned up in our train car and then at our French-owned Sofitel Hotel.

Mike and I got off the train, dazed, and must have looked like vulnerable tourists arriving at the Shanghai train station, where hustlers for the expensive cab ride circled us, barking out offers. They pretended to have a taxi, keys in hand, wanting you to agree to a price for them to escort you.

Mike tried to bargain, but after a few irritating confrontations, I spotted a hotel down the street. We escaped by walking a short distance across a couple of streets to a classy-looking hotel. We acted like we were hotel guests and got the doorman to put us into a cab. The cabs at the train station were asking ¥150. We paid ¥17, the fair rate, and I felt much safer as well.

Our loyal friend, Xi-fen, has been defending us from this hustle culture.

Again, we were so relieved to get out of the heat, and now the rain, too. We wanted to bathe, relax, and get away from all the people and noise. We ate at our hotel and watched the Asian version of CNN.

Shanghai

August 27, 1998

From my journal

We walked to the new Shanghai Art Museum, beautifully designed and impressive, a world-class museum. The shape was like the old bronze containers inside. The ancient bronze collection and the ceramics were fabulous. So many historic art objects were destroyed in the Cultural Revolution. On display were things uncovered after 1990. I bought postcards and jewelry as gifts. We weren't prepared for the pouring rain and had to run back to our hotel.

The evening was beautiful, clear, and not hot. We strolled down by the Bund and had dinner, looking at the beautiful lights around the harbor and across to the tower on the Pudong side. We checked out the Art Nouveau lobby of the Peace Hotel and admired the other historic buildings lining the water's edge. We talked about the old days, when the French and British ran this place, and the park sign that had said, "Dogs and Chinese Keep off the Grass."

August 28, 1998

From my journal

It was Mike's day to leave for the U.S. He had a 10:20 a.m. flight back through Narita, Japan, and then on to San Francisco. We took the hotel shuttle to the airport and got there in half an hour. Mike went to check in, and I waited for Xi-fen and Lu Ping. They arrived and waited with me for Mike to come back from checking in. Xi-fen and Lu Ping said a quick "goodbye" to Mike. She wanted to make sure he had his Great Wall wine. He promised to fax, write, and send me anything I needed. I had just enough time for a quick kiss and hug, and then I "demanded" all his money.

He'd paid his airport tax, and Chinese money is no good outside of China. He ran through the door to the airplane gate as the plane was now boarding. I think I am mentally prepared for this adventure. We have been married for thirty-seven years and have never been apart for three months.

As Lu Ping drove the two and a half hours back to Bell Economic School, Xi-fen slept, and I watched the scenery go by.

Bell School
Saturday, August 29, 1998, 9:00 a.m.
Fax from me to Mike
Dear Mike,
How was the flight? What do I need to know about managing the airport?

When I returned from seeing you off, I had a new, large mahogany desk. They delivered nightstands and a new, small round table and chair for my entry room on a "flatbed" of a bicycle. I lined my drawers with the gift wrap I bought at the Shanghai Museum. I can't decide if I should buy a bike. The traffic looks manageable at 6:00 a.m., but after that . . . ? I hope I can get used to the constant street noise, and I'm actually quite far from the street. See if you can send more Advil. I think I've figured out how to get to the Internet Café. Now, am I brave enough to get there on a bike?

My toilet broke this morning. I mopped the floor in all three rooms. What an exciting life!

Today we are supposed to see some "books" and tomorrow hear more about what students we will have.

I hid from mosquitoes all night but haven't seen one yet.

I know you'll enjoy Daddy's stories about China and this school.

FAX soon. It's a little cooler.

Love, Carolyn AKA Mom

Letters Back & Forth

Bell School

August 30, 1998

From my journal

It is Sunday, but you would never know it. China runs seven days a week, no rest, no religion, just push ahead with work. Xi-fen has gone to Nanjing today to smooth the waters for getting work visas for Don and Pam.

Xi-fen had her hair "fixed" last night. She went downtown on her bike to find a beauty shop. It took five shops before she found the right one. Many said, "Beauty Shop," and then were massage parlors. She was disgusted. She is relatively new to this city, as she has been living and teaching at a public school in Wuxi before working here with Mr. Chang.

Workers are working fast and furiously, getting this school ready for students. Parents and students will arrive tomorrow. The piles of weeds have finally been picked up from the central lawn area.

Our building is still dirty because there has been little cleanup at the construction site. The flushing mechanism on the brand-new toilet in my room doesn't work. My bathtub only has extremely hot water, not cold, so I run a bath and let the water cool. The countertops are beautiful marble. Mr. Chang is coming on the fifth of September, and all will be set straight.

California
August 31, 1998
Fax from Mike
Honey,
When getting on the plane, you need to have the little form for immigration. They are at the table to the right of the booths. I got stuck there and was almost the last guy on the plane. We were laid over for three hours at Narita—really boring. I slept after dinner, but my clock is still not running right.

Lynessa and the doggie, Muppet, are fine, but both were ready for company. Lynessa met me right away at SFO. She had a job interview in San Francisco, so I dropped her off there and drove home.

I sent you a package on Saturday. They have Global Express mail that takes five days, they say, and costs twenty dollars.

I called Linda and saw Gail. They are coming here for a Labor Day barbecue. I went by Bud's in San Mateo and showed him the pictures of the school.

We are getting along fine, but I miss you. Say, "Hi!" to your master teacher.

Love,
Mike

Lafayette, Ca

Tuesday, September 1, 1998

From my daughter, Lynessa

Hi Mom,

I hope everything is fine in China. Daddy and I developed the pictures, and the school looks great. Have classes started yet? What are your students like? How are the other teachers doing?

Picking up Daddy went fine. I had to have him drop me off in the city on the way home because I had an interview. The interview was for a computer school, not a very exciting job. The woman who was interviewing me was smacking gum the whole time—not very impressive. Daddy is recovering from four hours of dental work—and it's all still temporary.

I think you should definitely get a bike. Not that I know what it's like to ride a bike in China, but it would help you get around and explore stuff around the school. Plus, it's good exercise.

My friend Sarah, who stayed here last spring break, is in Santa Cruz, and I think she will come here to stay for a couple of days over Labor Day weekend.

I went to that Crayfish Party in San Francisco at the Swedish American Chamber of Commerce. It was given by some interns who work in the office. They are all brand new, so I told them that we should get together sometime. I think they are my age.

I interviewed at another place yesterday. I spent over three hours there. It was a really unusual organization. They do consulting with graphics to help companies work better on teams. They have some Swedish clientele, and that is why I got the interview. I spent two hours talking to the VP. There are only twenty people in the company, and then I talked to the woman who is the administrative assistant now. Although it is an AA job, it is only really straightforward administrative work for half a day, and then I would spend some hours in the afternoon helping with special projects. I really liked them. I kept liking them more and more, and who knows if I really have a shot? Anyway, it was an opportunity to learn about an unusual company in the Presidio.

Muppet is fine, but a little confused with Dad here and not you. She sleeps in my room and gets perplexed about what she should do afterward. I let her out in the morning. She is sleeping here on the floor right by me, waiting for some action. Maybe I'll take her for a walk before it gets too hot.

That's about it for my news. I hope everything is fine. Write back soon!

Love,

Lynessa

Bell School

Tuesday, September 1, 1998, 7:00 a.m.

Fax

Dear Mike and Lynessa,

Did you get my fax? Please fax back and answer my questions. How is everything at home? Is everything OK?

It's a little cooler here, but still just as hazy. Really awful weather. One day, for an hour from my room on the third floor, I saw the new bridge in the distance beyond Jiangyin.

I haven't been able to get a ride to the Internet Café. It's a problem. Tell people to fax, not email.

The electricity and water go on and off all day, sometimes regularly. It's difficult for the school, especially since the kitchen now has to feed the seven hundred kids plus staff, who all arrived yesterday.

Yesterday, we had neither hot nor cold water when all the parents arrived with their students. There were many in big, new cars and minivans. Students were on buses from the countryside, as some of them live far away. It looked like a younger college arrival with suitcases, quilts, and a few crying children among the preschoolers.

Within a few hours, the high schoolers had dinner, took showers, and hung out their wet clothes all in front of their rooms. They are responsible for doing their own laundry. The kindergarteners and first graders will be given a little basin and taught how to wash their faces, hands, and feet. Nurses will wash their clothes.

Today I have only two classes because half of the senior high school students are at military training this week. Next week, I'll have four classes a day. I walked over to the technical school and met the students. They were in their small wooden desks in straight rows. They are required to stand beside their desks when they respond to a question. This is what I will change when they come to my classroom in the English Center. Every day at ten, they do eye exercises.

They opened the new kitchen at the technical school. The food is fresh and better. As I walked by the preschool, I heard crying children again. They are only four years old, and I'm sure they miss their families.

I still haven't seen a phone. Xi-fen moved her office here to the English "Club," but she is isolated without a phone. She works so hard getting details done. The police chief visited yesterday to welcome us and check on our visas. He found a problem with mine, but we think it can be fixed with an extension here in Jiangyin. There are problems with Pam and Don's visas, but we knew that.

Please let me know what is going on at home. Lynessa, how is your job search? Please send faxes now. If it doesn't go through, wait a few hours. It means the electricity is off here. The fax machine, available to Xi-fen with her key, sits on a chair in a closet-sized room in the administration building.

Love, Mom

AKA Carolyn

Lafayette, California
Thursday, September 3, 1998
Fax from my daughter, Desiree
News from Mom! I will print out your fax and take it to Uncle Bud
this evening, so don't worry about that. Is there anyone else we
should send this to? It sounds pretty amazing.

Desiree

Jiangyin, China
Hi Desiree,
Well, I finally made it to the Internet Café. Amazingly, this small
city has this cafe. Paid internet access has just recently been
approved in China. I walked for one hour, not too bad, so if you
get this email, it will be a success. I didn't have the exact address in
Chinese, so I couldn't take a cab. I'll get someone to help me with
the address of the school and take a cab back. No one here speaks
English, but if I say Bell School enough times, they will figure out
where I'm from, and they will know the word taxi. The restroom
is unisex, with just a hole in the floor. It has porcelain where you
place your feet. The nearby buildings can see into the bathroom's
large glass walls, but it's China, so you can't worry about it. It
smells, so I try to avoid it.

Let me know you are receiving my faxes. My AOL account won't
work, so I will try out my new Yahoo address.

The subject of China is fascinating to me. I'm glad I have Xi-fen.
Of course, I'm only here because of Xi-fen. Jiangyin is considered
a countryside city. People stare at me, and I still haven't seen one
foreigner in town. I wore old clothes as a disguise to come here,
and they still stared. I reassure myself that the school is not like the
village in the *Secret Agent* TV show, and there will not be a giant ball
chasing me if I try to leave the grounds.

When I left the school campus, I had to walk beside the incredible, chaotic road in front of the school. It's worth your life to be on this road. Trucks, buses, some with chickens on top, cars, taxis, bikes, and scooters of every kind and description, all passing each other at the same time, "horning" as they overtake one another. They are building a new road at the same time, so there is huge equipment mixed in this chaotic scene.

I still haven't made up my mind whether I should buy a bike. It will get darker soon, and my free time will be after school.

Most of the teachers arrive by school bus about 7:00 a.m., and don't leave until 5:30 or 6:00 p.m. There is a two-hour lunch break at 11:30 a.m. Everyone eats in the cafeteria and then rushes to take a nap. The teachers who don't live here have beds somewhere on campus for this nap. Xi-fen takes a nap. She can't understand why I don't.

"Xi-fen, I just got up. I'm not tired at 11:30." I think I'm the only one here who doesn't nap.

This is an easy week for me. I only have ten classes and four groups, just half of my students. The high school students are well-behaved, and I am happy about the teaching situation. I'm glad to be an experienced teacher. The two teachers from Memphis have never taught and don't have any idea what to do. It's not Xi-fen's job to teach them, but she helps them a lot. They have no classroom management skills, and it's a problem. Their students are younger than mine.

I live on the third floor of the "English Club," just above where my classroom will be. Right now, I walk over to the students in the technical school building across this campus. That is where I will teach until we can get the club ready. I am taking over Xi-fen's students, so she can run the English Club, or English Center, as it really should be called. Xi-fen wants me to change my classroom, so the students do not stand by their desks and recite answers. I will have a different style of teaching. I will be teaching in a "Western manner." Xi-fen learned these methods while living with us and teaching at the junior high school in California.

Xi-fen is so frustrated. She says, "Our cleaning lady thinks she is too pretty to clean." She stands around in pretty dresses and mops a little with a dirty mop, no soap, and only cold water. She said she can't do windows because they are too high and too hard. Xi-fen's assistant, Susan, in our new English office near my classroom, sits at their desk and reads books. I don't see her doing anything else.

When Xi-fen told Susan to tell the cleaning lady to clean the bathroom near the office, Susan said, "Why should I care? I'm not going to use it."

It drives Xi-fen crazy. She is working so hard to get this all set up and is expected to teach classes as well. She showed me the lesson plans she must write out for every one of her classes. She has taught all these classes for years, but detailed, comprehensive plans are still required for each lesson. She is required to hand them in beforehand to a supervisor for approval for every class. I will not be required to write out this kind of lesson plan, thank goodness! Xi-fen would be the only one who could read them.

We are waiting for the arrival of Mr. Chang around September 9 or 10. He is the man Xi-fen worked closely with in building and planning this school. He is coming from Taiwan and is the only person who will do anything for her, the English Club, or foreign teachers. All the other bosses left for Taiwan, and so the school is in administrative chaos. It's funny to me, but horrible for Xi-fen. The weather is still hot, humid, and hazy, not good for photos. I'm hoping October will be better.

I am reading lots of books, but I would love letters or, better yet, faxes. Let me know what you are all up to. Note my new Yahoo email address—kcaroline[. . .], but I don't know how often I can get here. I still haven't seen a telephone.

Tomorrow is another day without electricity. The kitchen will have to feed over seven hundred, three meals a day. The water is still being turned off regularly, and no one knows why, so it's always a guess if we are going to have running water or power. We always have bottled water to drink.

I do miss you all, but this is a true adventure, a real cultural experience.

Love,

Mom, AKA Carolyn

Bell School

Friday, September 4, 1998

Fax from me

Dear Mike and Lynessa,

As expected, today we'll have no electricity. If we get hot water, I will wash my hair. Thank you for your faxes. Call Linda and see if they got my email yesterday, and ask if they could forward it to you. If they didn't, please tell me. I just received Linda's card.

Thank you for sending a package, Mike. I'll look for it. In the next package, could you send two jack-o-lantern "knives" from our kitchen drawer? I think we will do Halloween here.

Next week I will have twenty classes and eight groups, and I will still have to walk over to the technical school. The following week, I'll have my classroom here, directly underneath me on the second floor near the office. It will be easier, and I can decorate the classroom. We have no paper, large or colored, but their grammar books are OK. These students are Xi-fen's English learners and are far and away above the others, and they are not the highest-level class. Mr. Chang will bring special books from Taiwan for me to use so I can "teach in the Western way."

Xi-fen loved the "Hello" from Mike to my master teacher. She insisted she isn't my master teacher, but I insist she is!

Mr. Chang's arrival is unknown, and we all need money. Don and Pam should get food money, and I need my ticket money. Of course, I have traveler's checks, but I don't want to be stuck with yuan at the end of my stay. Mr. Chang is bringing our salaries, half in American dollars and half in yuan. We all may borrow from Xi-fen until he gets here.

I do now want to buy a bike because I figured out I could walk my bike to the roundabout. That takes about fifteen minutes, and I would be less worried about getting hit. Unless you have been here, you can't understand this traffic. Right, Mike?

Good luck with the job interviews, Lynessa. I'm glad Muppet and Bud are OK.

Love,
Mom

Bell School
Saturday, September 5, 1998, 8:30 a.m.
Fax to my daughter Lynessa
Dear Lynessa,
What is your email address? There is still no telephone here. Xi-fen may end up sending you three pages of fax today.

Is Daddy helping you work on the job situation? Is this Labor Day weekend? Have fun with your friend Sarah. I sent emails to Desiree, Michelle, and Linda. Did they get them? If so, Yahoo works. The desktop and keyboard on the computers in the Internet Café are in Chinese and English letters for pinyin and one word, Microsoft. I can get Yahoo by pressing the bottom key with the globe internet sign.

Today I'll cash a traveler's check in a bank in town without Xi-fen. Tomorrow, Xi-fen and I will buy a bike for me. I tell her that when I leave, she'll be a two-bike family. The all-new bike costs $40 plus locks.

The pollution here is terrible. It is combined with the hazy, humid weather and is never clear. When I can see into the distance, I see smokestacks pouring out black smoke. I think they are burning coal, and the steel industry is here, too. There is a leather tanning factory directly across the street from this school that I suspect is emitting noxious fumes that can't be good for children.

My upper-level students, Xi-fen's class, are especially nice. They march in and out of the room in lines.

We eat in the same place as the high school kids for dinner, but we go five minutes later, because it is so noisy. They all eat out of their own tin bowls. Last night at dinner, as the sun was dropping, I saw bats diving for insects.

Please give Muppet a hug.

XXX to you.

Love,

Mom

Bell School

Saturday, September 5, 9:00 a.m.

Fax to Mike, same day

Dear Mike,

Thank you for the fax. I was anxious to hear from you. The package isn't here yet. I'll keep track of when it arrives. Linda's card took nine days, not bad. Can you find out Gail and Axel's email for me? Maybe it will just be better to send things as a small package—it's a little cheaper.

I'm very excited about decorating my classroom. I'm so glad I brought the large maps. My map of the world has the U.S. in the center. Chinese maps have China in the center. I am going in search of some materials, like large paper and pens, etc. I think my new classroom will be fun. The students are well behaved and regimented. They all stand to speak. I'm working on an "American classroom," where they will just raise their hands. I will put their desks in a semi-circle. In some classes, I have twenty-six students, and in one class, I have forty.

Xi-fen is excited because her new apartment is supposed to be finished, and we can ride bikes out to see it. The politics here at school are a mess. Since the head of the board, we met him when you were here, left for Taiwan, there are only his relatives in charge. Xi-fen tells me they are incompetent. People here thought people from Taiwan should be more "Western" and not do the old Chinese way of hiring relatives but hire people for their competence. Complaints are that the cafeteria gives out different amounts of food to different people for the same money, the electricity and water go on and off, no one leads, no one decides, and everyone feels they are guarded.

XXX I miss you,

Love,

Carolyn

Lafayette, California

Monday, September 7, 1998

Fax from Lynessa at home

My friends did a group fax at the party on Labor Day, each telling me their news.

Gail and Axel, Linda and Frank, Desiree and Mike.

My dog Muppet put her paw print on the fax.

Hi Mom,

I hope all is going well in China. We love all your letters describing the details about getting the school together. How are your students? What are you teaching them? How is their English? What do they think of you?

Things are going well here. I got the job! The interview that I wrote you about went really well. This week will be a trial week to see if they like me, and I like them. It will be quite a commute to the Presidio, but maybe I can save up some money to move to SF in a few months. Desiree helped me get some new clothes for the job. I think it is going to be cold working in this Victorian house in the Presidio.

Daddy did most of the cooking for our barbecue today, but I think he liked that.

I was busy this weekend going to Golden Gate Park, seeing friends here from Oregon.

Write soon! And tell us what it is like there. Bud says hello and to tell you that he loves you.

Love, Lynessa

Monday, September 7, 1998

Fax to my uncle

Dear Bud,

I hope everything is OK in San Mateo. This is quite an experience. I guess Mike showed you the pictures, but what you didn't see is inside. There are so many things that would never pass building code standards. The faucets are the worst, and I still don't get hot water in my bathroom sink, only hot water in the tub. The shower pulses scalding water, so I only take baths by cooling the water first. Remember, this is all new. Thank goodness for the air conditioner in my room. I can escape the heat and be cool. Only the foreign teachers, three of us, have A/C; no one else. They know foreigners would not put up with how the Chinese have to live. The Chinese teachers do not have air-conditioning or heat in their rooms in the winter.

I taught three classes this morning and have two more this afternoon, one of my "big" days so far. Yesterday, Sunday, Xi-fen and I bought a new bike for me. It is metallic red, with a basket, a bell for "overtaking," and two major locks for front and back. The total cost was $43 U.S. We rode home with our baskets full of groceries from the outdoor market. We each strapped a box of fruit, one apple and one pear, on our bikes. It's amazing how much you can load on a bike.

I talked Xi-fen out of buying a live dove. She wanted to cook it for us in the illegal kitchen in her room. She wanted this bird because "It is good for my health." We will come back here again to take photos. Xi-fen said most of the food at the school is purchased at this local market.

The food here is quite good and healthy. There are lots of cooked fresh vegetables and occasionally a meat dish, sometimes strange meat, and of course, all the rice you can eat.

My students are awfully nice. They are so regimented that discipline is not a problem. They seem fascinated with me. I had the new, young high school group today. They are excited about me. When I walk or ride my bike somewhere, I practically cause accidents with people staring at me.

We still haven't seen any foreigners. There must be some working on this bridge. When it's completed next year, it will be the fourth-longest suspension bridge in the world. It looks like our Golden Gate Bridge in San Francisco.

Yesterday, we had a hint of a blue sky, and today, a little blue as well. There is a fog-haze here early in the morning. I can't see five hundred feet in the distance. The haze lifts as the day goes on, and now we have sun. The moon is usually behind haze as well. It's still hot but not as bad. Air pollution is a problem too—even on a bike.

I'll go tomorrow to the Internet Café and try to get more letters out.

Xi-fen and I will have next weekend off, so we'll go back to Wuxi (woo-she) and meet her brother. I hope to take a boat trip on the Grand Canal.

I'm soon going to decorate my own classroom downstairs from where I live. I'm so glad I brought large world maps and posters with me. I want the classroom to look like an American classroom, but there are few materials here. I did find some large chart paper and colored pens in town yesterday so that I can set up a class calendar. The students are not very worldly. I'm going to hang my large poster of Venice to see if someone can guess where it is. I'm not sure anyone will know. It's the "Bridge of Sighs" in Venice.

When the weather gets a little better, I can explore the countryside on my bike. I think I can ride to the Yangtze River because I can see the bridge in the hazy distance from this third floor.

I miss you and hope you are doing well. I wish I could solve the phone problem. I still haven't seen one here. I put a six-dollar phone card in a phone in town yesterday. I did get Mike, but the connection was bad. I'll try to call you next weekend.

Love,

Carolyn

Bell School

Thursday, September 10, 1998

Dear Lynessa,

Thanks for the long letter. Congratulations! I do hope you like your new job. I'll be thinking of you. Tomorrow I'll go and check my email. The Internet Café is difficult to get to.

Love,

Mom

Dear Mike,

Thank you very much for the faxes. I loved hearing from everyone, but I want to hear more from you.

The package you sent took nine days. You didn't send it Global Express unless you sent a package I haven't gotten?

Thank you. We are all poring through the magazines. I need more Post-its and 3 × 5 cards. When you send magazines, also send two pumpkin-carving knives from our kitchen drawer.

You have the negatives for the photos I took while you were here. Remember, I told you they are in the red ball boxes—our gifts from Guilin. I'll send you an email tomorrow.

We are all anxiously awaiting the arrival of Mr. Chang. We all need money, a telephone, and about one hundred other things.

I'm setting up my classroom downstairs. I'll walk the students from the technical school over here on Monday.

I got a beautiful card because today is China's Teacher Day.

Fax me more!

Love,

Carolyn

Jiangyin, Internet Café

Thursday, September 10, 1998

Dear Family and Friends,

Another eventful week in China has passed. We woke up with no electricity again, and now we have no water. Don, one of the other teachers, said when he saw the front fountain go on, he thought we might lose our water. We have had two weeks of school, so all the students, seven hundred of them, go home today at 1:00 p.m. for the weekend. The preschoolers have finally stopped crying, and now buses and cars are lined up to pick up students. Many students live some distance away in the countryside.

I have a full load of students this week—over two hundred high schoolers in eight groups with twenty, forty-five-minute classes a week. It's not bad, actually. The students are so regimented that they are easy to teach. Xi-fen says they are "duck fed." I am supposed to break them out of this mold and get them to think and speak English. There are some adorable students. The level one group has never had a "foreign teacher," and they treat me like a rock star, crowding around just to look at me. They are hoping I will say something in English— pressing food into my hands and asking me if I love them! They squeal and giggle. One student asked me in class, "Do you love me?"

"Yes, I love you," I said. Nothing else would do.

I walked them over today from the technical school and had them sit in a semi-circle in small wooden desks around the room, alternating boys and girls in the seating. They don't talk among themselves. When I mentioned to Xi-fen how unusual it was that they didn't speak to each other, she explained that boys and girls are not allowed to communicate. They are shy and quiet around the opposite sex. It makes teaching easier.

Yesterday was "Teacher's Day." My students gave me a beautiful card. The school canceled afternoon classes, and we had an "activity." Xi-fen and I went with the high school teachers and their wives in a school bus to a "Fruit Bar" in Jiangyin.

Translated, the bar is called "Meeting You at Midnight." The owner is related to someone at the school. It was newly decorated and played the most bizarre videos I had ever seen. We also did "Kara OK." That is what the Chinese call it. They love it. We were sitting upstairs in the bar, singing Chinese songs. They found Red River Valley for me, in Chinese, of course. The video with this song showed low-growing edelweiss flowers, at a low altitude in Lake Tahoe. It was better than the video downstairs that featured edelweiss with Amsterdam, blonds, and boats. They had jingle bells, I guess from an Australian Christmas point of view, with "horse" spelled four different ways in the same song, but they sang enthusiastically. Some of this was in English, sort of.

They carefully served me "wine." It looked like a Black Russian drink. When I smelled it—it was a Black Russian, well, sort of. I didn't drink it. They made Xi-fen a bright green drink with a red cherry and sugar around the edges of a long-stemmed martini glass. The stir sticks were clowns and teddy bears. It was a thoughtfully done party.

Last Sunday, Xi-fen and I bought my bike at a department store in town. Purchasing the bike and shopping took all day. On the way home, we decided to buy fruit in the local outdoor market. We stopped in front of a fruit vendor. Smiling, he looked at me and asked Xi-fen where I was from. She told him I was a foreign teacher.

"How much money does she make? Is she rich?" he asked Xi-fen in Chinese.

These questions are part of Chinese culture, but to Xi-fen, they are rude. She wouldn't tell him anything, but we bought a box of pears and a box of apples, which we strapped onto the backs of our bikes.

We were now loaded with our groceries, the fruit, and chart paper, and we went deeper into the outdoor market. I wanted to see where the live chickens were coming from. Xi-fen decided she wanted to buy a live dove in a large cage with other doves. She wanted to cook it in her dorm room. She has an illegal kitchen.

"With ginger and green onion," because, she said, "I need it for my health." I talked her out of it by convincing her that she didn't have time, and I really wasn't hungry anyway. It was a close call for that little bird.

While she was negotiating the almost sale, I looked up and realized that two feet above the chickens and birds were canopied beds—six of them draped with old, faded cloth. As we rode home, Xi-fen told me that these people were the "floating population," doing jobs no one wanted to do. They have to sleep with the chickens and birds to guard them. If you bring your watermelons in from the country, you sleep with your watermelons. The cloth around the beds was for mosquito protection. I don't know what they do in the winter.

I read at night. There is no TV. This weekend, Xi-fen and I will go back to Wuxi to shop. I will have to borrow money from her since Mr. Chang has not come from Taiwan yet to pay us. They are "adjusting" my passport, and I can't cash traveler's checks without it.

We are all anxiously awaiting the arrival of the infamous Mr. Chang. We all need him for money, and a telephone downstairs, and he is going to adjust all the problems in the school. Mr. Chang is also bringing books for my classes. Visa is unknown in our town of Jiangyin. There is hope that I might be able to use a Visa card in Wuxi.

We are poring over the magazines you sent, Mike. Thank you. I need more Post-its and 3 × 5 cards. I love getting all the faxes from friends.

The school politics are very complicated . . . but that's another letter.

Love, Carolyn

Jiangyin
Friday, September 11, 1998
Fax to my substitute teacher in Concord
Dear Charlene,
Our China tour was great, but it was definitely good to have my friend Xi-fen with us.

The school is fine. I have over two hundred high school students, eight groups, and twenty classes a week. The teaching is a pleasure. I am setting up a new English classroom of my own here in the new English building. I live on the third floor, and my classroom is on the second floor.

I need your help. Could you go to the educational supply store on Clayton Road and get me a set of the alphabet for above the chalkboard? I need it for the high school, so the animal one we have in C-19 would be great—nothing too "babyish."

If possible, I would also like two packages of the international flag trim we have in C-19. You would have to fold some of this, wrap it, and send it as a small package at the regular post office. I will have to pay you later. Save the receipts. We have very few materials, no colored paper.

I would really appreciate this. The fax here is 011-510 […]

Hello to everyone! I'll write more soon.

Carolyn

Lafayette
Sunday, September 13, 1998
Fax to China from Lynessa
Hi Mom!

I was nice to talk to you last night. I hope all is well and that you get your money soon. How is riding your bike? How are your students? Do they just wait for you to teach them rather than participate?

Your volunteer, Larry, called today and wondered how you were doing. I told him what I knew. He said that your ESL class in Concord was starting this week. I told him that you would probably communicate with the school somehow to let your class know how you are doing. I am sure they are curious.

My job at the Presidio is now permanent. That last week was really a trial week, but it seemed to be working out for everyone by the second day, so I'm not surprised. So far, the job has been a little boring, but unusual, as I got to work on chalking a poster for them. I can't wait for my first paycheck. The commute is a hassle, so tomorrow I'm driving again. On Tuesday, I think I'll take BART and then two buses. I heard on the news that they are opening up apartments on the Presidio for students as low-cost housing. At work, they said that this was available to people who worked in the Presidio as well. I'm going to check it out some more.

Well, write again soon with more info about the school and your classes.

Love,

Lynessa

Lafayette

September 13, 1998

Fax to China from Mike

Dear Carolyn,

We are having another hot weekend, but we should have cooler weather in the middle of this week.

The media is full of the Ken Starr report to Congress. He has finally gotten to say bad words in public. I just can't bear to hear it or read it. You are lucky to be missing this.

I'm about to send another package—pumpkin knives included. It will be Global mail. Tell us about more things you need. How about books?

Our Labor Day party was a big success. It was so hot we ate inside. The food got raves; they even ate a lot of watermelon. Gail and Linda are talking about going to Greece and meeting up with your art history teacher, Ann.

I was in trial last week. I used it to push around some other appearances, so maybe I won't spend all of September in trial. I am trying to be careful about choosing new cases. The old clients seem to be able to get into more trouble, so the work goes on.

I got my dental work completed. I spent a lot of time this weekend on my hand exercises for my wrist. I still don't have full movement. Lynessa watches me lift your weights that I found in the garage.

We seem to have the house under control. I have stepped in to help with watering the garden. Lynessa is cleaning regularly. I get my washing machine lesson tonight.

Missing you.

Love,

Mike

Chapter **9**

The Little Emperor

Bell School

From my journal

Lunch time in the cafeteria is always hurried. The students have hot soup for a liquid, no milk, and a rice or noodle dish. I avoid the chewy chicken feet. They are a norm in the soup. My students in California love them, but they are not my favorite. The teachers and students have scurried away to take their naps. I am never tired at 11:30 a.m. A man with a "fire hose" has begun to wash down the entire room.

The Little Emperor, what an only child is called, is five, four in the Western world. He has been dawdling with his food again today, so his "auntie" sat him on a table top. She directs the cooking, and when she's finished, she spoon-feeds him, wearing her waterproof apron and black galoshes that she wore to clean up the cafeteria. He eats after the other 470 elementary school children are fed and gone. Auntie occasionally has to play games to coax him into eating. He'd rather walk on benches and crawl on the long tables, smiling and laughing at the adults finishing their meal. She plays airplane with the spoon, shoving the soup or rice into his mouth quickly before he has a chance to say no.

He's a cute little guy with rare curly black hair and an impish grin. His dark brown eyes sparkle when he laughs. He's dressed in the regular preschool uniform of soft cotton printed pants, with a long matching jacket. The print looks like an American quilt design of teddy bears and hearts in red, white, and blue. He's learning English in preschool and loves to smile and yell, "Hello," to anyone who looks western.

His name is Leo, his family name is Liu, and the Chinese name for the number six. In China, six means "everything will go smoothly," a lucky number. His father is the principal of the school and one of the Chinese owners. Mr. Liu, also known as Mr. Six, is named for being the sixth born in his family. Mr. Liu now rules the school and is the "Emperor."

The Liu family lives in the most luxurious home in the city of Jiangyin. The three-story home is surrounded by gardens, fountains, night lights, and a concrete wall. They have cooks, drivers, and house servants to care for the families' needs. Leo has a room at home, but lives with Auntie at her house while the other preschoolers are boarded at Bell School. Many Chinese children sleep with their grandmothers. Leo sleeps with his auntie. She brings him back and forth to school each day. She pampers him with love and attention that boarding preschoolers don't get. He is the only student allowed to leave campus.

Auntie was employed as a nursemaid by this family a few years ago. It worked out so well they decided to give her the high-paying job of running the school cafeteria. She cooks, cleans, and takes care of Leo when his classes are over.

Leo's mother and father are factory owners and are becoming wealthy. Schools in China are owned by factories. Mr. Six owns eight printing factories that print labels for cigarettes and wine. He is an important businessman with factories all over China. He has little time to manage Bell School, which includes grades from preschool to high school and all the employees.

The Chinese gossip goes like this . . .

Leo's parents met a few years ago in one of these factories before the government decided to privatize them and let Mr. Six manage them. Mr. Six was a married man when he and Leo's mother began having an affair. They both had a child. Mr. Six's wife suspected and followed them to a rendezvous where she confronted them. Six months later, the wife died. People say that she died of a broken heart, but it was actually cancer.

The loving couple married. Since they both had children from previous marriages, the "one child policy" was in effect, and neither was allowed to have a second child. They had one anyway. When Leo was conceived, his parents kept it a secret. During her pregnancy, Leo's mother hid out with relatives in Shanghai. After Leo was born, they paid the large required fine that few can afford.

After the couple married, they moved into Mr. Six's home. Leo's mother was haunted by the spirit of the dead wife. She tried every Chinese method to exorcise the house of dead spirits to no avail and insisted that Mr. Six build them a home of their own.

Mrs. Six runs the house, servants, and owns a large department store in town. Mr. and Mrs. Six travel extensively. They have been all over the world. Mrs. Six loves to shop, so Leo has clothes and toys fit for "the little Emperor" that he is. Leo is not technically an only child, since he has older siblings, but he is a part of the new generation of "China's Little Emperors." He is doted on by his entire family.

Jiangyin

Wednesday, September 16, 1998, Evening

Internet Café

Dear Lynessa and Mike,

I gave Xi-fen a fax for you today because I didn't expect to get in here tonight. Don and I came in by cab to get groceries and then came here.

To hail a cab, we go out to the dusty road in front of the school, stand, and extend an arm with a limp wrist. It's kind of funny. I have made 3 × 5 cards with Chinese writing on them, listing different places I want to visit in town. Xi-fen wrote out the places in Chinese; the Internet Café, the grocery store, the Kodak store across town, the town center, and Bell School. Now I just have to show the cab driver the card, I know how much it should cost, and I am set.

My feet are killing me. I know it's the tile floors everywhere, and being on my feet four hours at a time. I've got to figure out a way to sit down some. I have twenty-two classes this week and eighteen next week because they changed the schedule, so we could get off next Friday.

Xi-fen and I will go to Hangzhou the first week in October. It's National Day, and we will have four days off. This is the only vacation I will have. We plan to go by boat overnight on Lake Taihu, then spend two nights in a hotel, and return by boat. The train ride takes six hours from Wuxi, which is an hour from here, so this way we save time and money. I do hope the boat is safe.

The route through Lake Taihu is part of the Grand Canal System, which started in 500 BC and has been improved and lengthened ever since. These hand-dug waterways, going north and south, have been needed since ancient times to connect China's largest rivers that run west to east. Lake Taihu is used as part of this canal system that starts in Beijing and ends in Hangzhou.

Mike should sign up for Yahoo email. I wasn't sure if this would get on the fax I sent. Your last fax ended with "the little gifts." Did you give Linda her birthday present? I got an email from her. Mike, are you able to figure out Quicken? I sure hope so. If you can't—just enter everything and don't reconcile anything.

Today is cooler. Don and I are thrilled. Xi-fen has announced that she is cold. The air is better, too. Maybe now I can take some pictures.

Don is easy to get along with, nice to talk to, and do things with. Pam is difficult. She is moody and still wears sloppy old clothes. She isn't doing well with her teaching either. Last week, she said she yelled "shut up" to her class. I told her that was not a good idea. This week she bought a whistle to use in the classroom. She has a real chip on her shoulder about her master's degree, but it doesn't help her in the classroom. Don can't stand her, but he is mellow and casual and hides his feelings so they can get along. They will be together for the school year. They both teach in another building, so I don't have much class contact with them.

Last week was Pam's birthday. I went into town and bought her a birthday present from all of us, and then at the end of the week, I went into town and bought her a birthday cake. Xi-fen, Don, and I had a little party for her with the gift, cake, card, candles, and wine.

She never said thank you, or even good night, when she went to her room. She said she had not had a party since she was eight. Hearing this, I tolerate her now but don't really care to include her in anything I don't have to. She has no social awareness or common courtesy. She is weird and moody.

This weekend, Don and I are going on a bike ride with a Chinese girl we met. She speaks English and wants to be friends with us. We are going over to the new bridge and perhaps meet an engineer friend of hers from England who is working on the bridge.

I hope this will open some doors for Don as far as friends go. Both he and Xi-fen worry about what they will do when I leave, still three months away. I need to expand my world on the bike.

Mike, take it easy with the work. Please pace yourself. We are anxiously awaiting news and magazines.

I need my "conversation cards." They are in the office with a rubber band around them. I need the easy ones, "Put up ten fingers," and the difficult ones, "What food do you like?" If you can't find them, please send four packs of index cards. I would love about fifteen plain manila file folders. There is no such thing in China. They have no file cabinets, just storage chests, newer versions of old Chinese furniture.

Don has declared Mr. Chang a "mythical character." We've all borrowed money from each other, and now I've borrowed ¥1,000 from Xi-fen. I don't want to have extra Chinese money at the end of my stay.

Love,

Carolyn

Bell School

September 17, 1998

Fax to home

Hi friends,

Last night, Don and I went into town to the "City Hunter Club." On Wednesday nights, young people meet in this bar to practice their English. This group calls itself "The English Corner." They are young adults with various levels of English, all working to pass their next level English test, the TOEFL test, a test of English as a foreign language. It is used to assess the English language proficiency of non-native speakers. The group is friendly and wants to chat. Don and I each order a glass of wine, but no one else drinks. It might be expensive for them, and many people here do not drink.

We met a new friend, Yang Li Ping. She has invited us to go on a bike ride with her and a friend, Ms. Fay, this Saturday at ten o'clock. She wants us to meet another friend, an engineer, Nagi, who works on the bridge. She says he is from England. We may ride over to the new bridge.

I think I need to practice on my bike, as she is talking about going long distances.

Lafayette
September 17, 1998
Fax from Mike
Dear Carolyn,

I had a court appearance in San Francisco on Wednesday night and an appearance in Redwood City Thursday morning, so I went over to San Mateo and stayed with Bud. He is getting around OK and has prepared breakfast for me. We watched TV and chatted for an hour before bed. He is wrapped up in the Clinton proceedings. He keeps the news on the radio all night. The girls have been good about calling and seeing him.

The papers here finally have the admissions from China that the Yangtze River floods this summer were caused by overlogging near the headwaters. The papers say the cost of the hydroelectric losses would more than pay for reforestation. China had better get green.

What temperature did it take to have Xi-fen declare it was cold? I hope that won't require any doves. Has the Chinese engineer whom we met at the Internet Café called on you? He might like to make friends with Don.

We got a letter from Nicoletta in Italy. I'm sorry to hear about her sister Louisa dying of MS. Please tell her how sorry we all are when you write to her.

I am concerned about you not being paid. Did you get money in Wuxi? Are the other teachers getting a handle on their classes? I'm sure they are not a "love-God like you"—a crane among chickens.

I'm getting the photos developed. I put your tiles out for people to see on Labor Day, and everyone thought they were quite marvelous. Tell me again who gets what gifts.

It is interesting that the people I talk to about the household situation observe that Lynessa must be taking care of me, while those she talks to think I am taking care of her. We are doing a good job of taking care of each other. Muppet is happy, but she is still looking for you.

September 18, 1998

Mike's fax continued. With more household issues he was taking care of . . .

I am signing up for Yahoo and canceling AOL.

Lynessa and her friend Katie, who is attending San Francisco State and qualifies for Presidio housing, are looking at getting into the Presidio housing program. This weekend, they moved the first tenants into the refurbished military housing.

Watering has its rewards. We are now eating our own tomatoes. The plants seem to be thriving—in and out. Lynessa is doing a good job with the housekeeping. I am doing most of the cooking since I usually beat her home.

Love Always,

Mike

Chapter 10

New Friends

Jiangyin

Saturday, September 19, 1998

Email

At 10:00 a.m., Don and I met our new friend, Yang Li-ping, from the "City Hunter Club," and her friend Ms. Fay for a bike ride. We met in town and then rode to a Confucius temple here in town. I will go back there, as it is a busy place with a bird, flower, and goldfish market around the temple. There were small rooms off the main temple, where private instrumental music was being taught to children.

We bought food for lunch at a small shop, then rode quite a distance out to a Buddhist temple on the top of a hill overlooking the Yangtze River. It was not clear, but I could see a ferry dock and some large ships lining the river's edge. Jiangyin is known as a shipbuilding center.

Ms. Fay is married and speaks excellent English. While we were eating lunch, I talked to her about her job and her family. The subject of the one-child policy came up. She told me that you cannot just decide for yourself when to have your one child. In each factory (a school is considered a "factory"), there is a person who carries out the government's decision on how many children can be born in that factory that year. If you miscarry, you must wait until it is your turn again. That person in charge is also responsible for seeing that women are using birth control. The workers are closely monitored. What we didn't talk about were forced abortions, which I know happen. Chinese families love children, so this is a huge sacrifice made by the Chinese people.

Yang Li-ping called her engineer friend, and we rode across town toward the new bridge to meet Naji George. I was surprised when we met because I didn't expect someone named Naji to be so decidedly English, with a British accent. He explained that his mother was Arab, thus his name. He works as a consulting engineer, traveling around the world for various projects. He goes back and forth to England every three months. He rode with us onto the new suspension bridge. I have been looking at this bridge in the haze from my room and was anxious to see it. It will be completed next year, 1999. It's an essential north-south link to get from Shanghai to Beijing. Now, people, cars, buses, and trucks have to take a ferry across the Yangtze or drive 150 miles out of their way.

We still have the same cleaning lady—"too pretty to clean." Mr. Chang still hasn't shown up, and life goes on at school.

There is a lot to be said about living above your classroom. I begin at 7:30 a.m. and only have to go downstairs. My classes take a lot of energy. Xi-fen wants lots of activities—all kinds of role-playing and learning games. My job is to make learning fun. Last week, I had twenty-two classes. I am a major celebrity to a couple of classes, especially with the girls. They want me to teach them to dance, they have all taken my autograph, and yesterday, they touched my hair and face. They also ask me about my jewelry. They are fascinated with me. They are awfully cute, with lots of personality, and are willing to try their limited English. I do have some boys who act up in some classes, but I manage to cope with them. I'm glad I'm experienced.

I'm excited about the emails and faxes you send, so please send more. Remember, I have no TV, radio, phone, newspapers, or magazines. So let me hear from you.

Love to all,

Carolyn

Lafayette

Sunday, September 20, 1998

Fax from Mike

Dear Carolyn,

I have located the cards you want and will send them from Martinez on Monday morning. The package will include the index cards, news magazines, and the pumpkin knives.

I am doing my second and third loads of laundry. Boy, that stuff does pile up. I am still getting a lot of washing machine guidance from Lynessa, who has now entrusted me to wash some of her stuff with mine.

My court appearance for the Wilson case was on TV. I ducked the TV cameras, but the *Contra Costa Times* and *SF Chronicle* have me saying wise things.

You will see from that the stock market is bouncing like a ball. Tomorrow, they are releasing the tape of Clinton's Grand Jury testimony. The media has gone nuts, and all pretense that there is going to be a non-partisan handling of the business is gone.

Love you always,

Mike

Lafayette
Sunday, September 20, 1998
Fax from Lynessa,
Hi Mom!
I hope everything is going OK. This will be a short letter. I am sending
you a letter from Kathleen and a new letter from Dad. (Lynessa filled
me in on how her life was going and news from her host family in
Sweden.)

I'm getting up at 4:45 a.m. tomorrow because I'm taking BART
and the buses. It's a two-hour commute.

I'm trying to convince Daddy to sign up for Yahoo.

Write soon.

Love,

Lynessa

Jiangyin
Monday, September 21, 1998
Email home
Dear Mike and Lynessa,
In Wuxi, we went shopping and to Xi-fen's parents' apartment for
dinner on Saturday night. I slept in her apartment and this time
remembered to bring my flashlight to light the six flights of stairs to
get to it. In the morning, she cleaned everything in sight until noon;
this is a tiny apartment, but it is clean and neat.

I wanted to call home, and it was getting past the time!! I did get
to make my two-minute call to you.

We then went from bank to bank to get what she said were checks
cashed. I finally figured out she meant CDs, so she could put her
money together for her new apartment near the school. It will cost
¥90,000, but that is only for the shell. She must add the electrical,
plumbing, kitchen cabinets, appliances, and everything to finish it.

She gets very nervous and flustered about money. It is hard for a single person in China.

We then proceeded to the department store at 3:30 p.m. to buy a TV. This took two hours, and her brother had already told her what to buy. I discouraged her from buying the microwave oven that day. It was getting dark, and I was afraid it would just take too long. This was exhausting—hot and humid, remember? We forced the TV into a small taxi and got it back to her dorm room here at school forty-five minutes later.

Don helped her install it in her room.

Love,

Carolyn

Jiangyin

Wednesday, September 23, 1998

To my students in Concord

Dear Charlene and students,

Thank you so much for your email. I was so happy to hear all your comments. Kuo Hao does have a beautiful hometown, Guilin, but it was very, very hot—even at night. Yes, Chun Pou, the Terra Cotta Warriors were spectacular. The whole archaeological site was huge and truly amazing. It will be several lifetimes before they uncover all the warriors.

I will send you photos of the school. It is fancy on the outside. It looks like a country club, but there are many problems on the inside. We never know if we are going to have water, maybe no water, maybe no electricity, or maybe no hot water. We always have bottled water to drink. We have a kitchen, but I don't cook much here. We have two cafeterias—with Chinese food, of course. Most of the time it is pretty good with lots of vegetables and rice.

Last weekend, I went with some new Chinese friends on a long bike ride out to the new bridge they are building. When finished, it will be the fourth longest suspension bridge in the world. Right now, the fourth longest is the one to the new Hong Kong Airport. This one looks like the Golden Gate Bridge. I met a British engineer, who is working on the bridge. There are very few foreigners in this city.

People stare at me and nearly fall off their bicycles. Children stare—and my students act as if I am a movie star. They crowd around me, give me food, take my autograph, want to touch my hair and face. Tonight, they are disappointed because they wanted me to teach them how to dance. Instead, I came to the Internet Café to write to you.

Next week is National Day, and I will take a trip. So I will tell you about it in the next email. I am very careful on my bike because the traffic is crazy.

Hello to all,

Your teacher in China,

Carolyn

Bell School

Wednesday, September 23, 1998

Fax to my family

We all met again last night with a group called "the English Corner." It meets every Wednesday at the City Hunter Club. The name for this "hole in a wall bar" was never explained, just a small neon sign on the wall with that name.

Tonight, there were about twenty young Chinese people in their twenties and only three foreigners: Don, Nagi, and me. Xi-fen came, too. I was glad Xi-fen could meet Nagi. She was curious to see where the infamous teacher Rachael used to hang out. I'm not sure why Rachael is considered infamous. I think she was just one of the first foreign teachers at Bell School.

Lafayette
Wednesday, September 21, 1998
Fax from Mike
Dear Carolyn,

I finally got off your Global Express. The whole notion of sending a package to China and maybe just the concept of Global Express proved too much for the least busy post office in Martinez. I easily handled it at Pleasant Hill. You will get right up to the latest muck on the Clinton thing.

Yesterday, while walking Muppet, I saw the big stag alone down in the canyon. The "For Sale" sign is still there.

Lynessa is over at Desiree's in Millbrae tonight. I guess the drive is easier going that way to work.

Muppet is pouting. It smells like skunk outside, and she is sure she missed something.

Love always,
Mike

Jiangyin
September 24, 1998
Email to Lynessa
Hi Ness,

Thanks for the fax from September 20 and the email. I am using Netscape Communicator at the Internet Café, and I like it. I will look up the news after I finish with all the emails home. Sometimes Xi-fen is too busy to send my faxes off that day, and sometimes she forgets to give me my faxes.

The Presidio housing sounds good. Katie sounds like a great roommate. Please check it out for safety.

I have a new way for you to call me. Xi-fen now has a phone in her office. I can't call out, but you can call me. The number is 011 86 […], then wait for all the Chinese to stop. It's a menu, then dial her extension, 8042. This phone sits on her desk in the English Center office on the floor just below me. Could you or Daddy call me Saturday night, 5:00-6:00 p.m.? I will wait in the office between 8:00-9:00 a.m. Sunday morning. This may or may not work. If it doesn't work, I will call you when I can.

Yes, I'm still a celebrity, at least to a couple of classes. They want me to teach them to dance.

I am here at the Internet Café with Don. We will now walk to McDonald's for dinner. You can tell I'm desperate. It's the only place we can eat in town. We just point to a picture to order. No one speaks English there. They have a clean bathroom, hard to find here. Then we'll come back to send more emails.

I miss you.

Love,

Mom

Jiangyin

Thursday, September 24, 1999

Dear Mike,

Thank you for the long fax. Now that Xi-fen has an office phone, I hope you and Lynessa can call me. I sent her directions on how to do it. If you call another time, you might just happen to find her in her office.

I hope to have a conversation with you. I miss you and wish you were here to experience this with me. Remember, Xi-fen says you can always come back. You could give lectures here on the laws in America.

I think Xi-fen gets cold at about 70 degrees. Now she is washing all her quilts. I have some quilts picked out in a store for myself, but

I want to wait until I get paid by Mr. Chang, the mythical character. He can't possibly be as good as his buildup.

I found another photo development place here, way across town. It has a new machine and much better development. I have a good picture of you with Lu Ping, our driver, and you in the garden of the "Humble Administrator" in Suzhou. I am taking photos of friends here. They do not have cameras or photos of themselves, so it's a way I can say thank you for things they do for me.

I didn't get money in Wuxi, I borrowed from Xi-fen, but I did cash another traveler's check here in town. I am living very cheaply. A yuan is about eight cents. Breakfast is about six yuan in the groceries I buy, lunch is two yuan, and I only eat two dishes for dinner, so it is only two yuan. It's pretty cheap. Xi-fen makes us rice porridge on Sunday nights when the cafeteria is closed. Tonight, I splurged with a fish burger here in town at McDonald's. I got the whole meal for ¥19.70, which is expensive for people who live here.

Mr. Chang had better show up before National Day next week. Xi-fen and I want to go on our trip to Hangzhou on Wednesday night. It doesn't say in my contract WHEN anything will be paid.

I have looked in every little shop in town and can't find anything to cushion my shoes. Could you send some Dr. Scholl's insoles like I wear in my shoes? Please, my feet are killing me. I brought some for each pair of shoes, but they have worn out! I don't want the thick ones in the closet. I need the thin ones that come three pairs in a package on sale at Longs, ladies' large. They would fit flat in a magazine. We are news-starved.

Last week, we had some people from Ireland visit the school. Xi-fen was told minutes before they arrived. She and Mr. Seven, brother of Mr. Six, who runs this school but isn't here, are the only people who can speak English, so they both met them. The next day, two more Irish people arrived. I guess one group was looking for exchange possibilities for their private school and college in Dublin, and the other was looking for places to put Irish investments. You and I saw the Irish Prime Minister on TV in Beijing, and I just saw him again on Xi-fen's new TV, when Don set it up for her. Xi-fen was sure there was no relationship, but they turned out to be part of the large Irish group after all.

Xi-fen finally got the letter off to her ex-husband and one to her son, just last Saturday. I know how upset she is with that situation. She has no idea if or when she will see her son. She has relatives here whom I don't know, and they keep telling her she should reconcile.

"I don't understand why they say that, Xi-fen. Don't they realize the situation? You have been divorced for several years now. Your husband took your son away from you," I said.

I can see it upsets her. She shakes her head and goes on with her work.

I tried looking at the news on Yahoo and found the Clinton topic, but there were so many articles from different newspapers that I was confused about which one to read.

China is shocked that all this is discussed in the news.

Please hug and tell Muppet hello. Some of my students couldn't understand why I didn't bring my dog to China.

The teaching is very active, but all there is to do is teach, so I really don't get too tired. I don't cook or do much but take care of myself.

Don, Pam, and I were called out of class and told to meet in a room in a building we had never been to. Our classes were canceled. It felt like a summons to the principal's office. It turned out that some dignitaries from the City of Jiangyin, who spoke no English, presented us with a very large presentation box of fancy Moon Cakes to welcome us to Jiangyin. We bowed, smiled a lot, and shook hands, and said, "Xie, Xie." There was no one to translate. It was a nice welcoming gesture.

These Moon Cakes, honoring the Moon Festival this time of year, contain a real cooked egg yolk inside to represent the moon. The ones I buy for breakfast just have preserved pineapple inside.

I am working with Don to get him some friends. You heard about "The City Hunter," where we go on Wednesday nights. The young people there are in their twenties and are really nice. None of them ordered drinks. They just want to practice their English with us. We met some kind people. The problem now is that Don has no money until "Mr. Chang gets back." He was supposed to be here on Monday but postponed his arrival.

There is a huge struggle going on with the Taiwan and Chinese bosses. This school is a joint venture between China and Taiwan. Taiwan wants involvement in this school as a business investment. China wants good educational opportunities for its children. Mr. Chang and Xi-fen are the only ones who want "Western things." The rest of the people in the school would prefer to do things in the Chinese way. The "Learning Center" at the elementary school is never used. It is just to show visitors, such as that group from Ireland. I did wonder why the pictures were hung so high for little children. I wonder if the English Center will be the same way.

The others in the school don't want to get involved with us; of course, there is the language barrier. The school advertises in their brochure, "WHY GO ABROAD WHEN WE HAVE EVERYTHING HERE?" Everything is us, the spoken English teachers.

I am sure I can find an international phone connection in a hotel in Hangzhou.

Write soon.

I love you and miss you.

Love and kisses,

Carolyn

Martinez, California
September 25, 1998
Email from Gail
"Calling Mr. Chang"
. . . calling Mr. Chang. Maybe he doesn't exist—a Chinese figment of the imagination—or perhaps absconded with the money! We could think up all sorts of scenarios, but probably it is just another one of those "livin' on Chinese time" events.

Two hours to buy a TV, even when you knew exactly what you wanted? Good grief!

I so much enjoy your descriptions of everything around you. You paint such wonderfully vivid pictures. I don't think I will ever know anyone besides you who will live and work in China and send me such interesting emails. Soooo, since that is probably the case, I will ask you questions, continually (none of which you have to answer, of course!).

What do you eat? Is it good? Do you think you will gain or lose weight or stay the same?

What do the Chinese do for recreation? Is going to the movies popular?

How many have TVs?

Is it possible to get any reading material in English?

Is anyone coming to visit you in the next few months?

How is the health care? What do you do if you get sick?

That's enough questions for now, I don't want to overburden you.

The biking sounds fabulous. What a great way to get around and really see things. Is the area hilly, and are there bike trails, or do you have to fight with cars?

I know I will have more questions for you.

Take care and don't fall off your bike.

Love,

Gail

Internet Café

Saturday, September 26, 1998

Email to Gail

Hi Gail,

I just got your email. We heard that Mr. Chang came back late last night from Taiwan.

Here are answers to your questions. I eat breakfast in my room. I have an electric kettle to boil water for tea. I have found "Moon Cakes" in the grocery store. They have pastries that are five inches across and filled with preserved pineapple. These cakes are the traditional food for the "Moon Festival" celebrated now all over China. I cut one in half and have half each morning with my British tea that I brought from home. Not walking over to the cafeteria in the morning saves time.

Right after my class at 11:30 a.m., I walk over to the cafeteria. There are three or four dishes and as much rice as you can eat. There is also soup. I pass up the kind with chicken feet. Soup is served from a big pot on the floor, which isn't very appetizing. It is their way to give adults and children a boiled liquid, and no drink. There is no milk for children, but there are not many cows in China. There are about seven hundred people, kids, big and small, and all the teachers and staff. I'm sure some of the meat is unknown intestines; I pass that up. There is some good tofu and usually some delicious cooked vegetables. It's a matter of how many dishes you want to pay for. Since each dish is eight U.S. cents, it is cheap. We eat with noisy children. Everyone hurries through lunch to take two-hour naps. If I eat dinner at school, we go to the cafeteria. We usually have a vegetable dish with meat and all the rice we can eat. It's healthy food.

I am losing weight because some of the eating situations are unappetizing. The room can be too hot, or it smells strange. There can be flies on the food, or some children are screaming. There is no wine, no cheese, or sweets. Don and I do have wine parties on Friday nights with "Great Wall Wine" that we get from one of the grocery stores.

We get tired of the cafeteria, so we go to a McDonald's in the center of town. McDonald's is popular in China, but not everyone can afford it. We can "point and eat." McDonald's has a clean bathroom. There is only one other "sit-down" restaurant in town that has a translated menu, but only Chinese is spoken. It's a bit dingy and dark, and it is safe, although not pleasant to eat there.

I don't think the people here would understand the word "recreation." I have seen the high school classes outside marching, but there are no games. The students go to classes on Saturday and Sunday, as well as weekdays. Everyone works hard. Xi-fen teaches on Saturdays, too.

There are no books in our library. No students ever leave the campus during the two weeks they are here. They go home every other weekend, many traveling a distance to the countryside.

There is a movie theater downtown. Most of the girls have seen *Titanic* and tell me it's their favorite movie. They smile and giggle when they talk about it. The *Titanic* theme music plays everywhere downtown. Small shops open to the street, playing loud music from radios that can be heard as you walk past. Going to a movie is not a common pasttime. I expect it's expensive.

TVs are rare. The wealthy have them, and I see TVs shared in neighborhoods. The TV is set up outside, and the neighbors watch it together. This works well in the heat.

There are no English reading materials here, perhaps in Shanghai.

No one is coming to visit.

I am told there is a health clinic here on campus. My goal is to avoid it at all costs. There is a hospital in town. If I had an emergency, I would go there. I will never let anyone put a needle in me while I am in this country. I would go home. Fortunately, I am healthy.

The "bike trails" are dirt paths that the farmers use between their vegetable plots. They have rocks, ruts, and smell like manure, but are generally good. I don't dare mix with cars. The highway in front is dangerous and chaotic.

Bye for now,

Love,

Carolyn

Saturday, September 26, 1998

Internet Café

Dear Kathleen,

Thank you for telling me what is going on in your life . . .

I am constantly trying to expand my horizons around here. I explained to Don, one of the young teachers here, that we need to expand his, too. We are making friends with some young Chinese people and trying to find someone to be his "tour guide," like Xi-fen is for me.

Today I had two friends, Yang Li-ping and Ms. Fay, come to see my rooms. They are our friends from the bicycle ride last Saturday. I showed them my photos, Lynessa's graduation party, the table of food, my house, and my friends. They were so interested; they had never seen the like. I showed them my book on California, and they commented on how beautiful it is. They were not just being polite. People put up with terrible weather here and don't know it. I know they couldn't believe our lifestyle.

Both other teachers had to teach classes today. I did twenty-three classes from Monday to Friday, so I had put in overtime and had the day off. The regimented students have classes all weekend, too. It's a little much. The high school students have been here for three weeks without a break. And can you believe boarding preschoolers? At 6:00 to 6:30 a.m. I can look out by the window and see their "nurse" walking them around the huge lawn area for exercise. The students all get to go home on Wednesday night of this week. Xi-fen and I will take a four-day trip.

Students in one of my classes are not happy with me. They wanted me to stay at school tonight and teach them how to dance. They treat me like a celebrity.

More later.

Love,

Carolyn

Jiangyin

September 16, 1998

Dear Mike and Lynessa,

I wish that you had tried a few more times to get through this morning. Xi-fen's phone didn't ring long enough for me to pick it up. Xi-fen insists that I need no card to activate it. I will call you from a hotel in Hangzhou.

We leave Wednesday night from here to Wuxi, where we will get on the boat and travel all night. We will arrive in Hangzhou in the morning. Xi-fen's brother is making the arrangements.

I do hope we have good weather. My photos are turning out so much better since I found the Kodak store on the far side of town. I can bike there. There is a bigger grocery store that has peanut butter, wine, chocolate, and other hard-to-find items.

Biking over there, I saw a man dressed in black clothes with bright-colored trim. He was carrying deer antlers. I asked Xi-fen about him. She says he is from a minority group, perhaps Tibetan, who is selling Chinese medicine on the street. His attire represents his business.

I am getting emails from my students, Juin and Chun Pou. They are very dear. I am emailing Charlene and my class. I have sent out other emails to friends that didn't go through.

I probably won't be able to write you until after next Sunday. I will teach fourteen classes in these three days. It's a lot.

When you send the foot insoles, could you send some Tetley tea in a Ziplock bag? I don't think my supply will hold out.

Thank you so much. I miss you all. I am looking forward to your fax.

Love,

Carolyn

Lafayette

Sunday, September 27, 1998

Fax from Mike

Dear Carolyn,

It was great to hear from you last night.

It rained, so when Muppet and I walked to get the papers in the morning, I could smell the rosemary.

Lynessa is doing the grocery shopping today, which may be a comment on the menu I selected for the week.

Desiree is coming over, and Lynessa is going out with her friends tonight.

Gail and Axel are taking their son Martin to start Davis today, so they will have an empty nest.

I will put foot insoles in the next package. I hope you have gotten the Global Express by now. Let me know as soon as they pay you.

Desiree is checking out our *International Travel* magazine. She is talking about going to Peru in November. If she does, Lynessa and I will just have a small chicken for Thanksgiving. It will be spring in Peru, and she'll be on a tour. We checked out the safety warning, and it appears the Peruvians are only shooting each other occasionally now, so tourists are safe.

I am not in a hurry for Lynessa to move out. Without her, I would miss you even more, if that is possible. Keep us up on your great adventures and take lots of pictures. We will keep the faxes and emails coming.

Love,

Mike

Lafayette

September 27, 1998

Fax from Desiree

Hi Mom!

I'm over here at your house hanging out. I'll drop you a line, though I think email is really the way to go. It was good to hear your voice yesterday, but it goes so quickly. It must be what a call for ransom sounds like.

Daddy and Ness seem to be doing well here together, taking care of everything. Dad seems to be doing a good job. He said he had no idea that cereal cost so much. Lynessa is certainly helping, too.

I hope it doesn't rain for my boss's wedding in October. I think she'll leave me in charge while she is on her honeymoon. Cool, huh?

Miss you much!

Love,

Desiree

Lafayette

Sunday, September 27, 1998

Fax from Lynessa

Hi Mom!

Thanks for the call on Saturday night. It was good to hear from you. I hope that everything is OK and that you get paid soon.

Here, everything is OK. My job is going OK. It just takes a lot of energy, and the days are definitely too short to get everything done. Even the weekends are too short.

Daddy, Desiree, and I went and looked at the place where I work, and then we went to Japantown for lunch. We went to a Vintage Kimono Show. I bought two that I'm going to change into jackets. I hope they are worth it.

I got offered an apartment this week in the Presidio, but it was going to be with a woman who was actually lying about her employment status to the Presidio housing people so she could qualify for low-income housing. It was too sketchy a situation to try to join. Now I have to explain that to the housing people and convince them that I am still interested without revealing that she has a job and is lying.

I'm fine with living at home right now. I would rather wait for a good situation.

It's been raining. We miss you!
Love,
Lynessa

Jiangyin
Tuesday, September 28, 1998
Internet Café, Email to my ESL class in Concord
Dear Charlene, students, and volunteers,
Everything is going fine here in China. My husband and I had a great tour to Shanghai, Guilin, Xian, and Beijing. We saw everything, including the body of Chairman Mao. We walked on the Great Wall and saw the huge buildings, millions of people, and cars in Beijing. The Terra Cotta Warriors in Xian were amazing. Guilin has beautiful countryside.

I like the city of Wuxi (pronounced Woo she) best. My friend Xi-fen and I like to shop in Wuxi. She has an apartment there, and her parents live in that city.

I have over two hundred students, in eight groups, with twenty, forty-five-minute classes each week. School goes all day with a two-hour rest.

The students are very nice and easy to teach. I have moved into a new English classroom just downstairs from where I live. This will be very convenient in rainy weather.

The English Center is a brand-new building. My living quarters are new and spacious. I have air-conditioning and use it often.

I bought a new red bike, so I can now ride into town and use the Internet Café to email to you.

In China, everything can be carried on a bike.

The best things about China are the nice people and my friend Xi-fen. The worst thing is the weather. It's hot, humid, and never clear.

I miss you all, but this is a great adventure. I hope everything is going well for all of you at school.

Best regards,

Carolyn

Jiangyin
Tuesday, September 29, 1989
Internet Café, Email home to family and friends
Hello from China,

After school, when the weather is good, I pump up the tires on my rose-red metallic "Hermes" bike and head out the guard gates of the school. I turn left and hold my breath as best as I can on the dusty path, avoiding cars and street traffic, and turn left past the rice field at the first row of houses.

I have a regular route. This narrow road starts out paved in concrete, but after a hundred feet, it turns to dirt and rocks. The dirt path goes along the side of the rice field next to the school. This is flat countryside. There are small patches of vegetables, bok choy, parsley, cabbage, and Chinese greens. I pass several tombstones all within sight of the school's see-through iron fence that surrounds the campus property. I pass by the little old lady with the three goats and continue west for about five minutes. I cross a canal and head out toward the "Army Barracks." At least I think they are barracks.

Yesterday, some of the army was out in uniform, watering their crops with neon green watering cans. They looked a lot less serious than the farmers, who are watering by long bamboo poles across their shoulders with buckets on the ends. The water comes from the many canals that run through the patches of vegetables. They waved and called "hello." Everyone wants to practice their English, even if they only know one word.

I found a small cemetery out there. People are allowed to bury their dead on their property. Xi-fen says it must be an important family since farmers don't usually have this kind of burial. It was about fifteen feet by fifteen feet, with a tall tree planted inside on a mound. It had a low cement wall around it with small lion statues to guard the narrow entrance. There were two stone tombstones with red and black Chinese characters. I must come back for pictures.

I continue my way to the road "where the chickens run free." The people look poor. There are cement houses in the dirt. The chickens are scrawny. Pigs are in cement shelters; none are outside like we saw in Guilin.

Great missed photos were of a little boy about three, naked and crawling on a brown bike with a wagon bed over the back two wheels. I passed an old woman on a bike with a gigantic, four-foot-high pile of sticks above her head tied to the back of her bike.

I go by too fast for photos. Some people run away if they think I am taking their photo.

These farmers tend their small patches of vegetables by hand and hoe. They have green produce, dry plants and leaves, bundle sticks for winter, and this week they are harvesting rice. They carry their picked vegetables in large baskets on poles across their shoulders. I think some of this produce is "eat some and sell some." In winter, this is covered in snow and cold.

The rice harvest has to be done in the space of about ten days. Fortunately, we have been having dry weather. The rice is cut and laid out in front of their houses in bunches of six since it was planted in sixes. It is collected and brought to a small, rented thresher. Many farmers transport the bundles tied to a long bamboo pole across their shoulders with the huge bundles tied on either end. Most of the threshers are run by old women, with scarves or straw hats on their heads for protection. After the stalks are put through the thresher, they are taken and blown by a rusty fan about two feet across to remove the last little bits of rice. This is all back-breaking work, but each family does its own. They have huge three-foot basket sieves to sort out the grains of rice.

I've named the "streets" on my route. There is "Canna Lilly Drive" with many individual farm plots. One day, I saw a small cow, a surprise in China. I go down "Billiard Boulevard," named for the billiard table under a red and blue plastic canopy. I follow this to the end, where there is a "bicycle repair shop." A man sits on a tiny box by the side of the dirt road, ready to repair tires and pump air. One day, he gave me free air. He pointed to my back tire. It was really low. I had no money with me and showed him empty pockets. He handed me his pump. People are nice to foreigners. This is not the first time I've gotten free air. I wished I'd had money with me to pay for the use of his pump.

I turn around at "the bike repair shop." It is so hazy that you can look at the sun. It is a huge red ball in the sky. If I ask my students,

"What color is the sun?" They will say red and not yellow because morning and night the sun is red through a polluted haze.

I return to "Canal Road," next to a canal with a boat that's not going anywhere. I suspect that people live on it. It has metal and cardboard patches. Some of the water smells stagnant, but women are washing their vegetables in it. There are a few ducks here, too. Children are walking home from the local school. Grandpas and grandmas are playing with their grandchildren.

Here, too, people are shocked to see me. Some stare in disbelief, and some smile in surprise. Some pass by me on a bike, turn to stare, and almost fall off. They rarely see a foreigner in town and never out by their homes in the countryside.

I finally reach the horrible highway being repaired in front of the school and bump my way home in the potholes. The whole trip takes an hour. It's fun to explore this area next to the school.

Love,

Carolyn

Wednesday, September 28, 1998

Internet Café

I met Mr. Chang in the office after school. He was pleasant and spoke excellent English. He brought books from Taiwan for my class, but they are at the printers and will be back in a few days. I don't know exactly what I will be getting.

After chatting a bit, he smiled and said, "You could make my dream come true if you would stay on and teach until the end of the year."

I explained I was happy here, but I needed to get back to my family.

Onto Hangzhou

Chapter 11

From my journal

While I'm here at the Internet Café, I thought I'd jot down some of the injustices in China.

Some years ago, someone, probably in Beijing, decided that people north of the Yellow River, north of here, could have heat. Construction north of the river includes heat. That person reasoned that south is south and therefore warmer and doesn't need heat. But a horrible situation was created, and people here have no heat at all. The only people here at our school who have heat are the foreign teachers and the bosses from Taiwan. Xi-fen has no heat in her dorm room. The temperature is the same inside as out. It froze last winter in her room, so she had ice crystals on her towels and in her water basin. None of the children or teachers living here has heat, and the classrooms are not heated. Fortunately for me, it has been unusually warm, and my classroom has a good exposure, so I haven't felt it yet. Some of the Chinese people reason that it is better to have air conditioning because you can always put on more layers in winter, but you can only take off a certain amount of clothes. Some Chinese choose A/C first; of course, it is not like ours, but it does provide a little cool air in this horribly hot summer.

Xi-fen just got paid for all her summer work, twenty-eight days in all. She worked hard setting up the English center, doing our visas, coordinating summer school, and regular school that went into July. It was a huge amount of work. Everything is difficult to do in China.

I met the big boss, who is now in Taiwan, this summer, but he wasn't friendly; he just paid her. She was paid ¥100, which is $12 in U.S. money. She was supposed to get ¥280, that is $10 a day. He shortchanged her. She has no recourse. It is insulting. He has no clue or idea of how much work it is to get and keep foreign teachers here. And without Xi-fen, this place would be hopeless for us.

I don't think she will stay here unless something changes. In two years, when it officially becomes a private school, she won't receive her retirement or health insurance. Teachers get a base pay and then an unknown "bonus" at the end of the year. The factory that owns your school pays out the money if the factory is doing well. This bonus depends on how well your students test. Of course, new teachers are given the most difficult students.

The administration has also decided to charge Xi-fen and others rent for their dorm rooms, but it costs more if you are single than if you are married. They will just levy this fee of ¥150 a month out of her bonus, and they don't have to tell her about it. We are paid ten times what the Chinese teachers make. The school has some major problems, but hey, things are looking up for the area. The province has just decided to let them build a junior college on the rice field next door and lend them the money interest-free for an indefinite amount of time. Well, it's China. Bye for now.

Jiangyin to Hangzhou

Wednesday, September 30, 1998

Firecrackers were going off early this morning, and we had dense fog.

This afternoon, Xi-fen and I left for our big adventure to Hangzhou. October 1 is National Day, their Independence Day. Next year it will be fifty years since the formation of the People's Republic of China. It also coincides with the Lantern Festival and Moon Festival, which celebrate harvest time and the rice harvest.

We gingerly waded through the mud to catch the one-hour bus to Wuxi, just out in front of the school. We took a cab to the dock in Wuxi. I was excited to start on this adventure. I felt like Michael Palin of PBS's TV Show *Full Circle* as we boarded the boat on the Grand Canal in Wuxi. All I lacked was a film crew to follow me and record this twelve-and-a-half-hour boat trip across Lake Taihu and through a section of the Grand Canal south to Hangzhou.

We checked our cabin. The tiny berths reminded me again of Michael Palin's China train berths. We started at 5:30 p.m. in the dining room. Xi-fen and I were envious of the fancier boat next to us with the outside cabins that we saw through the window. People were walking around on an outside balcony. Twenty minutes later, it was dark, and gigantic mosquitoes were plastered against our dining room windows. We were no longer envious.

We ate dinner at a community table. It was good food; Xi-fen had already inspected the kitchen. She uses me as her excuse to check for cleanliness. You must realize, as a foreigner, I am extremely rare. I never see other foreigners anywhere. People are interested in our relationship. They stare at me and then Xi-fen, when she speaks English. It isn't easy to travel around China, and I am so fortunate to have this deep cultural experience with her. There is no English spoken or on any signs in English.

Xi-fen said we should use the community bathrooms "before the rush." The floors and walls were covered in white tile. There was a one-foot tiled trench in the center that went from one side of the room to the other. I have so far managed to avoid these. This one had the canal water sloshing in and out of the trench into the lake—a terrible thought. There was a separate five-foot-by-five-foot room with two sinks. I decided to get my leggings to sleep in.

When I came back, Xi-fen announced that the "Chinese like to wash their feet."

She proceeded to wash hers with great flourish in the tiny basin, got everything wet, then washed her hands with toothpaste "to take off the oil," and declared herself ready for bed.

We went back to our cabin. I was in the top bunk with Xi-fen below. Our roommates, a middle-aged couple across from us in the tiny cabin, were helpless with the knob for the fan. It said, lo-med-hi. I managed to save them all from being too hot by turning it on. They smiled and nodded. The boat noises lulled me to sleep.

At 5:00 a.m., loud Chinese music blared throughout the boat.

"They want to wake us up," Xi-fen said.

I dashed upstairs with my camera to see if I could see anything out of the boat. It was pitch black. We docked at 6:15 a.m., and still no light. So much for photos of the Grand Canal.

When Chinese travel, they like the idea of saving money by having transportation and the hotel together. We had done just that. We got a taxi and proceeded to our "hotel." It was not a tourist hotel but a nine-story hotel for government officials called cadres. I was "smuggled in" because they don't allow foreigners. They didn't want my passport and ignored me.

This hotel had just opened after being redecorated, and everything was new and beautiful. We were so relieved. Xi-fen's brother's classmate works here, or we wouldn't have had a chance to get it, or even find a hotel in all of Hangzhou on this holiday weekend. Again, in China, it depends on who you know.

We settled into our room and immediately had to send for more toilet paper. There is never enough. They only give you a few sheets on a roll. We laughed and had to keep calling for more. I took a bath and noticed the label on the tub said, "American Standard."

We quietly inspected other floors of the hotel. There was a huge meeting room with gold walls and red velvet seats where members of the Communist Party met.

The city was packed. The Chrysanthemum Show had 20,000 people attend in one day. Other sights we visited had 10,000 people, and I saw every one of them. I saw five foreigners in the entire three days. I spoke to all "strangers" because we were the only non-Chinese. They were Australians.

This whole trip could easily have been called the "Misadventures of Carolyn and Xi-fen" if I didn't watch closely. Xi-fen gets lost and confused easily. Her brother had given her a three-page itinerary with all the sights we should see, complete with poetic descriptions of each place. She couldn't decide what we should do, so I looked around and decided.

"Let's take that boat ride on West Lake," I said.

Xi-fen checked the list, and it turned out to be precisely what was on the itinerary from her brother. It is pretty funny. She handles the Chinese, and I handle the travel common sense. The boat ride took us across the lake to a Museum of Indigo Dye and Fabric. It told Chinese history with indigo around the world. I bought a large round tablecloth, a wall hanging, and a blouse that had been stitched and tie-dyed with indigo in an interesting pattern.

We found it was impossible to get a regular taxi and ended up taking a bicycle taxi out to the Lantern Festival in a lakeside park. Beautiful old silk lanterns were hanging from trees and story displays. We saw life-sized dioramas made of paper-maché and painted wood statues of people depicting Chinese characters and legends. Xi-fen knew all the stories and myths. She recited a few to me. They are complicated, with lots of characters, some in heaven coming to earth to interact with people, and sometimes taking them back to heaven. There is always a display about the Monkey King and his travels. The story is an allegory based on a Monk from the Tang Dynasty (602-664 CE), who traveled to India.

We had to take a bicycle taxi back to our hotel. These taxis freak Xi-fen out. I think she may be more aware of the danger in them than I am when they just head out into the crazy traffic. We lived to talk about our crazy ride back to our hotel.

Hangzhou
Friday, October 2, 1998
The next morning, we caught the bus out to the "Soul's Retreat Temple"—the largest Buddhist Temple in southern China. The bus made crowded Italian buses look spacious. After an hour of standing up, we got there. Remember, it's hot and humid. Chinese don't wear or need deodorant; it's amazing. I don't think one could stand this hot bus ride in Europe.

The temple was fabulous. "Souls Retreat Temple" was rebuilt a few times. The large temple buildings had incredibly tall Buddhas in gold with deep blue and some red pillars as well as a multitude of other items on each altar. There were gold leaf statues of the eighteen gods of Buddhism and a huge statue of Guanyin, Goddess of Mercy and Compassion.

Many old women make pilgrimages to this site. There were hundreds of burning candles and lots of incense. Displayed here are three hundred ancient stone tablets that were carved with likenesses of ancient monks from India, who were "in charge" of many aspects of people's lives, not unlike Christian saints. Each was incredibly individual in a style I have never seen. Each one was supposed to look like the respective person. It reminded me of the idea of each of the terra-cotta warriors.

The rock sides of the canyon where the temple was located were carved with hundreds of Buddhas in niches. Some were six to eight feet high. There was also a "stone garden" with gigantic Buddhas, all carved out of rock, many twenty feet or more high. I was impressed with their incredible beauty. Xi-fen thought they had recently been moved there, but I can't imagine how.

After five hours there, we backtracked on the bus and went to the "Monument to the National Hero." This is for a guy who was unjustly executed about nine hundred years ago and has been essentially deified. Over the centuries, there were pictures, murals, statues, and various tombs constructed, and finally, this site was chosen as his final resting place to tell his story. It was packed with thousands of people. I couldn't understand all the hoopla, except that there really are not any other similar commemorations. It's a story that has stuck.

We then needed a taxi to get to the next pagoda. It was another case of too many people and not enough taxis. After losing taxis to seven or eight more aggressive people, Xi-fen flagged one down. She stood on one side of the cab and I on the other, and we pulled open the doors and commandeered the cab (very rude on our part). On the way to the pagoda, I suggested that we please hire this driver by the hour so we could see the planned sights and have a ride back to our hotel. A bargain was struck, relief, and at least the transportation problem was taken care of for a few hours.

Touring with Xi-fen is a continual "photo opportunity" for her. She has to have her picture taken at every sign, entrance, gate, or Chinese characters over one foot high. Every Chinese person wants to do the same thing. So we were constantly waiting for her turn to pose in the much-desired places. Preserving the scenery in photos is not important to her, only the fact that she was there. I can tell you this takes a lot of time. She loves looking at her pictures when I get them developed, so it's worth the time and effort.

The bus to get back to Jiangyin was going to take too long, so we needed train tickets for the six-hour train to Wuxi the next day. We waited in the crowded ticket office for an hour in line. At least now there is a guard to keep people from pushing ahead and cutting in the line—not the old Chinese free-for-all, the "no queue" situation.

The next morning, we went for a walk in a park along the famous West Lake. We imagined what this lake would look like in the spring with all its trees blossoming around the edges. Her brother had lovely poetic references to the beauty of this lake.

A reporter and a person with a video camera walked up to me. They spoke English and said they were from the local TV station.

They started filming.

"Hello, where are you from?" the reporter asked.

I told them I was from San Francisco.

"What is your favorite city in China?"

Of course, I said Hangzhou was my favorite city. Actually, despite the haze, it is the most beautiful city I have seen in China. Did you see me on TV?

To be continued. . .

Love,

Carolyn

Monday, October 5, 1998

From my journal

Yesterday we took the six-hour train from Hangzhou to Wuxi. When we got to the station with our tickets, we thought we were in the right line. There was a small TV playing a cartoon version of the Monkey King story. I couldn't read the signs, but watching the lines, I wasn't sure we were in the right one. I told Xi-fen, and she went over to ask. Sure enough, we had been in the wrong line. We got in the right line just as the train was boarding.

We stopped by Xi-fen's apartment in Wuxi for her to check on things. I walked over to the hotel in her neighborhood, owned by the Air Force, where Mike and I had stayed. I took the elevator up to their business office because I wanted to call home.

The young woman at the counter, attractive and in business dress, spoke English, but I "flooded" them with fast English that they couldn't keep up with. I smiled and said that my husband and I had stayed there, implying that I was still there, before I explained that I needed to call the United States. They said I could call and directed me to a small, private telephone room. I could pay for this through their business office. I got to talk to my family for a long time. I was so relieved to get through with a good connection. It was wonderful to talk to them.

Xi-fen and I were invited to dinner at her parents' home, so we took a cab to their apartment in Wuxi. We celebrated the Moon Festival, and her father made a banquet for us. This time at dinner, I got to ask more questions through Xi-fen. I asked her mother her opinion of Chairman Mao because they had lived through the Cultural Revolution from 1966 to 1976. She told me it was 70 percent good and 30 percent bad. I know this is the common answer now, but in reality, I think it was much worse. People are just relieved that it is over and don't want to dwell on the memory.

Her parents told me that during Mao's Cultural Revolution, Xi-fen's father lived with the children—Xi-fen, her brother, and sister—in the countryside. Her mother lived in the city and worked in the garment industry. She got to see her children occasionally.

We took a taxi back to Bell School to be ready for school starting tomorrow.

Saturday, October 3

Faxes from home

Dear Carolyn,

On Friday night Lynessa and I went out to dinner and to a movie. It probably didn't hurt to take some time off from our own cooking. Boy, has making the regular run to the market and writing the checks greatly impacted my sense of what things cost.

I wound up several of my cases last week. Things will slow down for a couple of weeks until I start more trials.

What should I do with the developed photos?

Michelle seems a little calmer about her job. She and her immediate boss are about to move to a new department, and she is looking at other jobs.

Lynessa seems to be finding her job interesting. She gets to use her Swedish at work.

It was great to talk to you on Sunday. I really don't like this no-pay deal. It just looks unstable. Thank you for telling Mystery Chang that you couldn't make his dream come true.

I am not surprised to hear what a popular teacher you are. You have always been my favorite. Please, don't "work like a horse."

Lynessa has been a great help. She is a great roommate. I am still taking laundry lessons. She was amazed at how much they took out of her paycheck. I think she will be able to work her way into Presidio housing.

I miss you a lot. I wish things were going better for you. Don't let them have you take over the school.

Love, Mike

Monday, October 5, 1998, Mid-Autumn Festival

Internet Café, Fax to home

Dear Mike,

I didn't get your fax until today. We got back from Hangzhou and Wuxi last night about 9:30 p.m. The cab ride took an hour because of the road work in Wuxi and the terrible construction in front of the school. For a few miles, it was even worse than when you were here. I hope to get to the Internet Café tonight, and I will email details of the trip.

Please sign my school papers that say, yes, I want to teach in the spring.

I have gotten part of the money owed me from Mr. Chang just in time for our trip.

I have not received any package. Martinez's mail is sometimes not delivered. Maybe "small package" is good enough. My feet are really bad. Shall I have a girlfriend send me the insoles? I would also like the British-style tea. Tetley's from Safeway is OK. I need the insoles!

Has Muppet been feeling OK?—No problems?

Can you please send the photos that you developed? I need the ones from Xi-fen's family dinner from when you were here so I can give them to them. They had me to dinner again last night. We had a banquet for Moon Festival.

Xi-fen took me aside into a tiny bedroom with one twin bed and a one-foot-wide space next to it and the wall.

"Carolyn, can I borrow some money?" she asked.

"Sure," I said. What's it for?"

"My brother, sister, and I need to buy 'death clothes' for our parents. Now is the time for them to get these so they are ready for them when they die."

I gave her the money she needed. Her parents are fine at this time. Chinese tradition is to have these clothes ready and to be paid for by the children.

My uncle sounds pretty frail. My sister had him over to dinner last week.

I hope everything went well with the Barbecue.

Love,

Carolyn

Lafayette

October 4, 1998

Email from Lynessa

Hi Mom!

I hope all is well. I'm so glad you got to call on Saturday night and got to talk to everyone at home from that hotel. It was nice that you could talk longer. I hope you got paid by Mr. Chang. Did you have a nice trip? I'm sure it was nice not to teach for a few days.

How is teaching going? Are they as disciplined as before? Are they as curious? Are they still fascinated with their American teacher?

Things are going OK. I'm not planning to move out anytime soon. I'm not ready to start giving half of my monthly rent to live in San Francisco . . .

We had a barbecue here today. I'm not as good as you at giving parties. We certainly missed you. Daddy wanted to invite twenty people, but I certainly wasn't up to having twenty people here. I can't handle that. Ten was more than enough. I cleaned the house for five hours.

Michelle likes to call me from Texas and talk about her job for hours. I think she should quit. She keeps trying to make it work, but the truth is, she's unhappy in Texas.

I don't have many exciting things going on in my life. Work wears me out since I'm leaving so early and getting home so late. . . This week we are having public workshops. Many people have signed up for our "Graphic Facilitators" classes to learn how to do their own graphics and facilitate their own meetings. I'd like to know more about our products and get more into the marketing part of our business.

I am sending you a fax with greetings from Desiree, Gail, and the other guests at the barbecue.

Anyway, that's about it for me. Write soon.

Love,

Lynessa

Wednesday, October 7, 1998

Internet Café, Email home to Lynessa

Hi Honey,

I got your faxes. I tried to send one to Daddy on Monday, but Xi-fen couldn't find the woman who had the key to the closet where the fax machine is kept. Yesterday, we had no electricity. Thanks for the email. I'll write more later.

I did get paid some of the money. Xi-fen is constantly pushing for us. Without her, it would be impossible. I am doing fine, but it's frustrating that I can't make long-distance calls from here. But what do I expect? Yesterday we had no water and no electricity. Today it is just no water. We don't understand why. I guess the answer is that it is China! What an experience.

More later,

Love,

Mom

Monday, October 5, 1998

Internet Café, From my journal

When we returned from Hangzhou, we had faxes from my daughter and husband waiting, as well as an email from my adult multi-level English as a Second Language students in California and their teacher, Charlene. Some of my older adult Chinese students have taken American names.

Dear Carolyn,

We were going to take a field trip to Golden Gate Park, but there was no bus to take us. The trip was canceled. I like going to school to learn to speak English.

Love,

Cathy

My house burned on September 11. Nobody was hurt. The insurance company is building a new one for me. I will have a new house in three months.

Love,

Shu Ying

I am happy I saw your email. I think you are a good teacher, teaching English in China. I know you will stay there, right? You have too much fine time.

Love,

Diana

I saw your email. I am happy you had a good trip. Wendy has back pain, so she has been absent one month.

Love,

Connie

I am not happy today. The bus driver was one hour late!

Love,

Yi Yon Hui

Thank you for your email. We were happy to know that you, an American, came to China to teach Chinese students English. That's a noble job. We all miss you and wish you to come back soon.

Love,

Antonio Cheong.

Do you come in contact with many Chinese persons? How many words do you understand?

Love,

Joe Chen

I saw your mail letter. I'm very happy. My bees are sleeping. They don't make honey now.

Love,

Kuo Hao Lai

I want to thank you for your lovely email. Your students and the others welcomed you. You are so beautiful, friendly, and outgoing. I'll suggest to you something as follows: 1. Don't go out alone by yourself. 2. Don't bring much money with you. 3. Be careful of your health.

Love, Juin

Thank you. Charlene gave us your email. I am interested in reading your email because you might stay in China and become a famous movie star. They want to touch your hair and face. I think Chinese people are lovely. We students miss you. We hope you will be back soon.

Love,

Yu Hsien

I hope you are full of interesting things to lead you back to the future. There is no electricity, no water, no car, no phone? But you can get all the food to eat and a computer to play with from a modern café!

Love,

Chun Pou

We enjoyed your letters and are looking forward to hearing from you soon! Everyone is working hard to learn English and have a good time. All the students and teachers miss you very much. Enjoy China, your Chinese students, and good health.

Love,

Charlene

Wednesday, October 7, 1998

Internet Café, Email to home

Dear Mike,

Thank you for the long faxes. I didn't receive the first one until Xi-fen and I got back from Hangzhou. Then the second one came in. I still haven't gotten the package. There is a rumor that there is a package in the post office in a town south of here, but no one knows the name on it, and they say it needs a signature. I don't know what this means. This is China!

I was sick yesterday; I'm not sure what it was, but the prescription for diarrhea saved me. It might have been one of the twenty dishes Xi-fen's father made for the Moon Festival dinner. I know one was eel, even though Xi-fen wouldn't tell me what it was. She knows I'm not crazy about eating eels, although she says they are delicious.

It's ridiculous that I can't get calls out of here. I would go crazy if I couldn't get to this email place. Don feels the same way. Thanks for all the news.

Life here is rather hysterical. What seems funny to me isn't funny to Xi-fen, who has to live it and not just visit. Xi-fen knows so many American idioms. She is saying again that she must "work like a horse." It's true.

I'm glad your barbecue went well and everyone had fun. Gail emailed me.

Michelle has emailed me, and I will send back some comforting words.

Xi-fen began pushing for the rest of our money again on Monday. On Tuesday at 4:30 p.m., we were supposed to meet with the accountant, but got a call in the office that she wasn't back from the bank yet. We waited. At 5:10 p.m., we went to see her. I got paid my ¥4,700, but not the U.S. cash or the plane ticket. Xi-fen will have to push some more. I think Mr. Chang brought the U.S. cash with him from Taiwan, as it's impossible to get here.

When you go to Safeway, ask at Customer Service if I can send MoneyGrams from China because I know I could send money to China from there. They will have to call the company. When they do ask about Wuxi, I think it is the Citic Bank and ask if I can send a MoneyGram to you in the U.S. from that bank in Wuxi. I am holding too much American cash. Jiangyin would be better, but I doubt it is on the list. In other words, can the money go either way? Please try to get the phone number in Wuxi.

I don't mind leaving Xi-fen money, but if I have a lot of U.S. money, I would like to send it home. There is not much to buy. I have lots of Chinese money now to pay for our travels.

I did buy some beautiful blue and white folk cloth in an Indigo Museum in Hangzhou. I also bought a jacket-blouse that looks great with my jean skirt.

Were you or your secretary able to put the address for the school job here in the Berkeley job listing? I hope so.

Tonight is "English Corner." Don and I will go. We haven't told

Pam about it.

School is fine. I have lots of stories. And I have to tell you about our big trip.

I am quite convinced that there is no one in China who can do what I am doing with Xi-fen.

I love you lots and miss you,

Carolyn

Thursday, October 8, 1998

From my journal

With Mr. Chang's return, we now have a wall telephone in the English Center. They punched a hole in the plaster wall for the installation, but it's in. I think I can use the two-minute international cards here, but there are no guarantees on the reception. I feel secure here, but I like the phone downstairs in case I need it in an emergency.

After my classes, I went to the English Office. Xi-fen was there with requests from Mr. Chang. I have been asked to teach two classes at another high school on two Saturdays at the end of the month. It seems the administrators are friends of Mr. Chang, and he promised them. They have not given me a subject, so I will have to improvise.

Now we are in full swing to put on Halloween. It's not known in China so I'm starting from scratch.

Upcoming Halloween 12

Friday, October 9, 1998

Internet Café, Email to Mike

Hi Honey,

I hope everything is OK at home. Don and I are here on the internet, and it's Friday night. We came into town to see if we could find Yang Li-ping and find out where I might get my hair cut. Do you think Judy could pop over and help me out?

We couldn't find Yang Li-ping. Xi-fen is super busy with Mr. Chang here, so I don't know what I'll do.

We are having a Halloween party on Thursday for half of the high school students and another party on next Tuesday for the second half. We are doing it early so Mr. Chang can see it. He is leaving on October 20, and according to Xi-fen, things are just not the same. I think the problem is that there is a power struggle going on between the bosses. Don't write things about the school in faxes, just in case someone might see it.

The Halloween party is a challenge because they have little paper and no paint. Don and I actually found balloons tonight in the little alleyway with Chinese items. The shop owner couldn't believe we only wanted orange and black. I am organizing English activities. Don and I searched again for Michael Jackson's "Thriller," but we could only find "Blood on the Dance Floor." Now that sounds appropriate for Halloween!

I still don't have the package from you. I asked Xi-fen to call the post office, but I'm not sure she had time. I think Global Express is too confusing for them to handle on this end. Maybe you could put a tracer on it, not ask for it back, and just find out about the delivery.

When you send the next package, could you send a roll of one-inch masking tape? It's the best thing I brought with me. I use it every day to hang things in the classroom.

My classes are getting better. I'm learning more about what the students know and don't know. Now I can help them more

I had a contest with the Mont St. Michel poster of France. I asked them, "Where in the world is this?" I left it posted in the classroom for a week. Only one boy guessed "correctly." He said he saw a "French house" in the picture. I think he was referring to the architecture—good thinking with limited English. I gave him a large chocolate bar and took his picture. He looked puzzled with the chocolate bar, so I'm not sure this was a great prize. I don't think kids are used to chocolate; maybe he didn't even know what it was. I searched all the stores, and this was my best idea.

Don't worry about sending me all the photos, just the ones of Xi-fen's family. They don't have any photos of themselves.

I am busy here with emails. My students at home and Charlene anxiously await every word.

How is your health? Has your wrist healed completely? I hope you are taking care of yourself.

At the end of next week, my stay will be half over. Then there are seven more weeks to go. Don thinks the days fly by. To me, a day seems like a week. I am still fine here and happy. It is a true adventure, unlike anything I've experienced. I still have more stories to share and need more computer time to tell you my adventures.

We went to find the English Corner last Wednesday night. It wasn't at the City Hunter Club.

When we walked in, the "hostess" said to Don, "I love to have many men here at night." He was a little surprised. He remembered her from before, so he introduced me to her. I don't think that's what she wanted. Naji George showed up. He was leaving for England the next day and was trying to return a pink bicycle to a girl who had left for Beijing. It was funny. What to do?

Don was desperate to buy deodorant and asked Naji where to buy it. The Chinese don't need it. It's really scarce.

The Halloween party will keep me busy for a few days. It's also hard to do because nothing is efficient; everything is difficult.

I still haven't been paid my American money or the airline ticket. Xi-fen has done everything she is supposed to do. Everything has been "chopped," but I guess I have to push her again. She will have to try them again, a total waste of time for her. She gets so frustrated with the administration. There is no way I would get involved with the student exchange with this group. Xi-fen's teacher recruitment job is difficult enough.

Mr. Chang seems to be trying to remove himself from the daily struggles at this school. It's true with him that everything gets done, but now he is leaving again. His new idea for me is to teach the junior high students.

Xi-fen says, "We can't leave them out."

Please send the insoles. My feet are a real problem. I know it's the tile floors, but I can't do anything about them.

My schedule is better. They changed all the classes again. Now I start at 7:30 a.m. on Monday and have five classes, but on the other days I start at 8:30 a.m. and have four classes in the morning, except for Friday, when I have three in the morning. When I asked Xi-fen when I would do all the new extra activities, Xi-fen said, "Well, you will just teach the junior high on Sunday."

I said no to Sundays. I don't think she was really thinking, although I think that is what they would tell her. I will figure out a time I can do this, but not on Sundays.

They have added new landscaping by placing chrysanthemums in small pots in the planter area. This seems to be how they "plant" new flowers. It does make them easy to change out when they've bloomed.

The weather is still quite warm, and the road in front is worse, if you can believe that. Today it looked like a dust storm in the desert. Everything at the school is getting dusty. I truly think they add fine powdered dust each night. I don't know what is worse, dust or mud.

Email soon. I'll try to write more tomorrow. Please print my emails and save them. I can't print here.

Did you put in the ad for a teacher in the Berkeley job listing?

Love,

Carolyn

Lafayette

Sunday, October 11, 1998

Fax from home

Dear Carolyn,

I am getting off another package that will include insoles, cards, books, Time, and your sample ballot. I will not send this via Global Express. They are trying to trace your package.

Downtown Pleasant Hill is leveled for the new buildings for redevelopment. The Cal Fed Bank is all that's going to be left standing. By the way, the tellers always ask how you are doing in China. Lots will look different when you get home.

We just got your email that you got the package. I still propose to send the next one as I did the first. Monday is Columbus Day here, so it can't go out until Tuesday.

Love,

Mike

Lafayette

Sunday, October 11, 1998

Email from Lynessa

Hi Mom!

I hope things are going OK. It sounds like you will be happy to come home. I am going to try to email more this week.

Things are going pretty well here. Dad and I seem to be getting along fine, although it is looking like I might move out soon with Katie to the Presidio. If we get our application in quickly, we will be able to choose a three-bedroom apartment.

I'm a little worried about leaving Dad. I actually think he will be OK. I may do a half-and-half stay here. Katie and I will not have a TV, nor do we have much furniture. The apartments are huge.

Well, it will be another week of work. We are doing workshops now. On Friday, there was no one to help with the phones. The woman who usually takes orders left to go on maternity leave. I work nine hours with a ten-minute lunch. I was going nuts with the phones. Tomorrow will be better, and I don't think that will happen again.

Michelle is worked up about her job. She calls and talks for hours about it. Now I guess her friend Bruce is moving to California. She should leave if she is miserable. She is obsessed with moving to England.

Uncle Bud started his therapy again and is only eating vitamins. I talked to Mary Jo, and she has been getting on his case about eating regular food. I think he has started to eat a little.

Muppet hasn't been sick the entire time you have been gone. I haven't had time to take her on walks, but today we walked to

Baywood. She got to meet her doggie friends, Kiku and Lockey. Pretty exciting.

Daddy is happy about his cartoon. He's been working hard on it. He's doing OK. He gets excited about making dinner and grocery shopping. It's nice to have someone making dinner. I'll miss it a lot when I move . . .

I hope everything is fine with you.

Love,

Lynessa

Sunday, October 11, 1998

Internet Café, Email from Don to my family

Hi Mike and Lynessa,

Carolyn asked me to write to you because I was not concerned with the mud and was coming into the Internet Café regardless. The following is her note.

Don

Hi Mike and Lynessa,

I got the Global Express package. I'm sorry I didn't get a call out. It poured last night, so the road is muddy. I have to work with the students this afternoon for the Halloween party. I'll call soon.

It's pouring now.

Love,

Carolyn

Home, Lafayette

October 11, 1998

Fax from Mike

I have had it in mind to make up this enclosed cartoon since I got home. I had to do a lot of research at the library to get the right chicken and a crane. Fortunately, Gary Larsen helped me out. I have not titled it, but I think you will recognize it right away.

Give Xi-fen a copy.

(The cartoon is in a chicken house with chickens on the floor looking at a large crane with wings spread standing in front of them). I didn't get your joke. At first, I thought it was about chicken feet. I'm not sure it all came through clearly. Does it mean "A Crane Among Chickens"?

Lynessa has gone to look at a three-bedroom apartment at the Presidio. It has an ocean view. She and her friend Katie have faxed the bank statements and will wait to hear. If it comes through, I'm sure she and Katie will have a great time putting it together. Many of their neighbors will apparently be he-he couples.

We are definitely having fall, as it's cool at night. I finally gave up on help and cleaned out the garage so two cars can go in. I got the refrigerator in my office just in time for hot drinks instead of cold.

I have just been grocery shopping. We are spending more than the twenty-five cents a meal that you are. I have learned to shop on the Safeway "club" card. I have started to learn that it is wise to replace the used contents of the pantry.

Love always,

Mike

Monday, October 12, 1998

Internet Café, Email sent to my family with copies to friends

Hi Mike, Hi Lynessa,

I hope you got the message I sent through Don yesterday. It rained so hard the road was really impassable for me to get to town or even get a taxi. I also had to prepare for the art class that came Sunday afternoon to make Halloween decorations for the Halloween party on Thursday. They did a fine job, but I worked on scrounging up the paper goods to use. I searched every paper store here and in Wuxi. They didn't have much.

On Saturday, Don and I shopped for balloons, candy, and music. Don is in charge of music. We went to all the paper stores and little shops in the alleyway off the main square in the center of town. Don wanted to find Michael Jackson's "Thriller," which he said has Vincent Price and Halloween sounds. We had to face facts that it just isn't here. He'll have to use something else.

These kids lack a lot of common vocabulary and know nothing of Halloween, but that's not unexpected. Today I did five classes about Halloween with all the drama I could muster to show a witch, ghost, scarecrow, pumpkin, jack-o-lantern, and mask.

I told the story I used to use in primary grades about the "little old lady who sat and spun" while various body parts rolled into her house. At the end of the story, a jack-o-lantern head rolls in. In a quiet voice, almost a whisper, you ask, "And do you know what he said?" Wait and then in a loud voice, you say, "BOO." I made some of them jump and scared a couple of boy "troublemakers" in the class. It was fun!

The students are making word skeletons by learning various body parts. Words will make up the skeleton bodies on paper with jack-o'-lantern heads. We'll put them up on the walls around the party room downstairs. At the party on Thursday night, we will have Halloween bingo with Halloween vocabulary and other games. We will have dancing.

These students, here for two weeks at a time, are so controlled and programmed. I think this party will be lots of fun for them.

We want to carve pumpkins at the party, too, but so far, I have only found a few at the market. I've explained to Xi-fen what we need. Xi-fen spends hours chasing and re-chasing things we need in the English Center. I needed scissors for the class. She went to the man who sat by a locked door and had to "argue and fight" with him about borrowing class scissors. Each person has a job here, and his is to "protect and defend" supplies. Everything is an argument. It's a real waste of time, but it's the Chinese way and is expected.

I finally got the $500 U.S. Xi-fen says Mr. Chang has just "chopped" (signed with his Chinese chop) the paper to refund my airline ticket. Doing things in a timely manner does not seem important, but they expect it of Xi-fen. She works so hard, and they keep piling on jobs for her to do.

"I'm working like a horse," she says. It's a favorite expression of hers, and it's true.

"Can't you tell them, no?" I asked.

"I can't do that. They will just say, 'We have twenty people in line behind you that can take your job.'" Xi-fen is such a hard worker and so talented in teaching and languages. I know this is not true. She is unique in her skills and is unappreciated.

Mr. Chang is leaving again on October 20, which is why there is a big rush to do this Halloween activity for him.

Last week, I was in the English Center, and Xi-fen told me she is going to do a school newspaper. Last week it was just for the English Center, done in English. Today it is going to be translated into Chinese—remember it doesn't exist yet—and gotten out by Monday, now to the whole school and community.

Xi-fen keeps putting more and more pressure on me to do things for her. I don't mind helping but . . . there is no escape when you live right on top of your job.

I am teaching the two classes at another high school in town. Now she says, "We can't leave out our school. So would you teach our junior high school students on Saturdays?" I agreed to teach them two Saturdays when we will not go out of town. As my "agent" she has negotiated $12 per hour, a high rate for China. I know Mr. Chang is requesting these classes.

You can see why the Internet Café is my great escape. It's like phone calls home. It makes me feel close to all of you.

Everything is still fine here, still warm. Don is doing OK with his teaching, but Pam is struggling. A supervisor from Memphis University is coming to see her. Maybe that person can help her.

It's difficult to get to this Internet Café now because the rains have turned the roads into thick mud.

Send me news from home.

Love,

Carolyn

Letters to Friends

13

October 12, 1998

Internet Café, Email to Gail

Hi Gail,

This Internet Café, which isn't a cafe at all, has an empty glass coffee carafe but never coffee, and it is where Don and I hang out. It is our escape and keeps us from feeling so isolated. My students in Concord email me with their limited English. Charlene, my friend and their substitute, uses the stories I send in easy English for class lessons there.

Chinese life is quite different from what you might expect. Almost everyone lives close to their job site. Transportation for this many people is limited, and all they do is work. Their houses are small, so upkeep is minimal. Most have few possessions and don't worry about whether their home is in good condition. Xi-fen is an exception. Work, at least at this school, is stretched out so many hours. If you live here, you work round the clock like Xi-fen. That doesn't mean you get more done. It isn't efficient. She has to "fight and argue" with everything she tries to do or needs for us or the English Center. She doesn't want to admit that this is the Chinese way, but it's what I see. She also has to fight to get our bottled water delivered.

People I meet do not seem too interested in the world, and they don't know much about it. It could be that they don't have extra time. It seems like most have TVs, even the teachers who spend almost twelve hours here. There are no reading materials, newspapers, or magazines. Some teachers sleep at their desks for the two-hour lunch, and Xi-fen tells me they have beds here at school. Xi-fen's room is in a building across from the English Center, where I am. I can see her window across the grassy area from my room.

Every minute of the student's schedule is planned for two weeks at a time, and there is no free time. Students get a local TV station in their classrooms but only occasionally see some sports shows at night. The school has applied for a satellite dish, but it will be months before permission is granted. The people here seem content with this local lifestyle. The people I have met don't think about going out or traveling. It is costly and out of reach on their salaries.

I am not required to take Chinese language lessons like the other foreign teachers because I am not here for a year. If I were to study Chinese, it would be Mandarin. I wouldn't be able to speak to people in town as they speak "Jiangyinese", the local language. Reading Chinese writing is the same for all, but speaking is different from town to town and sometimes village to village.

Answer to your health question: No health care for me. For some reason, Xi-fen "doesn't have it yet."

I just can't get sick. My friend Naji George, the bridge engineer, gave me a phone number to call his company for a hospital referral in Wuxi if I ever needed it.

There is no English reading material unless we go to Shanghai, two hours away. There is supposed to be a store there, but I have no idea how big it is or what it has.

Don and I use Yahoo news. One sentence tells the whole story. It sounds worse than awful there at home now.

It is still quite warm even though it rains and turns the dust to mud. I used my air-conditioning unit last night and am still chasing mosquitoes and wearing repellent to bed.

I love hearing from you. Say hi to Axel.

Love,

Carolyn

Thursday, October 15, 1998

Internet Café, Email home to Mike

Hi Honey,

Did you get my letter? My eyes went blurry, and I couldn't tell if I sent it to you. Just let me know, and I'll write it again. Thanks for the report on Bud. I can't tell you how much I appreciate your going by and checking on him. I think Lynessa did talk to Mary Jo.

Mary Jo was going to get on him about eating. I sure hope she did. If I were there, I would tell him he'll land in a convalescent hospital to get better if he continues to treat his body this way. I also think Mary Jo should get him to see a doctor at Kaiser—one for geriatrics that can evaluate his condition and get him off that "therapy." I spoke to Mary Jo about this before I left. She knows the Kaiser system and hopefully can do this. I sent Mary Jo two emails and haven't heard back. I'm not sure if they received them.

I'll write more soon,

Love,

Carolyn

Martinez, California
Friday, October 16, 1998
From Gail
Hi Carolyn,

I think what you are acquiring on this extended trip is patience, patience, and more patience.

But no, sad to say, I didn't see you on TV. Did you see yourself on TV? They should put Xi-fen on TV, as she seems to enjoy seeing herself. Maybe all the photos she has taken of herself is a way to prove she has been in those places. Maybe it has some spiritual significance, good photo karma.

I enjoy reading about all the trials and travails of living and traveling in China, as well as hearing about all the historical stuff. I do love your scenery and weather descriptions.

You sound happier, maybe because you were on TV?

Our trip to Greece is moving forward. It's two weeks from tomorrow. Ann wants me to rent a car, as it's cheaper from here. I spent an hour on the phone and found a wide spectrum of prices. I settled on Auto Europa. Linda has talked me into getting drachmas ahead of time, so I'll track down the American Express office in Walnut Creek.

I keep seeing Mike's name in the paper. The paper mentions his client, the pregnant woman, and her underage lover. Poor woman. Mike is doing the best he can. We are all rooting for him to find her a halfway house so she won't be in prison when her baby is born.

Your Halloween preparations sound great! Too bad you didn't find "Thriller," but it might have been too scary.

Love,

Gail

Saturday October 17, 1998

Internet Café, Email home

Hi Gail,

Thanks for your email. I always love hearing from you. This email saved my sanity.

Don and I agree and laugh at the reports that say the internet is isolating. It sure isn't for us.

Xi-fen likes to memorialize herself in the "scenic spots" because it is a big deal to travel. People in this area do not think about going anywhere but the few miles around where they live.

I have been teaching for seven weeks and I have seven weeks to go. I have never been unhappy here. I just try to report it in a realistic way. If I were unhappy, I would be home in a minute. Xi-fen is so grateful to me for coming. I am helping her personally and with this English Center. I feel like she "sent for me," and it was meant to be. I'm grateful I had this opportunity to experience this culture.

Xi-fen has an uphill battle here at school trying to promote the English Center.

I do use the lovely journal you gave, but I like to record more in my emails. I use the journal for quick ideas and impressions.

I don't get any details on Mike's cases. We have limited communication.

It can be boring here, but there are diversions.

We have one more Halloween party on Tuesday night. Halloween is strange here, but the students are fascinated by it.

Hi to Axel.

Love,

Carolyn

Saturday, October 17, 1998

Internet Café

Dear Mike and Lynessa,

I am so distressed. I just erased my entire finished letter to you and must start over. This keyboard is tricky.

I'm so glad I got to talk to you. It was great to hear your voices. I'm glad to hear things are working out for Lynessa and Katie. I think it's a good idea to be able to go back and forth a little until I get home.

I told Lynessa that Xi-fen had me lined up to give a lecture to students and teachers tomorrow at the highest academic high school in town. She wants it to be on the American school system, complete with a handout, so they would understand me. I told her there wasn't enough time to do it—meet with our students, get candy, cakes, do all the Halloween decorations, get apples, and teach five classes on the same weekend. She changed the date. I also explained that it's Mr. Chang's last week, and he isn't going to care about this other school event. He is just too busy. She pushes me when she thinks it will please Mr. Chang. That's her job.

The Halloween party was a success, with the Halloween bingo game, jack-o'-lantern word people, bobbing for apples, and pumpkin carving. The students in art classes made their own masks. Somehow, those teachers had access to orange paper.

It was a job, as I had thirty kids hanging the decorations when our cleaning lady, "too pretty to clean," who is completely ridiculous, started mopping the floors under our feet. I nearly tripped over her bucket. By 8:00 a.m. the next morning, she had thrown out all the corn stalks and the pumpkins. We dug the cornstalks out of the garbage, but the pumpkins were gone.

They managed to turn off the water just as the party started so we had no water for bobbing for apples or the bathrooms. Xi-fen made three panicked calls to Mr. Chang, and water was turned on thirty minutes later! Well, this is China . . . Everything is difficult.

I think the local TV station is going to come and film the next party, Tuesday night. More later . . . I probably can't get to the internet until Thursday. I look forward to your faxes.

We are also looking forward to the package. I am fighting a bladder infection with the medicine I brought. I just have to drink a lot of water, which is a real challenge if you need to use these horrible, smelly toilets!

Yesterday, we went by school car to a Chinese Water Town two and a half hours away. It was our reward for doing the Halloween party and not taking overtime pay. It was much better than money because we couldn't travel on our own and would never have been able to get to this unique village.

It was sort of a "Chinese Carmel," small homes and shops from a bygone era lining the canals, which were like Venice, in a Chinese way. There were students, artists, shopkeepers, and old women watching life go by, sitting on chairs, talking to their neighbors. We went for a boat ride with a woman, poling our way to see the famous ancient bridges the town is known for. There were many domestic tourists and seven foreigners. We got back at 9:00 p.m. It was a fun day.

Pam drove us all nuts! She is unbelievably self-centered. All she talks about is herself. She corrects everything you say, even for events where she wasn't present! I will never criticize Don for not going on an outing where he has to spend the entire day with her. She drove Xi-fen crazy, and our driver, who doesn't speak English, told Xi-fen to leave her home next time. She is a strange person.

I miss you all,

Love,

Carolyn

Lafayette
Sunday, October 18, 1998
Email from Lynessa
Hi Mom!

I hope your Halloween parties went well. Did you get all of your supplies? How does everyone like Halloween? Do they like bobbing for apples? I guess you can find apples in China. Did Mr. Chang like the party?

As you know, I got the apartment in the Presidio with Katie. We are both excited about moving into it. We are hoping to choose which one we want, and of course, we want an upper one with an ocean view. I may even be able to ride my bike (your bike) to work. We are planning to move on Sunday. Katie has furniture from her grandmother's house. It is old and heavy, so we will need help and a truck.

Work is going smoothly. They are hiring a new full-time accounting assistant, who will also do admin part-time. That makes four of us doing admin, which seems unnecessary when it is only a company of twenty-one people. I have the perfect amount of work and enjoy the sales part of my job. I have a business email, so now I am in the loop for the marketing team.

I don't understand where the money comes from to hire new people all the time, pay for benefits, and buy new lighting. I like the people. Most have kids and families.

Daddy invited his brother over for lunch today and barbecued all sorts of stuff for him and left me out. Sometimes he can be very frustrating.

I'm hoping to make new friends in the city now that I've cut three hours off my commute time. I miss my friends from college in Oregon, and I miss going out with them.

I don't know what we'll do for Thanksgiving. Desiree will be in Peru and Michelle in England. It may be just Daddy and me.

I will try to see Bud this week.

Take care and write soon!

Love,

Lynessa

Tuesday, October 20 and Wednesday, October 21, 1998

Dear Carolyn,

Well, I was tired, but my face was again on channel seven on the Wilson case, which is about finished. What a sad comment on what we are fed as "news." So here I am becoming famous while you adventure around China.

I am continuing to work out for my wrist with your weights that I found in the garage. It is much better, but it is still not all healed. The doctor is pleased, so I guess it will work out.

Muppet continues to thrive. I have been amazed at how often I have been able to get home for lunch and let her out. It will be tougher when Lynessa leaves.

The package I sent should be about to arrive. I just sent it by airmail. No more Global Express.

Have you finally been paid?

October 21, continued

I am already starting to plan events for your return. It may not be as quiet as yours, but I will soon be leading a very staid existence. I am trying to picture cooking for one when Lynessa leaves. Maybe I will go on the mooncake diet.

At the end of next week, Gail and Linda will meet Ann in Greece. I plan to have Frank and Axel over for steaks and beers.

I have wound up several big cases, but I have return clients who are in trouble again. All the stuff in the papers doesn't hurt.

Bud is doing well. Lynessa will see him on Thursday or Friday.

We think several of our rugs are over there. Lynessa is anxious to cover her linoleum floors.

Please let me know what else I can send you. Do you want books? Is there any point in trying to send paper so that Thanksgiving doesn't look like Halloween?

We are having great fall weather. It sounds like a sea of mud there when it rains.

I love you,

Mike

Wednesday, October 21, 1998

Internet Café, Email home

Well, the Halloween parties are finally over. Thank goodness. We did two, one last Thursday and one this Tuesday. We split the high school group of two hundred or more into two groups. It was crazy and exhausting, and that was just the preparation.

Our cleaning lady, "too pretty to clean," threw out all the pumpkins last week after the party. One of the teachers, a good friend of Xi-fen's, went door to door in the countryside asking the farmers for pumpkins. She found enough white ones—they don't have orange—and saved the party. The farmer asked us to save the seeds and return them to him to plant next year. Xi-fen told me that they weren't the kind you can eat, but I assured her that it was fine with us. The pumpkin carving went on as planned, and the seeds were returned. "Too pretty to clean" threw out all the cornstalks we had for decoration, but we were able to go through the garbage and retrieve them for the second party.

This party was important because we had the local TV station coming.

We went through incredible grief to get receipts, with the appropriate "chop," to get reimbursed from the school for the small cakes we ordered. Nothing is easy or convenient. This whole project took hours and hours.

The "teacher," Pam, was horrible. She slept last week as we all rushed around hanging decorations, working with students, and setting up music and the stations for the student activities. It's hard to describe her. She assured us she would help this week. She showed up as the party was getting started. The students had fun "bobbing for apples" and playing Halloween bingo. They had never done these activities. They did not hesitate to put their faces in the large pan of water to try to bite the apples. Many danced to the fast music. I danced with Mr. Chang.

The TV station was there recording it all. It was great. Xi-fen was very proud of the event and rightly so.

Afterward, upstairs I opened a bottle of red wine and offered Don a glass to celebrate. He had done all the music and acoustics. Pam saw it and asked if she was included. Remember, we were all exasperated with her.

I said, "Well, actually, I am feeling like 'the Little Red Hen.'"

I asked her if she knew this classic story. She said no, so I explained the story to her. She was fuming, turned on her heel, and announced that, "She had tried to help." And we said, "Hello, are you with it?" She is not speaking to me, and I hope it stays that way.

Today, Wednesday, I had eighteen teachers, friends of Xi-fen, who came by school bus from her former school in Wuxi to observe my teaching in the classroom with a full class of students. They stayed the entire period, listening to everything. Fortunately, it was Xi-fen's class, and they could be asked to cooperate. The class was so good. I must figure out a way to treat them. After class, I met for an hour with the Chinese teachers who asked me questions and listened to my English.

Finally, at 4:00 p.m., Don and I came into town here. We'll eat at McDonald's, shop for groceries, and try to find the English Corner. We have lost contact with our friends Yang Li-ping and Ms. Fay.

We can't call them on the phone. Maybe they will be at the English Corner tonight.

This weekend, I will teach two junior high classes. I have set it up to be easy for me, and hopefully fun for them. If the weather is nice, I can go for a bike ride to the other side of town. I will try to get to the international hotel—it's not the one I thought it was, but I want to check out if I can get AT&T and phone home.

Xi-fen's "probably trainable" assistant (the jury is still out on this), Susan, continues to mess up. She just lost all the original papers for the English Center News. She opened up the back of Xi-fen's camera and exposed all her film from Hangzhou All that time taking photos of her posing in front of sights was wasted. Fortunately, I have other pictures in my camera. It drives Xi-fen crazy. I like Susan, but she is a little flighty.

I am still waiting for the package. All of us are complaining about our feet. These floors are so hard.

Hi Lynessa, Thanks so much for your emails and faxes. How is your job going? I'm so happy Muppet hasn't been sick. Please give her and yourself a hug from me.

Love,

Mom

Dear Mike,

What have you found out about Money Grams? I really need to know so I can plan for this U.S. money. I don't want to keep it here. Anyone can come into this building. Do you want me to ask someone else to find out for me? I need help on this. You have to start the research there. It's impossible here. I've asked.

Love and kisses.

Where is my fax from you?

Wednesday, October 21, 1998

Internet Café, Email to Gail

Dear Gail,

You are so good to write so often, as I know how busy you are. Thanks for the news about your trip. I will have to keep track of the days you are gone in Greece. You should see Delphi early in the morning. Mike and I took a bus trip, and our guide knew the places along the way where the Greek myths were set. She had studied all the Greek plays and could tell us the stories. "Remember, the oracle is always right. Do you want to know what the baby will be? A boy or girl? The Oracle says, 'boy no girl.'" The comma must be interpreted. Boy, no girl or boy no, girl.

It's getting cooler here. I need a sweater at night. Right now, I am removed from issues at home. I wish I could exercise more here. We could use a video player with videos, but it's not an option.

The floors are tile. All of us are complaining about our feet.

Now Don and I are going to McDonald's to eat and then to the bars to try and find the English Corner tonight.

I'm excited about your trip. I'll write more soon.

Love,

Carolyn

Martinez, California

October 21, 1998

Email from Axel at home

Dear Carolyn,

I just finished the book *London* that you lent me. It took quite a while, but it was also worth it. I've always liked these comprehensive types of books, very Mitchenerish. Do you even have time for reading? I gather that they are working you quite hard. Send us an average day's work itinerary.

I got a chuckle out of your going to McDonald's for supper, so American, and then heading for the pub later, so European. How are these months going to change the way you spend your time, or will you immediately revert to the prior routine? We always think we'll do all these things when we return from a busy and stimulating trip, and then end up slipping right back to the same old. We briefly talked about canceling our cable TV since our son won't be here, but it won't happen.

I can hardly wait to hear all about your adventures when you get back.

Love,
Axel

Thursday, October 22, 1998

Internet Café, Email to Gail and Axel

Hi Gail and Axel,

Well, it will be easy to slip right into my old ways at home and be very happy about it. There is little that is familiar to our culture, or to those in Europe, a food or a custom. I will miss Xi-fen and my friends here.

Today is actually a pretty day. I rode my bike to get here. It's Friday, so with the new schedule, I finished my classes at noon. I had hoped to take pictures on the canal, but the boats were all docked.

I do read a lot. I finished *Aztec*, the most grisly book I've ever read. I need more to read and may have to resort to reading Don's fantasy, which I don't like. I have only one book left and no way to buy more. I'll figure something out.

I have five classes on Monday, 8:30 a.m. to 3:10 p.m., with a two-hour lunch break, when they sleep. Tuesday through Thursday, and Friday, I have four each day. This Saturday, I have two, and Sunday

I have one class. Xi-fen talked me into doing these as favors for Mr. Chang. This week, I will have twenty-three classes. Most teachers here have fourteen and complain. I don't have to stay overnight with the boarding students for night duty like they do or write out the comprehensive lesson plans.

I am paid ten times more than the Chinese teachers.

Thanks for writing.

Love,

Carolyn

Martinez, California
Friday, October 23, 1998
Email from Axel
Hi Carolyn,
Just a quick note to a celebrity. Let me know what kind of books you like to read, and I will go to Bay Books, over next to the Capri Theater, and buy a few second-hand novels for you. Bay Books has a great collection of all kinds of books.

Reply ASAP, or the books will arrive after you have left.

Love,

Axel

October 24, 1998
Internet Café, Email to Axel
Hi Axel,
Thanks for the offer to send some books. I would like that. Mike is not reliable about sending me anything, and he is so slow! I like historical fiction, but anything you think is good is fine. I read all kinds of things. You should wrap them with brown paper, tape them, take them to the regular post office, and send them Air Mail as a small package. It

should take nine days to get here, just like a letter. Thanks so much!

Just another word about McDonald's. It's hard to understand this place, but other than Kentucky Fried (yucky food), it is the only place we can eat here. I can't even recognize the Chinese symbol for rice. Every restaurant has only a Chinese menu. The food stalls on the street are not a safe option. Xi-fen and I found some indoor fast-food places the other day, where I could just point to what I wanted, but they are far away across town.

Thanks in advance for the books.

Love,

Carolyn

Martinez, California

Friday, October 23, 1998

Email from Gail

Hi Carolyn,

You will have to give us your autograph when you come back! I have a few more questions for you. Who cut your hair? Are there hair salons? What if you wanted a perm? Did you bring enough clothes? Have you bought any new ones? Will you bring back any clothes?

I got Greek drachmas, $200 worth. It looks like a lot more. I got a passport holder, a map of Greece, and a Greek travel book. We are set. Next week at this time, we will have been on our flight for half an hour. I wish the travel part were over. It takes a whole day to get there.

Love,

Gail

October 24, 1998

Internet Café

Hi Gail,

You are such a faithful friend to write so much and so often. Thank you. I am kept busy here at the "Café" answering and writing. It's good.

My friend Don is twenty-eight, like my daughter Desiree. He is mellow, nice, and easy to get along with. The young woman who came with him on the same program from the University of Tennessee is difficult, and no one wants to be around her. They are with a program based in Shenzhen. They came when Mike was here. Neither has any experience. Don is doing all right with his preschoolers, but Pam has an out-of-control classroom and is not teaching much. She thinks she is doing fine. She is clueless and does not have the personality for teaching elementary grades.

I got my hair cut last week in what was considered the "best salon in Jiangyin." Susan, Xi-fen's assistant, recommended it. "Energetic" is how Susan described my haircut. I went to a nice-looking young man and had Xi-fen translate for me. The salon was a bit messy, with hair piled up in corners. I probably won't have to get it cut again. I wouldn't attempt getting a perm. They don't have reliable products.

Shopping on my own one day in town, I did find a pants outfit that fits. It's kind of funky. Xi-fen says it's "Taiwanese style."

On another day in town, I was walking around, and a man in a black car started following me. He kept motioning me to come over to him. I ignored him, and because I was walking, I could easily duck around corners and lose him. It didn't scare me too much because Xi-fen assures me here people are expected to be good to their "foreign friends."

I'm excited about your trip to Greece. I emailed Linda.

Can you imagine how to explain the Clinton debacle here in China? It is all over the news here and kind of disgusting.

I had a long phone call with Mike this morning. Xi-fen and I found a good telephone in the wholesale local market, where people sleep with their chickens. I got through to AT&T. I just need to make a local call to AT&T, and they connect me, but it doesn't always work.

My clothes are fine here. Xi-fen is wearing wool, but I am not cold and am wearing my summer clothes with light sweaters. As I expected, I am wearing my clothes out. I hand-wash everything. My shoes are a problem because I am having so much trouble standing on my feet for hours on the hard tile floors. Mike was supposed to send me insoles, but it has been three weeks, and they haven't arrived yet!

Happy packing.

Love,

Carolyn

Chapter

Celebrity Status 14

Saturday, October 24, 1998

Internet Café, Email to family and friends at home

Stepping out of the car sent by the high school in Jiangyin today, I felt like I was Princess Diana, with my new short haircut and my celebrity status. This school sent this car for Xi-fen and me. I was to be their guest lecturer for a specially selected group of fifty high schoolers at the highest scholastic school in Jiangyin. These students were tested in junior high school and were in the top 1 percent of all students in the area. Public schools are grouped strictly according to test scores.

These students have never had a foreign teacher speak at the school. I was treated like the president, a big deal. All they lacked was a red carpet for me. Whenever I feel the need to be a celebrity, I will come to China.

One girl came rushing up to me and said, "I saw you on a corner in town and couldn't believe what I was seeing. Now I actually get to meet you."

I had put together an outline showing how our government is set up and how the U.S. education system functions. I went through it, explaining more as I went.

I opened for questions and called it "Interviewing the Teacher." They were certainly an appreciative audience. I walked with the microphone up and down to reach the students in the terraced aisles. I felt like Phil Donahue, doing this on his TV show. They laughed at my jokes and asked great questions. I learned as much about them as they did me.

The students asked questions I didn't expect.

"What kind of childhood did you have?" "What did you do after school?"

I told them about Girl Scouting, taking piano, and dancing lessons. They were amazed and told me they had never seen anything like this. I told them I used to walk to the library in my town and check out books. They couldn't believe that our libraries are free for anyone to use. They told me here you must pay to use a library, so people don't use them. I told them I could check out books and bring them home.

Here, no one is allowed to check out books, "because no one would return them."

I told them we were on an honor system, but we do pay a small fee if the book was late. I told them about after-school sports. They were amazed. They have no sports. I could tell they feel that their life is too regimented, competitive, and stressful, with no "free time." They were envious of my childhood. It seemed idyllic to them. There is great family pressure from parents and grandparents to succeed. They asked me about President Clinton.

I will go again next month. I assigned "homework" for them to think about their short-term and long-term goals. I'm not sure what I'll do with it next time, but I'll think of something.

They took about fifty photos, gave me a bag of gifts, and will pay me as well.

My morning was spent at my own school, teaching two classes of junior high students. Their teachers came with them. They looked like our American fourth graders. They were so cute and enthusiastic. They were happy and excited, as this was their first English lesson. We practiced "shoes," and then "socks," and learned, "I am wearing shoes and socks." They tried so hard; it was just adorable. I loved it.

It's Saturday night, and Don and I are at the Internet Café. We'll probably walk to the "City Hunter Club." I will go from celebrity to bar fly in one day.

Sunday, October 24, 1998

Internet Café, Email home

Dear Mike and Lynessa,

Mike—How is your wrist? Have you found out any information about Money Grams yet?

I have to put someone else on it if you don't help me. I have to work on this now because everything is so difficult to do here, and Wuxi and Shanghai are far away.

I wrote a long letter to you last night and somehow lost the whole thing!!! UGH.

But now I'm back. It was good to hear your voices this morning. I hope Lynessa's move goes well.

I will ask Xi-fen to check the fax machine. I am still waiting for that package.

It was so much fun yesterday morning to teach the junior high students. They were so excited about learning English; it was absolutely adorable. I did two classes and will do two more in two weeks.

As I mentioned in the email, it was quite unbelievable how that other high school treated me. I was such a big deal to them. They were gracious and welcoming.

Next weekend, Xi-fen and I plan to go out of town to visit Ming ming Ayi, another exchange teacher who taught in Oregon at the same time Xi-fen lived with us. It sounds like it will work out for us to go by bus to Nanjing.

At the English Corner on Wednesday night, Don and I met four friendly Chinese women: one an art teacher, an army officer, a translator for a shipping company, and an executive in a hospital. They spoke excellent English.

I met two men from California here at the Internet Café on Thursday. They were having retrofits made for the toll booths on the Carquinez Bridge near us in California. I helped them set up Yahoo accounts. They were happy about that.

They were saying how hard it was to get anything done in China. They have a box of equipment that has been in customs for a week. They are nice guys. One of them will be here for six weeks.

When I said I had a bike, they couldn't believe it! This guy, six-foot-four, said he was afraid to cross the street. I told him I used to be that way but was used to it now.

Write soon!

Love,

Carolyn

Sunday, October 25, 1998

Fax from Lynessa

Hi Mom!

I am starting this letter a little early because of the time change. I am tired though. We moved me to the Presidio today. On Friday and Saturday, we had a retreat at work. There are so many people who work at the Grove that I don't know because they travel so much. . .

Sunday, we moved. Katie's parents rented a van and picked up furniture from her grandmother's house in Walnut Creek. We picked up a bookcase and some chairs from here. Our apartment is on the second floor, so it was quite a process. Daddy was a great help. I will stay there tomorrow night by myself, and Katie will come on Tuesday night. I think it will be pretty lonely on Monday. We are looking forward to having more time without our commutes. We can both take the bus from there.

I hope you make it through the Thanksgiving parties now. You don't have much longer to go! We all miss you here. I seems like you have been gone a long time.

Love,

Lynessa

Lafayette

Sunday, October 25, 1998

Fax from home from Mike

Dear Carolyn,

We are sending this with last week's fax. Sorry you didn't get it. It was really good to talk to you on Saturday night without the feeling that the card would start beeping any second. It sounds like you are enjoying being a "star." When I tell people we got started walking around Jiangyin, they don't understand.

Lynessa and I have just finished dinner and have given Muppet a bath. She is drying on my lap. After Lynessa spent two days in San Francisco, Muppet started sleeping with me upstairs.

Lynessa and I, along with Katie and her parents, spent a large part of the day getting the girls' furniture moved into the new apartment. It has a view of the water from the deck. Katie and Lynessa will now spend the week arranging the furniture into the spacious rooms. They have neighbors who seem pleasant and have two friendly pit bulls.

We had a pretty big rain here on Saturday. The leaves are turning colors, and it is getting cool at night.

I am starting to count down to your return.

Love,

Mike

Dallas, Texas

Monday, October 26, 1998

Email from daughter Michelle

Wow, Mom!

I never considered the option of just going to China to be a princess! Sounds wonderful.

I can't wait to see the short hair. It's great that you can ride your bicycle. I'm trying to walk at least a mile every day and four on the weekends. I'm also going to my yoga gym.

The weather is nice now here in Texas. It's over seventy degrees for the high and fifty degrees for the low.

I can have the windows open. The heat this summer caused a cricket infestation. There were crickets EVERYWHERE. The worst was having them fly into my hair at restaurants. Well, that's over, and the next thing is apparently a moth infestation. This isn't as bad, but I hear worms are next. I really do want to get out of here! (smile)

I have found some jobs on the internet that sound perfect in San Francisco. I am sending one a resume this morning and crossing my fingers that it will bear fruit.

I'm getting ready to have a little Halloween party. That's good, too.

Love,

Michelle

October 27, 1998

Bell School, Fax to home

Dear Mike,

The package arrived yesterday. It was not double-wrapped. It was put together with flimsy tape. It contained two thick insoles, one magazine, no photos, and two empty tea bags. You mailed it on October 17. I told you in mid-September that I was desperate for the shoe insoles. What was it about "desperate" that you didn't understand? It also contained deodorant. I did not ask for deodorant—do not want deodorant—a total waste. Are you reading what I write? I did ask for masking tape. Did you get that message?

You cannot send such a flimsy package to China. You need to wrap it in heavier paper or buy the plastic envelopes at the post office or at mailboxes. You must tape the seams. We have packing tape at home in the kitchen drawer.

This is all you have to do for me for three months. I'm not even costing you money.

I need six pairs of thin insoles. Those thick ones you sent are OK for my slippers and sandals but not my regular shoes. I can't walk without these pads. I am on my feet now for five hours at a time, teaching with aching feet.

I need:

1) 6 pairs of Dr Scholl's thin insoles

2) Tea would be nice; seal it in a zip lock bag

3) 1" masking tape. We have some in the kitchen drawer

4) More magazines

5) 3 packs of Post-its

I guess the photos of Xi-fen's family were inside the packet, too? They are gone.

Please answer these questions:

1) What is the information on the MoneyGrams?

2) Did you put the ad in the Berkeley job listing?

3) How is your wrist?

4) Have you had your doctor's check-up?

I hope to hear from you soon. Take care of yourself.

Love,

Carolyn

Lafayette

Wednesday, October 28, 1998

Fax from home

Dear Carolyn,

Lynessa and I have just returned from having dinner with Linda, Frank, Gail, and Axel. It was a send-off for Linda and Gail's trip to meet Ann in Greece. Linda is worried about her hip. Gail has reserved a car to go to see the monastery at the top of those funny mountains. Linda really misses you.

Lynessa will be here for a few days. We are getting the wheels aligned on her Buick.

She seems happy with her new place, but they don't have hot water and need lamps.

I have been very busy at work. The receptionist at the West County Jail asked me, "Do you work every day?" I told her she wouldn't see me in December.

October 29, 1998

Dear Carolyn,

Well, now you have the *Time* magazines that are all about the Clinton thing. Congress voted for an impeachment inquiry this week. The fate of the whole thing probably depends on the results of the congressional elections. The public sure doesn't want it. There is a lot of dirt being thrown around. Barbara Boxer and Davis are both in tight races here.

Lynessa is here doing her sewing while I write. She and I are doing our laundry. I am on to it now, but I will have to wash a lot more dishes if she moves out. I have found that doing the cooking for dinner is not only practical but also puts work out of my mind when I get home.

Continued fax
Friday, October 30, 1998
Dear Carolyn,
Muppet and I are going over to San Mateo to see Bud today. He is anxious to see Muppet. I will go to a car show with my brother and probably stay in San Mateo overnight.

Desiree and I, and hopefully Bud, are going up to the Presidio to see Lynessa's digs. I will try to get some of the food organized for "the presentation." We should have plenty of leftovers to leave for Lynessa.

The election is on Tuesday, and campaigning is more negative than ever. Boxer has now pulled ahead. Davis looks like a landslide over Lundgren. Clinton picked the Republicans' pockets on the budget and is now looking very presidential. Unless the Rs pick up a lot of seats in Congress or the Senate, the impeachment business should die before Christmas.

Speaking of Christmas, the stores are decorated for that event already. Lynessa thinks it is disgusting. Me too.

Love,
Mike

Continued fax
October 30, 1998
Dear Carolyn,
It rained here a while ago. We are definitely into winter weather.

The news today is that Gingrich is resigning as Speaker of the House. The Republicans are depressed. Hopefully, this means impeachment will die.

I folded the laundry and have done some cleaning. I have all the bills current. What a good little house husband I am.

Love,

Mike

Martinez, California

October 28, 1998

Email from Axel

Dear Carolyn,

I went to the post office today and mailed off some insoles and some books from the second-hand bookstore in Concord. I found some historical fiction that you said you like.

The post office personnel did not inspire confidence, so make a mental note to keep an eye out. Let me know when and if they arrive.

Love,

Axel

Internet Café, Email to home

Dear Axel,

Thanks so much for doing this in a timely manner. If things are wrapped well, they will get here in nine days. I brought seven books with me, but I'm on the last one. It's a horrible detective story about chopped up body parts. It's gruesome to read at night. Of course, I could be writing postcards instead.

Thanks again, Bon voyage to Gail! I wish her a fantastic trip.

Love,

Carolyn

Wednesday, October 28, 1998

Bell School, Fax to home

Dear Mike,

I finally got your faxes from October 21 and October 25. The fax lady with the key to the "room," actually a closet, did not tell Xi-fen they were there.

I'm glad Lynessa got moved in. I'm anxious to see the apartment. Lynessa has a new email address so I will be emailing her there.

Are you getting my emails? Maybe I should just forget about sending them to you and send faxes instead? What do you think?

This place is beginning to seem normal to me—funny how one gets used to things.

Today I am starting "Jeopardy" in some of my classes. I need this kind of activity to supplement the English "books" Mr. Chang brought from Taiwan. They had fifty copies made—all on copy paper and stapled. No one here considers copyrights. The problem is that the cultural differences and lifestyles between Taiwan and China are huge.

One lesson talks about playing tennis and going to the tennis club after school. These students have no idea what tennis is let alone a "tennis club." I have to pick out things they can relate to. We can do "giving directions," such as, "walk three blocks, turn left, and then turn right at the corner." I use copy paper on the floor for them to use as blocks and buildings.

The weather is nice but hazy. I use a little heat from the A/C unit they installed when you were here because I get up early. I'm still wearing my summer clothes with light sweaters.

Does your brother Tom have email? I could be sending stories to him and your mother.

Take care,

Love,

Carolyn

Martinez

Thursday, October 29, 1998

Email from Gail at home

Hi Carolyn,

Tonight, we had dinner with Linda and Frank, Axel, me, Mike, and Lynessa. Linda organized it, and we had lots of fun, though missing you. There was chatter about Lynessa's job (she needs stuff to do!) and her new place in the Presidio. It has huge linoleum floors and an ocean view that makes it all worth it. We will, maybe, visit after we come back.

Linda and I chattered on about travel stuff, what to bring, vitamins, long flights, her hips, etc. We are bringing our bathing suits. I feel like we are in a movie about three middle-aged ladies seeking thrills and adventure in exotic Greece. But of course, we are anything but your average middle-aged ladies: an art historian, an artist, and a technical writer/scientist. (I am the boring one.) If you were with us, you would be the missionary, as in China, bringing our language and culture— just kidding. You would be the teacher/traveler.

I hope you get the package. Axel did not sound very hopeful when he returned from the PH post office. He had to talk to several people before anyone had a clue. I hope you get it. If not, I hope the books have a good home and hopefully not the back room of the PH Post Office.

I am being careful in my step and aerobics classes so as not to hurt myself and end up hobbling around Greece. Linda will just have to be cautious and not walk or climb when she doesn't want to. Ann has me dragging around; that's why I'm being careful.

I've rented a car, and they told me I didn't need an international license. Now they are saying I do. I hope Ann can help with the driving. This is not sounding like a break from my long commute.

If you don't hear from me for a couple of weeks, you will know where we are. We will send you a postcard, and hopefully, you will receive it sometime in this lifetime.

Just think. Next year you will be back in Italy, and we will be in England, Germany, and who knows where else. Our little "feet just can't be still."

Take care,

Love,

Gail

Thursday, October 29, 1998

Internet Café, From my journal

With Halloween out of the way, Xi-fen is now talking about Thanksgiving. She wants to have a traditional meal like she had at our house in California. Her plan is that I would teach all two hundred-plus high school students western manners as they are eating dinner at the long tables in the cafeteria.

"Xi-fen, I don't think I can do that! We teach our children manners at our family table gradually over time. I can't see this working out with so many students." The problem I saw was getting and keeping their attention since some did not understand English. She wanted me to address the "spitting on the table" among other things.

"We need turkeys," she said.

I had never seen a turkey in China. Xi-fen had stuffed turkey in mind with mashed potatoes, maybe cornbread, and cranberry sauce. She acknowledged that she may have to give up on the cranberry sauce idea. She began to put her plan into operation.

The students go home tomorrow, so this weekend we are going to Nanjing to see Xi-fen's friend, Ming ming Ayi, who was an exchange teacher in Oregon while Xi-fen lived with us. We will stay overnight with her, her husband, and her son.

Nanjing & Yangzhou

Monday, November 2, 1998

Internet Café, From my journal

Xi-fen and I took the bus to Nanjing, and Ming ming Ayi met us. We stayed with her and her family. Xi-fen, Ming ming Ayi, and I had fun touring the famous sights in Nanjing.

We went to a tiny island on an inlet along the Yangtze River to see Shen Banqiao, a poet's retreat. Remnants of old walls, with aged yellow paint on his house, were all that was left. He was most famous for his calligraphy and orchid paintings that were hung on the walls.

I bought an orchid print of his work. We will find someone in Jiangyin to mount it on silk and make it a traditional Chinese scroll.

Lafayette
Tuesday, November 3, 1998
Email from Mike
Dear Carolyn,

Lynessa has just re-sent my last fax. I didn't know it didn't go through on Saturday. She is over to vote. The folks at the polling place all knew you are in China. See, you are famous here, too.

Wednesday, November 4, 1998
The Democrats did very well in the elections, especially here in California. Boxer and Davis won big. The Ds picked up seats in Congress and stayed even in the Senate. Hopefully, it will mean that the impeachment inquiry will die an early death. Lynessa is slowly getting more things for her apartment. She will come over Saturday and Sunday, and it will be good to have her here. I made meals with lots of leftovers to send home with her.

November 5, 1998
I have been chasing everyone to call Bud more often. He seems weak but upbeat. I met the housekeeper last weekend, and she is very nice. I will take Muppet over to him on Friday, and Lynessa will pick her up on Saturday morning. Bud needs company.

I am off to attend my seminar this weekend in Monterey. I may have to do one more this month. I am adamant to get them done before you return.

Frank and I went out to dinner and a "shoot 'em up" movie. Gail, Linda, and Ann are going to Crete before their return on Tuesday.

Muppet is fine. She will get a haircut tomorrow. She still looks for you. I think she is taking me on walks rather than the other way around. When I came home for lunch this week, I left the front door open. After I sat down to lunch, she got back into her bed. Suddenly, she started growling and ran out the open front door. She chased a deer up the hill, and when she came proudly back, she was covered with stickers.

The fax continued. . .

Sunday, November 8, 1998

Dear Carolyn,

This will come with my last letter. It was to be sent on Saturday but didn't make it.

Lynessa is visiting here and shopping for lamps. I'll make us a pot roast so she will have leftovers to take home. She talked to Michelle in Texas yesterday for two hours. I guess Michelle still has lots of complaints. Michelle is going to England for her job.

Bud was blustering over the election when I saw him on Friday. He seemed pretty spry. He was happy to have Muppet for almost a day while I went to the seminar.

I had great fun watching a video with Lynessa last night. Lynessa has been cleaning almost all day.

I sent a package to you that you should have received by now. I hope it is more successful than my last attempt. They are grading the clerks at the Walnut Creek Post Office, so maybe that will help.

Write and tell me about the things you want to do when you get home. I think about it a lot, but my ideas may not be yours. Let's have FUN! I am starting to count the days.

I will write again soon.

Love,

Mike

Thursday, November 5, 1998

Bell School, Fax sent home

Dear Mike,

I just received your faxed letters dated October 28 and October 30. Did you receive my two faxes from last week? Should I resend them? You didn't answer any of my questions. They were important to me. I already knew where you went to dinner; Axel told me last Friday. The election is not very important to me, as I'm not there. *Time* magazine and the other things I need are.

Are you in a fog? I'm worried about you! I tried to call you four times this morning at 10:40 a.m. here. Do you have the phone unplugged, or were you just not home?

Do you read anything I write?

We are isolated here, and your non-response is upsetting. Please respond.

My sister is doing what she can for Bud. She wrote me a long letter saying she was getting him healthy food. He is taking a cure-all, Chinese medicine that, coincidentally, my students at home use and sell.

Please take it easy at work. I hope you have a good time in Monterey this weekend.

Love,

Carolyn

Martinez

Friday, November 6, 1998

Email from Axel

Dear Carolyn,

Gail and Linda flew to Greece last Saturday. They met Ann in Athens. Gail said she walked around the Acropolis on Monday in good weather, though it wasn't hot. There were only a few people on the Acropolis. I would love to be able to go there in the off-season.

The next day, they were scheduled to rent a car and drive to Delphi and then Meteora. Instead, after seeing how crazy the driving is and how difficult it is to even decipher the road signs, they decided not to rent the car but take tours instead. They took a tour to Mycenae, Corinth, and that area. They flew to Iraklion in Crete. Gail called me from there after they toured Knossos. She said the museum was fabulous, with lots of Minoan artifacts and pottery. From there, they are going island hopping to Santorini, then Tinos, back to Athens, and home. I miss her a lot.

Everything here is pretty mundane. I'm at work a lot. Mike, Frank, and I were to go to the movies, but I had seen the movie and had to grade papers.

This week, Frank is in Monterey taking kayak lessons. Mike is in that area, taking some classes for his continuing education. I'm at home. Martin just walked in from Davis. He almost had to do his laundry at Davis! Unfortunately for him, I'm not his mother and won't do his laundry for him.

I hope all is well with you. You must be seeing the light at the end of the tunnel now. Gail will fill you in with her news next week.

Love,

Axel

Friday, November 6, 1998

From my journal

At five o'clock this evening, Xi-fen and I left by taxi to catch the ferry that would cross the Yangtze River to go to Yangzhou, known for its beautiful park. We got on the ferry and then had to take a bus to the city.

A man in the back of the bus was questioning Xi-fen. She turned to me and told me he wanted to know what I thought about the Clinton debacle. I put my hands up to hide my face, as if I were embarrassed.

He told Xi-fen, "We know our leaders do the same things, but we don't hear about it. We have a velvet curtain. You have a transparent one, so everything is seen. I think that is better."

Days are shorter now, and it got dark as we got in a taxi, the next leg of our trip. We rode through dark farm land with no lights in sight. The taxi stopped suddenly, and a woman opened my door and began shouting at me—she pointed to a mini-bus and pulled on my arm. Someone else started yelling at Xi-fen and opened her door. I was led onto a bus and watched as Xi-fen got out of the taxi. I watched through the window and plotted how I would rush to get off if she didn't make it on the bus. She got on and we were driven to the city and found our hotel.

The next morning, we went to the ancient Buddhist Temple and the old marketplace with old men standing around. I picked out a white jade piece from a low table and unsuccessfully bargained to get a better price. The old man in the Mao jacket was insistent, and since I hadn't seen any before, I paid his price. I think they looked at Xi-fen and me and decided we wouldn't be there if we didn't have money to spend.

We walked around acres of gardens and lakes in Yangzhou Park. It was lovely. Now we wanted to eat.

This restaurant was supposed to have noodles and fried rice. I looked at the Chinese characters as if I could read them. I still can't even recognize the character for rice; it changes.

We sat down, and Xi-fen announced that she was going to check the kitchen. She got up and went out the open doorway, down a bamboo-lined path to the kitchen. She returned a few minutes later and said it looked clean.

"There are a couple of middle-aged ladies with big woks doing the cooking," she said. "I told them I wanted them to rinse our plates with boiling water. They told me I could do it myself."

"Can I help you?" I asked Xi-fen as she quickly collected our few dishes and carried them over to a basin across the room. She poured boiling water from a thermos over our plates and sat down.

"Miss Interpreter, Miss Interpreter, excuse me. Who is that foreign woman sitting next to you?" a man called out to Xi-fen from the table next to us.

Xi-fen whispered the translation for me.

"I'm not her interpreter," Xi-fen said and turned around to face me.

"Well, who is she? You must be her interpreter," he insisted.

"I am not. We are traveling as friends."

"Where is she from? How can you be friends?" asked the other man sitting next to him.

"She is from America, and she's my friend," Xi-fen said.

"He just can't believe we are friends," Xi-fen whispered to me.

I knew the two men at the table were looking at us again. I have been in China for three months and was almost used to this staring. Xi-fen and I created quite a spectacle wherever we went. People gathered around us to watch me shop and listen to hear her speaking English to me. They gawked at us with open mouths when we laughed and chatted like best friends.

We do make an unusual couple. I'm tall, large, and "Western." She's petite. My travel clothes are comfortable with shoes for walking. Xi-fen, on the other hand, dresses for how she will look in photographs.

This morning in our hotel room she chose a fitted red plaid wool jacket, with a black fitted skirt with nylons and high heels, checking herself in the mirror as she dressed. She looks darling. Now she is hot and her feet are sore, but the pictures I took of her in front of all the "scenic spots" we walked by will turn out great.

"Carolyn, do you want your picture taken here?" she asked as we walked along.

"No, thanks, Xi-fen, but how about we take yours?" Her favorite poses are leaning against statues, sitting seductively on a bank, or looking through hanging vines. Another pose is with a parasol. She calls it "Japanese style." Too bad she can't take my picture. She either moves the camera or can't manage the auto focus. Cameras confuse her.

I tried to ignore the men next to us by looking through the open carved walls of this old Chinese Pavilion. The calm water of the lake and shore beyond showed through the carved ebony fretwork wall. The walls rose twelve feet, opening up to the clear blue sky. Today was the clearest sky I had seen since coming to China.

The lovely old fretwork was chipped and needed refinishing. As I looked up and around, the whole place was a bit shabby. The cement floor was spotted and dirty. The table tops were well-worn wood. We sat on loose, squeaky chairs. But thanks to Xi-fen, we would have clean dishes and hopefully good food.

No one came to get our order, and finally, Xi-fen went over to a young woman sitting at a desk in the middle of the room. She told her what we wanted to eat, and the woman wrote it down on a notepad. The woman spoke to an elderly man in his seventies who had just arrived carrying a large, round tray with dishes of food on his shoulders. He was wearing a blue jacket with a mandarin collar. He nodded when Xi-fen explained our order. Xi-fen came back and sat down across from me.

"Xi-fen, are those blue Mao style jackets some kind of restaurant server uniforms? I noticed other elderly people outside wearing the same thing."

"Oh, no. Those old people are wearing their clothes from the seventies. They think they are still in good condition, and they don't want to be wasteful. There was a time in China when everyone dressed like that."

"Miss Interpreter," the first man called again. "How old is your American friend? My friend here and I have a bet on."

"How old do you think she is?"

Xi-fen is always loyal to me, never telling my age.

"I think she is fifty-five," the first man said.

"I think she is forty-five," the other man said, "But Americans are always younger than they look, so I will say she's thirty-five."

Xi-fen translated the exchange to me. I laughed. I know she hates to get into these conversations about me. These are the common questions for foreigners. The Chinese respect and welcome age. We Americans want to stay young. They had more questions.

"Is your friend rich? How much money does she have? What does she think of President Clinton?"

I heard the name Clinton and realized they were quizzing her on the latest scandal in the news. Xi-fen was trying to discourage conversation by leaning over and talking to me.

"What do you think of this place?" she asked.

"I think it's a lovely pavilion from old China, not rebuilt like we usually see. It's wonderful that it wasn't destroyed in the Cultural Revolution. It could just use a little spiffing up. That's all."

"What was that word you used? Spiffing—I don't know it. What does it mean and how do you spell it?" She quickly opened her purse and pulled out her tiny book for writing new English words.

"I think it might be slang, or maybe I just made it up. You might not find it in the dictionary." I explained the meaning. She diligently writes down new words and definitions. When we get home, she will look it up and ask me about it again.

We started talking about going back this afternoon to our school in the next province.

"After we leave here, we'll get a taxi to the train station," Xi-fen said.

"We can't do that. Remember, we crossed the Yangtze River on a ferry last night?"

"Oh, I forgot."

"This is what we'll have to do. We have to find a taxi to the bus station here in Yangzhou, take a bus to the ferry to cross the Yangtze, then get to the train station in Zhenjiang on the other side. Then we'll take the train to Wuxi, find a taxi to your apartment to pick up those blankets. Then we will find another taxi to take us back to school." If all the connections went well, it would take about six hours. It is getting cold at night, and I know she needs those blankets. Her room at school is freezing with no heat.

"I don't know how we are going to get on the ferry. We don't want to pay too much. A taxi on the ferry will be expensive; a bus is cheaper."

"Don't worry about the money. I'm paying. I've got to spend my Chinese money here. It is not usable in America. We were lucky last night finding a taxi driver from the ferry who knew where to meet a bus that got us to this town. But I was a little worried when the cab driver stopped in the middle of that pitch black road and the woman opened the cab door, yelling at me to get on her bus."

"I know. I didn't understand what was happening either."

Oh dear, I thought Xi-fen understood what was happening.

The food was taking a long time. Just as Xi-fen got up to check on our order the old man wearing the Mao jacket arrived and put our food on the table.

"I don't think this food is hot enough," Xi-fen said, closely inspecting the food.

Our waiter took the food back to the kitchen. He returned promptly with the reheated food. It still wasn't really hot, but we decided to eat it anyway. We were running out of time.

"Miss Interpreter?" It was that voice from the other table again. "Please tell us how old your friend is. We have to settle our bet."

"I'll tell you which one is closest, but I won't tell her age. You are the closet," she told the man on the right.

"Oh, good. I win the bet, and he'll have me to dinner at his home. You and your foreign friend are invited, too."

"Thank you, but we have to be off now. Where is our waiter?"

We paid our bill and walked a long way back to the park entrance to find a taxi to begin our long journey home.

Monday, November 9, 1998

Internet Café

THANK YOU

Dear Axel,

Thank you so much for the package. It was postmarked on the 27th and arrived last week on the 4th, a record seven or eight days. I was so happy with the books and insoles for my shoes. Relief at last. I will reimburse you when I get home. It was a lot of money to send it, and I truly appreciate your thoughtfulness.

Thank you for the update on the travelers in Greece. I'm glad they got to Crete. I loved it all. Their trip is short, so they will want to go back. Then you will get to go.

Thanks again for the books, insoles, and news.

Love, Carolyn

November 9, 1998

Internet Café, From my journal

Xi-fen and I were invited to dinner at the home of Mr. Six, the man in charge of Bell Economic School. His brother, Mr. Seven, picked us up in his car. Mr. Seven and his entourage, his brother, wives, and children, had just returned from Australia, where they saw Xi-fen's former husband and son.

Mr. Seven is a friend of Xi-fen's ex-husband and was very persuasive in getting Xi-fen to sign the papers to let her son go to Australia with his father. Mr. Seven insisted that he did not know of their plan to stay in Australia and not bring Xi-fen's son back to China. Mr. Seven brought her son books from Xi-fen on his last trip.

We were invited to dinner to talk about their trip and meet Mr. Seven's family, who reside permanently in Australia, even though he runs a cigarette, wine label, and printing factory next door to the school. He also has a silk flower company close by. Mr. Seven is very personable, with a smooth, mellow voice, and he speaks perfect English.

Mr. Seven has a likable eighteen-year-old son who is attending a university and an adorable four-year-old daughter, Kathy. She was very concerned about getting a new hat for the Ascot Races in Melbourne.

Seven years ago, when he and his wife immigrated to Australia and became citizens, they decided to have another child because the one-child rule no longer applied to them. His wife and daughter live in Melbourne, and Mr. Seven lives in China and travels between both countries.

Mr. Six does not speak English. He is about my age and learned Russian in school when those countries were friendly with each other. His parents do speak English and reminded me of my students at home. They are about the same age, in their eighties. Mr. Six is the business brain of his successful eight-branch printing company that prints labels for cigarettes and wine. He has become a millionaire in the last ten years.

At the first meeting of teachers and workers at Bell School, as the principal, he told them that the school existed to make money, and that was their purpose. It is a case of a businessman running the school, and he is definitely not an educator. Business decisions come first.

The school suffers from significant unhappiness and disorganization. Mr. Six is never there because he travels to his factories all over China. His business office is in Jiangyin. He is the owner of the Chinese part of this private Bell Economic School. His factories support the school.

Dinner was a huge banquet with double dishes of delicacies, including blue river crabs and turtle soup with dead floating turtles, their heads up in each terrine. I tried not to let it upset me by avoiding their gaze.

Mr. Six is an intense man who likes to gamble. He left shortly after dinner to play mahjong even though there were ten guests. His wife was not happy with him.

Lafayette

November 8, 1998

Fax from Lynessa

Hi Mom!

How is China? I hope things are going well. You have less than a month left. You are probably looking forward to coming home.

I am here with Dad today. My job is fine, but I keep wondering where they get their money. They have hired another artist. I like keeping busy.

Desiree leaves for Peru on Thursday. She is excited about it.

My apartment is shaping up, but I get a little bored there. We have a TV, but we don't get any channels. Katie doesn't want to pay for cable. I may be willing to in about a week. I'm hoping to learn about my neighborhood and find things to do.

I bought some lamps today so at least I have light to read by.

I hope everything is OK. I can't wait for you to see my new place.

Love, Lynessa

The Commune 16

November 9, 1998

Internet Café, Email to friends and family at home

I was surprised to hear that there was a commune here, about a twenty-minute drive from school. Xi-fen and I went to visit the village called Huaxi (pronounced Wha she). It is in the countryside close to where Xi-fen grew up during the Cultural Revolution.

Since the 1940s, the people from Huaxi have been known as industrious and hard-working. They wanted to improve their rice and other crops, so they decided to level the hilly land and rid it of rocks, a tremendous feat. The surrounding villages in this poor, rural area thought this was a crazy idea. Life for everyone was already hard.

Through persistence and determination, they succeeded, and their agricultural production improved. Now, they have charts to prove it. Through each decade and through the Cultural Revolution, they continued to improve their production. A leader emerged in the 1960s, Wu Renbo, who continues to guide the village today. Wu Renbo is a secretary in the Communist Party.

After Mao's death in 1976, Deng Xiaoping took over. Deng began to promote more businesses for China. He thought the way to help the Chinese people was to put factories in the countryside. People could still farm, but they would have factory jobs to improve their standard of living. Huaxi has taken this idea and developed a planned community with communist principles unlike any other. Everyone in the Huaxi village pooled their money into the village funds.

Now there are many factories, steel and iron works, clothing, wine production, and other products. The government started all of these, but they are run and controlled by the village, and essentially developed by Mr. Wu.

Each family was given a large new home of their own, with several floors to accommodate the typical extended family. Each family was given a car, clothing, a modern kitchen, refrigerators, telephones, air-conditioning, and many items the average Chinese family couldn't possibly afford. Each person works in a factory for the commune seven days a week and enjoys these material comforts. Money goes back into the commune, and a family can ask for what they need. Each family has differing amounts of money, depending on their position in the various factories.

Our school has a few students from this commune. There is a huge new pagoda with a large department store on the first floor, selling all the products the village makes. People can visit here to see the outstanding progress.

Within the living grounds, there is no dust or mud, a common condition in China. The detached homes are connected by covered walkways inspired by those in the Summer Palace in Beijing. There are different-sized houses depending on the size of the family, but all are modern, spacious, and well-maintained. People grow flowers and have backyards with wells, water cool in the summer and warm in the winter.

On the same large living grounds is a vast complex, three stories, and stretching for blocks. This apartment house is for the "floating population," China's homeless. It is Huaxi's way to help those less fortunate than themselves. The people housed here do work in the factories. There is no crime or related problems. The needy people have a grocery store right in their apartment building.

Close to this huge apartment building is a Peasant's Park, with a Chinese Garden and Pavilions dedicated to older people, sort of a "Longevity Monument."

The walls of the covered walkways display the history and old photos of Huaxi. Above the portrait of each family are pictures of all the things they have, including a telephone and a refrigerator. Each display is the same, of course. The display shows a picture of bank certificates and tells how much money every family has.

This "First Village" of China is the envy of the villages around it. People feel very fortunate if their son or daughter can marry into a Huaxi family.

With our same car and driver, we went to see Xi-fen's girlfriend in the TV studio. It is small and just getting started. We saw the equipment they used. Her friend has just started to work there.

November 9, 1998

Internet Café, Email from Don

Subject: The City of Jiangyin

English teacher at Bell School, a view from my fellow foreign teacher

What follows is my muddled attempt to describe the town I live in. Expect no order because I am making it up as I go along. Search for a plot and you will find none. If you give me grief about my spelling, I'll never write to you again. To me, grammar should be a four-letter word, so I try to ignore it. You have been forewarned.

Ahh, the fabulous city of Jiangyin. It lies about two hours west of Shanghai. This region is supposed to be one of the more prosperous areas of China, but sometimes it seems close to a third-world country. Of course, I have never been to a third-world country, so what do I know?

As far as China goes, Jiangyin is a small city. I think there are about 500,000 people here. This is only a guess, but I think it's close. During the day, the city bustles with activity—people going about their business in a busy but relaxed fashion. I must say that the people here are really friendly. I have always been treated with more respect than I deserve. If the people in the city make the city what it is, then the people of Jiangyin have made their city a fine place to live. I think the people who live here could give Memphians a few lessons in Southern hospitality.

Like Memphis, Jiangyin is built next to a major river. It has grown up next to the great Yangtze. As you may or may not know, the Yangtze is the third largest river in the world, I think. Damn, where's an almanac when you need one?

Bicycles rule the road here. Very few people have cars of their own. People of wealth have mopeds. The minority, but supreme dictators of the road, are the taxis. Bicycle vs. cab. The bikes have the numbers, but the cabs have the advantage of size and armor. The cab drivers push and cajole their way through traffic, honking at anyone foolish enough to veer into their path. It seems as though one is expected to honk at every opportunity, no matter how slight.

True terror is driving in China. The Chinese employ a tactic known as the fish in a stream theory. If there is room for a bicycle or a car to go into a specific area, they go. The lanes on the street appear only to be suggestions. Driving into oncoming traffic is standard policy. Fear not, least ye be run off the road.

The bicycles are the cruiser type. The front wheels are extended forward more than your basic mountain bike, and the handlebars are raised. This makes a person on a bicycle sit up straight. All the better to see the road with, my dear.

For some reason unknown to me, Volkswagen has won the race

for preferred car in China. Most of the taxis and privately owned vehicles are VW Foxes or Sonatas. I'm sure the Germans are pleased.

The city itself is kind of dirty. Not that there is any trash about, but the buildings are just dirty. This city often reminds me of Juarez, Mexico, which is the border town to El Paso, where I grew up. Environmental degradation is a fact of life in China. The factories here spew out noxious crap day and night. Rare is the day that I can see more than a mile or so through the constant haze that the people here call air. The long arm of the EPA doesn't reach Jiangyin.

Often, when I ride my bike, I get a nagging headache from the pollution. My "hotrod" is the standard Chinamobile—a Shanghai-made Phoenix. The tires don't hold air very well, and my bell and the right pedal have fallen apart. I fixed the pedal, but the bell remains in pieces. Otherwise, it is a fine machine.

One thing that makes me homesick is the lack of trees. Jiangyin has a climate very similar to Memphis, but here the trees are small, scrawny, sad-looking things.

I have about six bars to bar hop to; it's nightlife in the fast lane. Beer is cheap and life is low, but all in all, it's a fun time. I have mastered the art of ordering a beer and asking for the check. Beer in Chinese is easy to remember because my transliteration of the word beer is pee joe. I think of a guy named Joe who needs to use the water closet.

There are a few discos, but I have shied away from them. The music is bad, and unlike clubs at home, you have to have a partner to dance with. In addition to this annoyance, the discos have a weird dance show and silly contests before everyone else is allowed to dance. I say dance show, but that's a misnomer. They have a half-dozen girls walk out in random configuration, wearing skimpy outfits. They slink on stage and give smoldering looks to the crowd, then turn around and return from whence they came to change into other skimpy outfits to do it all over again. This can go on for some time. Interesting but not really entertaining. Well, heck, who am I to judge?

There is a movie theater, but of course it's all in Chinese so I avoid it. They have a bowling alley, but it's not fun bowling by yourself.

Then there are the public toilets. Oh, my gawd. The only toilet that I can go into without holding my breath before I enter is at McDonald's. Yes, no land is safe from Mr. Ronald. There is also a Kentucky Fried Chicken, but I've never gone in. As I was saying, the bathrooms are truly disgusting. They have no toilets, just a hole in the floor that one must squat over if the call of mother nature is too strong to allow a hasty retreat back to the school. When I come to the Internet Café, I usually have to walk over and close the door to the men's room because, although my computer is a good twenty yards away, the oh-so-pleasant aroma of urine makes its presence known.

One of the bars I go to has so many of those mothball things in the urinal that it makes my eyes water to stand there and do my business.

One interesting thing about this town, and maybe all over China, is the small outdoor restaurants that spring up like mushrooms after a rain. Just as the day gives way to night, people bring out portable tables and propane grills to ply their trade. At first, I thought to avoid these bacterial playgrounds, but now hunger has won the battle over good judgment. You see all the restaurants close by eight o'clock or so, but the little portable places keep cooking until late into the night.

My first experience with the roadside restaurants was with some friends of mine, one American, David, his Chinese girlfriend, Grace, and a Chinese guy named Dao Mail. David asked me if I have ever been sick in China, and I told him no. He proceeded to tell me a story of how he drank some beer from a bag with some cab drivers in a city north of here. He claimed he had seen many people drinking this bag-o-beer and thought it was OK. He was mistaken and became quite ill from it. By the time he finished his story, we arrived at one of the little cafes on a canal bridge.

We ordered fried noodles. Heat is good. I got mine without meat. Our meal turned out to be quite tasty. The cooked vegetables with our noodles were fresh. The cook even gave us cigarettes when we finished our meal. I don't plan to eat at these places often because the stakes are high once you get sick. On occasion, it's OK.

My narrative has gotten longer than I'd planned. Stay tuned for the next glance in China, but don't hold your breath.

I should be working on lesson plans now.

Take care,

Don

November 11, 1998

Bell School, Fax home

Dear Mike,

Thank you very much for the package. You mailed it on October 29, and it arrived on November 6. I got it on Sunday, November 8. We all appreciate the *Time*, and my feet have more relief. I ration my tea to one a day, so I have a few more days. Axel sent me some insoles last week, along with several books.

I was very concerned about you. Did you have a nice time in Monterey? After the people at home, I miss all the beautiful places in California: Tahoe, Carmel, and our mountains.

I have asked a friend to help me with my financial questions since I have had no response or questions from you. Did you not get my email about five weeks ago asking for your help? I need the information about MoneyGrams. I don't like having all this American cash in my room. I am getting to a desperate state because everything is so difficult to do here. Do you read what I write? You never comment.

I am busy now writing tests for all my students' levels. I want to put them into percentage scores for their grades.

Everyone has been sick but me. I hope to keep that record.

The students wrote compositions, and some chose to write about me, "their favorite teacher." One said I had the "prettiest classroom in China."

Yes, let's have fun. What about Las Vegas at New Year's? I would like to stay at the Mirage. What do you think?

Love,

Carolyn

Lafayette

Friday November 13, 1998

Dear Carolyn,

It was great fun reading all your stories. I really think you should turn them into a book.

I'm glad you got the last package intact. I will send all future packages from Walnut Creek.

Count on Las Vegas for New Year's. I have made some other plans also, but you tell me what you want to do, who to see, what to eat. Make a list. Also, I have conferred with the girls, and we need your Christmas list before you return.

We have it settled that Lynessa and I will have Bud and Desiree over for Thanksgiving dinner on Sunday. On Thursday, Lynessa and I will take a meal over and help Bud watch football.

Muppet is doing fine. She had a strange morning because of a weak battery in the smoke detector. She is still looking for you. Lynessa came over last night, so we are keeping her confused over where to sleep.

The trip to Monterey was less than great. It rained the whole time, which did make it easier to listen to all the lectures. I thought you might call Saturday night and hurried back.

I think I told you, Lynessa and I watched a video.

I am off to Yosemite for the last of the continuing education for my specialization hours. It will be cold. Two of the guys from Monterey will be there, and we will have dinner and drinks—not the same without you.

Bud liked having Muppet for the weekend. He is happy to come here for Thanksgiving.

Think of some more things you would like to do.

Love,

Mike

November 15, 1998

Internet Café, From my journal

Friday, the students went home for the weekend, and Xi-fen and I had plans. On Saturday, we took a school car and driver out to see a factory that Xi-fen thought I would be interested in.

A classmate from junior high school runs the factory. She told me he had been a naughty boy and was a terrible student, but after high school, he became a member of the Communist Party, where he moved up the ranks. The government rewarded him by giving him a factory to run and collect profits.

We toured the large factory. He did not speak English, but he and his family were most hospitable, with Xi-fen doing her amazing translating. It was a "melt blown factory" that manufactured non-woven cloth like we might see in hospital gowns and other one-use products. It is made of small plastic pellets that are blown and melted into the making of this fabric. I saw the huge machines, imported from Germany, large bins of pellets, and wide, long rolls of finished fabric in many colors that would be exported around the world.

It was evident that he was making lots of money when we saw his beautiful office, conference rooms, and enjoyed a delicious lunch with his family served by his staff.

We then went farther out into the countryside and saw where Xi-fen grew up. Only one partial cement wall of her home was left near the stream where she said she used to pick shoots for her family.

"What kind of shoots were they?" I asked.

"Oh, I don't know the names. They are just shoots. Chinese eat all kinds of shoots growing by our houses. No one pays attention to the names."

She showed me where the Red Guards had painted Mao's sayings in large black letters on the outside wall of each house. People in the village could read them when they walked by.

We stayed overnight in a local motel rated less than three stars, which is required for foreigners. They ignored me and my passport. Xi-fen's and my room had plain cement walls. It had two beds. I laughed when I walked into the bathroom and saw the toilet seat had that paper strip across it saying it had been sanitized. I guess they were trying to be assuring that it was old and dismal, but clean.

The next morning, we went to visit some of Xi-fen's countryside cousins. They were friendly and nice, as usual. I smiled and nodded a lot since no one spoke English. It was another time I wished I had a film crew with me to record what was going on. As I sat around the table with everyone, I daydreamed that perhaps if I were in a movie, I thought Jaclyn Smith playing my role would work.

They were eating dry, brown soybeans in pods on a wide, flat, circular woven tray.

Laughing, one cousin said, "We are the soybean generation. This generation is the chocolate generation."

I watched out the window as two children maneuvered a houseboat with a long pole in the stream close to us. I asked Xi-fen about the family having two children. She told me people in the countryside were allowed to have two children.

After our visit, we were driven to other friends of Xi-fen's, who had asked us for dinner. They had a two-story new home in the countryside. In the center of the house was a wide circular stairway with a huge chandelier suspended from the ceiling of the second story. I decided the chandelier must have plastic "crystals," as it would be too heavy if they were glass. It was a dramatic entrance.

Delicacies were placed in the center of the dinner table. There, on a platter, were a dozen of the barbecued quail on long skewers that I had seen in the market. Poor little birds. I told Xi-fen I couldn't eat them. I had to think fast. I couldn't eat them because they were my "California state bird." She translated, and they said they understood. Whew, what a relief.

Since my time here is going by rapidly, Xi-fen and I are trying to fit in all we can. She is most anxious that I experience many aspects of the Chinese culture since she knows how interested I am.

Money Sent

Chapter **17**

Lafayette

Monday, November 16, 1998

Dear Carolyn,

Here is the latest of the continuing saga to send you money. I was finally led to a mailbox office in the Payless Shopping Center on Monument. The money portion had a window with triple bulletproof glass. This seemed excessive, as it was located right next to dark windowed Concord Police sub-station.

Try to imagine my joy to look through the glass and see behind a well coifed Chinese lady of mature years wearing a white silk dress. I listened attentively as she urged the Mexican girl cashing a check ahead of me to study computers.

First, I had to fill out a form. It looked great until she couldn't seem to pronounce, after several lessons by me, "Jiangyin." Holding her funds on her side of the glass, she got on the phone and spoke to someone whose pronunciation was obviously more hopeless than hers. Finally, the words, "No can send there."

"How about Wuxi?" I wrote Wuxi. She made another call—yes!

Now to the computer. I saw the reason for the urging earlier about computers—lots of worrying and she doesn't want me to lose the $30 transmission fee. Pointing to the computer screen, which can hardly be read, as it is five feet away from the heavy glass, she turned, pointing, and said, "Whooshi?"

I said, "Wuxi."

She said, "Whooshee!"

I said, "Wuxi."

She said, "Who is Carolyn Oliver?"

While having an out-of-body experience, I saw my stunned self, saying, "My wife." We now had a crowd of all races and sexes who had never seen money going to China before. I started to think this was a Chinese Opera, and they are the audience.

Now the lady was interested in the personal side of the transaction rather than my losing $30.

She asks, "Is your wife in danger?"

"No," I said, "not as long as she gets this money."

I decided that since I gave Lynessa money this morning and paid the wagered $30 with $2 worth of quarters and dimes, I would cash the last traveler's check I had been carrying. After three times of pointing out that it says "either signer can cash"...

She said, "Go to a bank."

The computer sent $500 to the City Industrial Bank in Wuxi. It is a MoneyGram. The bank is to call you. The secret Swiss number for you to pick it up is 05029778. I hope it is easier to receive than it was to send it

I will write more news soon.

I am fine, but Muppet and I are missing you.

Love,

Mike

From my journal, Bell School

After class, I walked into the English Center office and saw Mike's fax on my desk.

I read the first paragraph, skimmed the letter, and screamed, "Oh no!!"

I rushed to my room to retrieve my emergency two-minute international phone card that would hopefully get through to home.

I rushed downstairs to use the local phone on the wall that Mr. Chang had installed and dialed the numbers required by AT&T to reach my home number, praying it would go through.

Relief—as Mike picked up. "Mike. What were you thinking? Why did you send me money? I wrote to you that I was trying to send YOU my U.S. money. You didn't read what I wrote to you! Go get that money back. I don't need any money!!!"

I couldn't believe he put all this time and effort into this. Mike never asked me about this, and then he got it all wrong. He only had to ask my question at our local Safeway.

Wednesday, November 18, 1998

Internet Café, From my journal

I've had a reprieve on doing Thanksgiving. Even if Xi-fen can find turkeys, which is doubtful, we could use chickens, but there are no ovens in this city to bake them. She has checked around, and the only oven in this entire city is in the International Hotel and not available to us. Food in this part of China is steamed or cooked in a wok. They don't bake. This area does not use much wheat flour. It's a rice-based diet. Whew!! That was a close call. Now they want me to stay for the Christmas Program, but my ticket is set.

This evening, Xi-fen told me we are invited to a wedding reception for one of her relatives. We talked about what to wear to the dinner, as the wedding has already taken place. She says there will be about four hundred people there.

"You will have to drink. That is the custom."

"What is the liquor?"

"I don't know, but they pour you a shot, say 'bottoms up,' and you drink it. Then they pour a shot for themselves, and you keep drinking with them."

"Xi-fen, I can't do that. Can't we just say, 'I don't do that I'm a lady?'"

"No, you can't. That would not be polite. It's expected."

The reception was in a large meeting room not far from our school. There was a white banner with red Chinese symbols of "Double Happiness" behind where the bride and groom sat. People were seated at long tables with white tablecloths. No one spoke English, so I smiled at people a lot. I wanted to look friendly since I was the only foreigner. A man came over to our table with a bottle and shot glasses. I smiled, acted coy by tilting my head to the side, and said, "No, Xie, Xie."

Thank goodness they didn't push me! This is an advantage of being foreign. They don't quite know what to do with you.

The first food to be served were those small blue river crabs that everyone seems to love. I don't really see the point, as they barely have any crab meat. I have learned to suck on the tiny legs like everyone else, and I pretend that I am eating something. I can now do this for twenty minutes, which seems to be the required time. I was offered the extra crab, as they were being polite. Again, I said, "No, Xie Xie." The banquet continued.

We left soon after dinner. It was a school night.

Lafayette

Sunday, November 22, 1998

Fax from Mike, did not see until December 1.

Dear Carolyn,

I was so glad to talk to you the other night. Hearing your voice is a reminder of how long you have been gone. See you soon.

I am still looking for your plane reservation stuff. Give it to me again.

I went to see the Dragon Lady at Mail Boxes. It's very difficult to send money from China. I have thought about your money dilemma and can't offer much help. A bank account is OK, but devaluation could knock it in half. Buy Christmas presents.

Desiree is coming home two days early from Peru. Altitude sickness is the complaint. We will have her at our postponed Thanksgiving dinner here on Sunday. We will also have Bud and Kathleen.

Bud seems to be doing somewhat better. His trip to the doctor ended with an alternative medicine stand-off. Lynessa and I will take over dinner and watch the football game with him on Thursday.

Lynessa was here on the weekend. We have lots of empty closets now in the back bedroom. It was nice to have the company, but poor Muppet doesn't know where or when to sleep. Doggie is fine. We have been having some big rain storms, but we walk her religiously between them. She is still growling at things at night.

The "For Sale" sign is still up in the canyon. Our neighbors, the Morimotos, have sold their house. A house on Kelly Ann Court is for sale at $449,000.

Michelle is about to return from London. She did not sound very optimistic about getting a job there. She is talking more and more about coming back to the Bay Area.

I am really looking forward to a short week. I have been busy, but I am trying to pare down December. I keep thinking I have this case in Truckee about to start, when something always goes wrong. Oh well, maybe we can use it as an excuse to go up to the snow. Lots of snow is falling, and we are due for a big rain today.

Stay a crane among chickens.

Love,

Mike

Thursday, November 26, 1998, Thanksgiving Day

Bell School, From my journal

We taught a normal day at school today. Don and I invited Pam to come with us for Thanksgiving dinner. Our only choice was McDonald's. We traveled by "card" in a cab together from the front of the school. I had a chicken sandwich, and we pretended that we had the usual food on a Thanksgiving menu.

"Please pass the mashed potatoes."

"Would you like some cranberry sauce?"

"How about some pumpkin pie?"

"How is the turkey?" We joked around with each other.

"Would you like more stuffing?"

It was a lighthearted conversation; we laughed and all got along.

Jiangyin

Friday, November 27, 1998

Email from Naji

Hi Carolyn,

I have been back from England for about two weeks, but I am laying low, as my arm is in a sling. The sling should be coming off today, as it has been six weeks to the day that I had an operation in England on my left shoulder.

I believe you shall be going home next week, and I hope we can all meet—maybe in the City Hunter, but you are welcome to come to my place.

If it is on, I shall give you the address and directions. You would probably like to invite Xi-fen Hua—I presume she is the Chinese teacher I was once introduced to. Of course, I would like Ms. Faye, Don, and young Yang Li-ping to come, too.

I have not had any beer except one small bottle of Tsingtao the first week I was here because of the medicine I am taking.

Regards,

Nagi

Saturday, November 27, 1998

From my journal

Trip to Wuxi to buy last minute gifts

Xi-fen's brother told us we should visit the antique and book market. It's located in an old section of the city and has beautiful old Chinese shops constructed of wood, many with wooden fretwork. I love Chinese antiques, but I find I take photos of what I like since many are thousands of dollars.

I saw gemstones of all colors under the glass counter in a small shop and asked to see them. The shopkeeper showed me rubies and sapphires. She assured Xi-fen and me that they were authentic. She said the rubies were man-made in Russia. I bought one for myself and each of my three daughters. They were $6 a piece, so I figured if they weren't real, I wasn't out much money. I bought a few sapphires as well.

Xi-fen wanted to get "pearl powder" for her health, so we taxied to a shop over by Lake Taihu. Xi-fen bought the powder, and we ordered a tea made with this powder and hot water. Since it is crushed pearls, it must be like taking calcium. This is supposed to balance your chi.

We went to a large department store, and I bought more gifts to take home. I was trying to spend my Chinese money. I bought Xi-fen a leather handbag. She didn't want anything else.

We were staying the night at Xi-fen's apartment. I was trying to change a lightbulb for her above the bed. I tried the bed, and it seemed sturdy, but it fell apart, and I fell on the floor, breaking my glasses, and getting a black eye. Now I couldn't wear my contacts, and I would have to teach the remaining days with this black eye and my taped-together glasses.

Lafayette
Sunday, November 29, 1998
Fax from Lynessa
Hi Mom!

I hope everything is fine in China. It must be getting cold now. It's getting cold here, too, but it's probably nothing compared to China.

We just finished Thanksgiving dinner. I'm going to watch *The X-Files* and drive home. I'm afraid if I stayed tonight, the traffic would be really bad in the morning. It's much easier to take the bus to work from my apartment.

We are looking forward to your arrival next week. I'm going to make a grooming appointment for Muppet. Otherwise, it may be hard to get her in.

We'll see you next week!!!

Love,

Lynessa

December 1, 1998
Fax from Mike
Dear Carolyn,

We have just finished Thanksgiving dinner. It came off pretty well. Lynessa insisted on fresh cranberry sauce, which she made. I gave away as much of the turkey as I could, but I will probably be eating leftovers until you arrive home. I'll save some turkey soup. Bud was in a good mood and ate a good meal. He brought pumpkin pie. Kathleen always seems in such wonder that men can do more than open a can.

Lynessa went to the Swedish party in San Francisco and had a good time. She bought some Glogg, which maybe we can help her drink when you see her new apartment. She has lights and rugs solved.

We had some excitement on Saturday night. A bunch on teenagers were drunk and making a lot of noise at the bottom of the driveway on Gloria Terrace. It turns out that they threw the "For Sale" sign on the lot to the other side of the street. Any joy from watching it down was abated by its having smashed our mailbox.

I think you are right that we should have New Year's with our friends, but let's go to Las Vegas in January. I have made some plans that I think you will like for December.

Tuesday, December 1, 1998

Fax from Mike, continues from dated Nov. 22

Dear Carolyn,

Your upgrade is confirmed. Business class arriving at 11:10 a.m. in SFO. You have window seats 11H to Japan and 14H to the US. I sure want to see you comfortable and happy on Sunday.

Love,

Mike

My Days are Limited

Chapter 18

Tuesday, December 1, 1998

Internet Café

Hi Gail and Axel,

My time is getting short here. It is going to be difficult to leave Xi-fen, my students, and all the friends I've made.

The students were disappointed that we were not able to come up with a Thanksgiving dinner for them. I did the next best thing. I showed them how to make peanut butter and banana sandwiches. They had never tasted peanut butter and thought the sandwich was really unique. "Why bananas and not jelly?" you might ask. I wanted to teach them the word "slice," and you can't do that with jelly. Remember, I'm not teaching gourmet cooking!

Last week, as I was giving the final tests, I spotted four boys cheating. I could tell it was the true/false section. I spoke to Xi-fen and told her I did not want these students getting away with this. She agreed that they should be retested. I wrote another test where the true/false looked just like the previous test but was in a different order. They missed them all. They have not been strong students and have trouble learning English. I left each student with a percentage grade from their tests that the school could use.

I finished teaching today.

These last four days, I will be taking care of things I need to do before I leave on Sunday.

Xi-fen is busy with Mr. Chang, who gives her more work each day. I have other friends to help me. My friend Alice is going to go with me to buy the paintings I have picked out at the art gallery. She will help with the bargaining and my directions for removing them from their frames and rolling them so they fit in a cardboard cylinder for me to carry on my back for the airplane.

I rode my bike across town to pick up my last photos from the Kodak shop. I will pass them out to all my students and teacher friends.

Love,

Carolyn

Wednesday, December 2, 1998

Bell School, From my journal

I am no longer teaching my classes, but Xi-fen and I went over to the other high school that I spoke to a few weeks ago. This time, I went through the American government, explaining the various parts and levels. I also gave them the word "homogeneous" and explained how our society compares to theirs. I know it's a bit difficult for them to realize how many different groups of people we have here in the U.S., compared with everyone being Chinese with a similar culture and expectations.

My visit was again a huge success. Talking to the 125 people, I once again did my Phil Donahue rendition as I walked up on wooden risers, answering questions from the students. I love interacting with the students in this way. They are curious and ask great questions.

Internet Café, Email from Naji George

Subject: Yes, I'm back, but I may be going.

Carolyn,

I told Yang Li-ping and Ms. Faye when they visited me last Sunday that I was planning to go to Pugi in Hubei Province, a three-hour drive south of Wuhan, for business related to one of our jobs in Nepal. It was planned for tomorrow and Thursday; however, the Chinese contractor from Beijing informed us that the test I was going to witness is not ready. This may be delayed until the weekend.

Therefore, I could come to the City Hunter, but I am so busy with my colleague on leave that I don't think I can make it.

On Monday, I started physiotherapy at the People's Hospital in Jiangyin. I hardly slept a wink on Monday night; however, I have already started to feel the benefit, as I can move my arm into a bigger arc parallel with my body. The physiotherapist tells me that after three weeks, I may get 90 percent of its use. You told me that you have stopped teaching. Why don't you come to the hospital if you can spare the time? I am here for about forty-five minutes. Jenny, Alice, and Cindy know the location of the hospital. While all sorts of things are done to my left arm you can hold my other hand.

If we don't meet before you go, I wish you the best for Christmas and the New Year.

My regards to Don. Tell him these come from his Arab friend. Regards to all my friends at the City Hunter.

Have a good time,

Yours,

Naji

Email to Gail

I just realized that this could be my last night at the Internet Café.

Mr. Chang came back again. He has invited me, Xi-fen, and I don't know who else to dinner tomorrow. We were supposed to go tonight, but he had to change the plan. So that just leaves Saturday night, which I guess I will spend with Xi-fen and probably Don.

Don will miss me since the other teacher is difficult. There is a possibility that the school may get a young guy who is already in China and is of Don's age. You wouldn't believe the red tape that has to be done on visits here. Xi-fen is going out of her mind with work and frustration, and then Mr. Chang told her today all the new things he wants her to do. It keeps her so busy and so upset that she doesn't have time to worry about me leaving. This is good because we are such close friends. We will miss each other terribly. She relies on me for help in the English Department.

I had a fall at Xi-fen's apartment last weekend, but I was soooo lucky it wasn't worse. I have a horrible "black," actually purple, eye. I put on double makeup, but I'm afraid to see the photos.

There will be Christmas here. They do a big program, especially at the elementary school. My high school kids may be left out. They were shocked that I wouldn't be here to celebrate Christmas with them.

My students are bringing me gifts hourly. You can't imagine what students think makes great gifts, and I need to bring it all home. I am taking more photos of them to give something in return for all the gifts. The girls love coming to my room and looking around at my books and jewelry.

It will be hard to leave Xi-fen. I have told her how much I have learned and how much I have enjoyed being with her. Yesterday, I was sentimental and sad about leaving, but today I'm ready. I'm trying to pack. I just didn't expect all these gifts. Let's hope I can get it all on the airplane.

It has been rather nice to just take care of myself!

See you soon.

Love,

Carolyn

Shanghai Airport

December 8, 1998

From my journal

I'm sitting on a 747 in first class in the upper story of the plane. It's a different world. I just said goodbye to Xi-fen. I hugged her quickly without a lot of talking because it was difficult, and I knew she would cry, and I would cry if I let it go on. She is such a dear friend, and we have had so much fun together. It is sad for me to leave her, but as my mother used to say, "Nothing lasts forever," words that are hard for me to accept.

It feels so luxurious in this big, soft seat with room to stretch. I've got a long way to get home, but this is relaxed comfort. I was too hot, wearing the five layers of clothes to keep warm, so I took off three and it's better. The older lady sitting next to me isn't looking in my direction, so I assume she doesn't speak English. I am asked to pick a dinner from the menu, pick a wine, pick a TV station. I wrapped up in a soft blanket as we took off.

My dinner arrived. It's huge shrimp, no spitting here, thank goodness. There's a salt and pepper shaker on the tray with heavy silverware and a cloth napkin. I haven't seen or thought about those things in a while. I've become a little sensitive to soy sauce, and there is a tiny bit on the salad, but the food is good.

Matt Lauer is on the TV. I'm news deprived. He has uplifting stories about people triumphing over their disabilities. It seems to me that only in the Western world do we feature these stories.

Chapter 19

Home

December 9, 1998

Fax to Xi-fen

Dear Xi-fen,

I arrived home safely. Greeting me at the San Francisco Airport with balloons were Mike, Desiree, and Lynessa. It was absolutely gorgeous weather as I arrived at the airport. I could clearly see all the way across California. I went to see my uncle. He's fine, and he's so happy to have me home.

Mike cooked a delicious dinner. My friends have been calling and saying they are happy to have me back. Everything in my home seems so strange; I guess I will get used to it tomorrow.

It was a real culture shock, especially on the airplane with the luxury of first class. It was wonderful to have airline points to cash in for my seats.

I spent over five hours in the airport in Japan, so it was a long trip. I don't feel tired, but my eyes are tired. I hated leaving you in China. I will miss you so very much, but we both must look forward to meeting again.

In the end, I left all my American money with Xi-fen. She put it in a bank account to use it for her new home. I left most of my clothes so I could fit gifts in my suitcase. Xi-fen assured me she could find people who could use them. I told Xi-fen to give my bike to Mrs. Su, the wife of a teacher at school, who had had us to his home in the countryside for a delicious multi-course lunch that he had cooked himself.

I wish you lots of luck with buying your house. If the yuan I left is not enough to cover postage for the things you will mail to me, use the other bank money. I hope you will use the bank money I gave you for your house and all the extra things you must buy.

You are my special sister. I hope things at Bell go well and the English Center prospers. Remember, you can always send an email to me through Don or a fax to my house.

I have a lot of work to do to get my home ready for Christmas. Don thought that the school was OK on songs and music for the Christmas program. If you want me to buy and send anything for Christmas, let me know at once, and I will quickly send you what you need.

Please do say, "Hi" to everyone.

Love,

Carolyn

Tuesday, December 8, 1998

Email from Don in China

Subject: Howdy partner

Hey,

I'm glad to hear that you made it back OK. I always worry about people when they have such long trips.

Yes, I'm still here. The internet place is still cold, but they must be running some kind of heat, because it's not too bad right now. I saw Cindy and told her I had a picture for her from you. I'll give it to her tomorrow at the English Corner. As far as I know, it's still a secret from Pam. Maybe I can make it all year. It might get tough when new people come, but if I can make it that long, it won't really matter anyway.

I keep forgetting you are gone. I walk home from classes, and I think about telling you something or asking if you want to go into town. Then I think, oh yeah, she left. Dang!

Pam had to move into my old room because of her leaky pipe. She told me about it at school and bitched about it all day. I told her it's not that big of a deal and that she was making it worse by complaining so much.

When I got home, and was moving into your room, all three new teachers were there helping Pam move her stuff. Remember that my old room was connected to her room. She didn't have to move but a few feet. While I watched, Pam never moved a thing. She just directed the teachers around. Incredible! She doesn't even have that much stuff.

One of the teachers from our office invited us to her home for wontons. About twenty of the elementary school teachers, non-English speakers, went. Somehow Pam never showed up at the proper time so she didn't go. Lucky break. Anyway, I had a really good time. The house was cold, but the wontons were great. I laughed at them, and they laughed at me. The women I sit with at lunch made fun of me all night long, and so I put watermelon seeds in their drinks when they weren't looking.

Xi-fen has already sent your package. You know how industrious she is. Did you know that there is central heat in her dorm, but they never turn it on? What is the deal with that? Xi-fen said it was expensive—you'd think they would turn the thing on. Sometimes I wonder about these people. Heck, most of the time I wonder.

Pam has still not washed these dishes. I'm waiting to see just how long they will sit before she does anything about them.

Well, I'll leave you with the same thing a friend left me with. There are two rules for ultimate success in life:

1. Never tell everything you know.

Your pal,

Don

Friday, December 11, 1998

Internet Café

Email from the Don

Subject: Howdy

Hello,

Yes, I still think time is going by quickly, though the cold is making it go by a little slower than before. I just got a heavier coat, a new sweater, and a shirt, so things are not too bad. As far as sending things to me, I think I'm in good shape. As you know, I have "thermal" underwear on the way, and another friend is sending me some music. One thing I would like, but don't need, is a hacky sack. I see all these kids kicking the feather thing, and I would like to show them we do the same, but with a small bag we call a hacky sack.

Oh yeah, don't forget about sending the U.S. flag for the wall at the City Hunter.

I have a good "Pam is a dumbass" story. Today, Friday, the parents of the kindergarten and pre-school came to watch classes and see a show by the kids. The school had put a lot of pressure on us to make sure that everything looked as good as possible. Thursday, we had a special rehearsal/practice lesson that was watched by Xi-fen, the principal, and our teacher partners. My class was first, and then Pam's. I think mine was OK, not great, but OK. Xi-fen gave me some good tips today that helped. Pam's class on the other hand was painful to watch. She just doesn't interact well with people or kids, plus she had not taught them much. She looked bad because she chose to wear jeans and tennis shoes. Xi-fen and I talked about it later, and she told me she had asked Pam to dress nicer.

The next morning, we were both up early to get ready for the parents' arrival. We were in the kitchen doing the early morning kitchen thing, and Pam said she would wash the dishes later. I told her that she needs to because two weeks is too long to leave her dishes. She claimed that some of them were not hers, including the strainer. I said it must be hers because I have never used it, and you, Carolyn, always washed your stuff right away. She said she has not used that thing since forever, and I said, "Yeah, it's been dirty in the sink for over two weeks. Besides, that is only one thing."

"Well, we haven't had water," she said. I told her I have managed to wash my stuff almost every day. At this point I let her off and changed the subject to the parents coming to watch our class.

She started off badly: "Yeah, I didn't need Xi-fen telling me how to dress."

I said that since she knew Xi-fen and the principal were coming, she should have dressed better. Anyway, she says that she didn't have many clean things to wear. Well, whose fault is that? I thought this was a sorry excuse because the water had been on almost a week, and she could have washed something the night before. Besides, I wear my outer layer at least twice before I wash it. So does everyone in our office. I notice them wearing the same things for several days in a row sometimes. Pam always makes some excuse before she ever looks to herself to blame.

Well, as far as the dishes go, she should be in control for a while. I stuck it to her hard, and she couldn't say much. That should keep her in line for a couple of weeks anyway.

I know all of this is trivial and petty, but you are the only one I can share what's going on with her and who will understand. I hope it's not too boring for you.

Later,

Don

Tuesday, December 19, 1998

My email to Don

Good to hear from you. Believe it or not, my mind is still in China. I think it is because I don't "give up" friends easily, and I am trying to remember everything and everyone. I am going to write a book. I've got a title, Email from Jiangyin. This book idea is confidential at the moment. I think I will have flexibility with this title, but of course, I now have to do it.

Today, I will pick up my new ring with the stones I bought at the antique market with Xi-fen in Wuxi. It is gold with rubies in the center and three small diamonds on each side. The jeweler says the four stones I bought are each 2.5 karats and worth about $700 each. He said they are like the man-made Chatham rubies made here in California. The shopkeeper in Wuxi told me these were from Russia. I did not tell the jeweler that I paid $6 U.S. for them. I will give each daughter one for Christmas and let them choose the setting for a ring. If you can find the antique market in Wuxi, it might be a way for you to get some money.

Just a warning: The envelope that contained cards for me from Susan and Li-ping was slit open completely at the bottom, so I can't tell if that is all it contained. The envelope paper was thin and flimsy.

I'm really surprised the Christmas program was canceled, but you were asked by the school to be Santa? Hummm … have fun. Wish I could get a picture of that!

Speaking of pictures, the development here is so much better than that place in Jiangyin. My pictures look so much better. I haven't started to put my photos together, but I've bought the albums.

I'm really not in the mood for Christmas. It's not as much fun without little kids around. All my grown girls will come for Christmas. Later today I will pick up my daughter Michelle from Dallas.

Gosh, furniture in the lobby? Have you gotten the promised ping-pong table yet?

Tomorrow, Mike and I will go to the mountains. Mike has a court appearance near Lake Tahoe. The problem is that it is snowing like crazy, making it a difficult trip. We had unseasonably warm weather last week and now have a freeze!

I'm glad Susan is enjoying the English Corner at the City Hunter Club. It is her only chance to stay out "late."

I absolutely agree that you should do your school plans during school time, and preparation is of primary importance. I can't stand to be unprepared either. If Pam is doing a poor job, it will come back to haunt her later.

It was so good to hear all the news; as I said, my mind is still in China—even if I've stopped eating Chinese food.

Merry Christmas,

Love,

Carolyn

Write soon. I can't get Yahoo to send or do anything—maybe too many shoppers online.

Lafayette
December 23, 1998
Dear Xi-fen,
Your Christmas card and letter arrived yesterday in plenty of time for your Christmas greetings. I loved your beautiful card and thoughtful letter. You must remember that you haven't lost me. I am always here for you. There are just a few miles separating us! I miss you, too. My mind is always thinking about China . . . What is happening? Is this or that working out? I think of you so often. It was such a wonderful opportunity for me to come and teach and be with you for so long.

We have a beautiful tree up, all decorated, but I haven't decorated the entire house like I usually do. Every day, I put up a few more decorations. I also have many packages to wrap and lots of cooking to do before tomorrow. I hope you will one day be here for Christmas dinner. But remember, we can have Christmas dinner food any time of the year.

Thank you for mailing all those things. I don't think the countryside basin will break. I am happy Mrs. Su is riding my bike. Please tell Mr. Su "Hello" from me.

You tell me in your fax that you are very busy at school as usual. Mr. Chang certainly has big ideas. I hope there is enough time in the day to do them all!

Please tell Susan and Li-ping that I received their lovely cards and messages. It was very thoughtful of them to write to me. I promise to write to them soon. I miss them both.

Winter is here, and it's cold. I had to cover my outside orchids with blankets.

I will send the music for "We Are the World" so your class can hear it. Tell them "Hello" and that I will write to them at the beginning of 1999.

Happy New Year to you all! May all good things come to you in 1999!

Love,

Carolyn

Lafayette

January 10, 1999

Dear Xi-fen,

How is the new year? I hope plans for your new apartment are going well. I'm happy for you, even though it will be a lot of work.

We had a nice New Year's Eve here at our house with friends for dinner, and then Linda and Frank stayed overnight on Thursday. When Linda goes into the hospital for a hip replacement operation, I plan to visit her a lot.

I am just taking down the Christmas tree today and putting away all the decorations. It's a big job. I'm putting my photos in albums. I had to have some reprinted because some are missing, so it has taken a lot of time.

School started again, and I have a few new students in my English Language classes. My students here are very interested in the pictures. I am also writing about China and all the things I learned. I know Don told you about the value of the rubies. It's quite unbelievable. I gave one to each daughter, and each is picking out a setting for a ring. Everyone loves the miniature teapots and stands. I gave one to each daughter and one to my sister. I have kept the two biggest for myself, at least for now. If a daughter admires mine, I will gladly exchange a small one for a big one. My brush holders from Turtle Park for holding beads are beautiful in my living room with all the lovely beads from China. All the freshwater pearls were a big hit, too. Everyone thought they were gorgeous. My girls loved the huge lavender pearls, and my sister and sister-in-law loved the apricot-colored ones. I'm very excited about getting my two paintings framed.

The Lifelong Learning Department of my school district has asked me to teach a travel class. The class is called Cultural Studies for the Traveler. I asked what I should teach and was told to just talk about my travels and show my photos. I will talk to the participants and see what they would enjoy doing. So far I am planning to have an hour of "travel talk" and an hour of a video to show on a large screen. I will need to find videos about places around the world.

Please tell Susan to tell my student Angela in level one, class four, thank you for her New Year's fax. Three days later, I received her card and letter. I think it took over a month to get here. I will write to her soon.

I miss you all. Please tell the students hello for me and I wish all of them a very Happy New Year. I miss them too. I'll write more later, but this fax is easier than writing a letter.

Love,
Carolyn

Continuing Friendships

Chapter 20

Lafayette

Tuesday, February 22, 2000

Dear Yang Li-ping,

Thank you so much for your surprise phone call. I am happy you had a good trip to America. Did all your translations go OK with your associates? I hope next time you can come up to San Francisco. You must realize that Las Vegas is a fantasy world. Next time you should see how American families live. I am still teaching English and travel classes now. I am taking a class myself in ceramics. I'm learning how to throw pots on a wheel. It's fun but difficult to start. We are getting our spring rain now. Take care and write when you can.

    Best regards,

    Carolyn

Jiangyin

Tuesday, February 22, 2000

Dear Carolyn,

Thank you very much for your letter.

I am now busy communicating with those customers I met at the fair in Las Vegas. I shall try my best to ask them to place us an order. It is going on well.

The sunshine is very nice. The trees are very green. The sky is very clear; the air is fresh. The road is very clean. The people are very kind. Every family has a nice yard, lovely flowers, and a house with good decoration. The Chinese food is very delicious and the same as Western food. I like California very much.

But it is very expensive in the U.S. I took $1,000 U.S. to travel for two days with a guide in Las Vegas. During the four-day fair we had dinners every night. Every dinner cost more than $300 U.S., which doesn't include tip. After dinner once, we paid $40 for a taxi from Chinatown to our hotel.

This year, we went to Hollywood and Las Vegas. Next year, we will go to Disneyland. I hope to go to see the Golden Gate Bridge with you.

I did a good job during the negotiation in the U.S. I am applying for a visa to Frankfurt to take part in a music festival from April 12 to 16. I am not sure about getting the American visa. Maybe I shall go to America this July, but it is up in the air.

Looking forward to hearing from you soon.

Best regards,

Jessica Yang

P.S. I got an American name, Jessica. Do you like it?

From the time I left China in 1998, Xi-fen and I had been corresponding by letter, fax, holiday cards, and an occasional call from me. Now with an email connection installed at Bell School, it will be more convenient for Xi-fen to write letters.

Bell School, Jiangyin
Thursday, June 8, 2000
Dear Carolyn,

I was so excited to find that I got your email, and you got mine. It is so convenient for us to communicate now.

I couldn't wait to email it to you yesterday. But they cut off the electricity from 7:00 a.m. to 5:00 p.m., and I had to leave the office to take the school bus by then. I feel very sorry about that.

Carolyn, I wholeheartedly apologize to you for not writing to you until now and making you so worried about me. Actually, I have intended to write since I got your last fax, but there was always something that kept me busy and prevented me from sitting down to write a long letter to report all about my work and life here. I felt guilty about this, especially when I realized that I hadn't even sent you a birthday card.

Carolyn, I was kept busy all the time since we had eight foreign teachers here last semester. There is always something troublesome happening both in their teaching and life here and had to be handled as fast as possible. As you know, at the end of last semester, three British teachers left, and I was kept busy, recruiting three new foreign teachers, and going through all the application procedures before they could come to teach. Fortunately, I finally had three to take the place in time. However, the three new ones have no teaching experience at all, so besides getting them adjusted to the life here, I had to train them to handle the spoken English classes. That was a lot of work, and it's not easy to get them into teaching, as you know. One can't be a good teacher without a half or one year teaching practice at least. That's really the hardest part in my work, as foreign teachers usually want to stay teaching here only for one year. Some for only one semester, and they are mostly foreign people without any teaching experience.

This semester, my own teaching kept me busier and gave me a lot of pressure, too. I had to prepare my students to take the examinations for colleges and universities. I had to teach more periods per week; I needed more time to plan my lessons. The students who took the exam are the same students I have had for three years, and you taught them for three months and gave them credit as the best cooperative class. They all worked very hard, enjoyed my teaching, and gave me high credit, too. I like them a lot and did enjoy teaching them for all these three years.

At present, we don't know how many can pass the exams; however, two of my students, one boy and one girl, are going to Switzerland for further study. Both of them are excited. I am excited, too, as I helped to get all the procedures done. On the day they had to leave school, we had class pictures taken, and everybody cried, including a few boys. It moved me to tears, and I cried, too. Now all my students have left school, and I miss them a lot. They also miss you, too. They said that you are the best foreign teacher they ever had in the three years at Bell School, and they told me to say "hi" to you.

Actually, all the technical students you taught miss you a lot. Many times, when foreign teachers couldn't handle the class, I was summoned to help them out. I tried to give them moral lessons. Some bold students would ask me this question.

"Miss Hua, can you recruit foreign teachers like Mrs. O or just have Mrs. O come to teach us again? We like her teaching us and we will show our best behavior."

I was really happy to hear that, but where can I recruit a teacher like you? It's really a hard question for me to answer. Both students and the teachers had a really good impression of you. They all admire me that I have you, such a good and helpful friend, as I always tell people whenever I talk about my experience in America.

At the end of last month, I finished all my teaching. I feel a bit relaxed. However, we have eight foreign teachers here. Most of them don't really know how to teach, plus they don't put their heart into teaching. They just come here to get the money to travel and have a place to stay. It really upsets me, so there is a lot of work for me to do. Carolyn, there is always some problem either in their teaching or living. This makes me feel frustrated and stressed almost all the time. Fortunately, there are one or two of them that are qualified and often try to help me with some problems in their living situation, too.

Just ten days ago, I had to deal with two foreign teachers' special and unexpected cases. One of the young male teachers, only twenty-four years old, had an operation because of his lymphoma last summer. After he came here, he actually had his blood tested each month in Shanghai, and we didn't know about it. This time, the blood test report on May 28 showed signs of cancer coming back, so he had to leave for America right away for further examination. For two days, I had to work out everything and arrange his leaving. Thank goodness, these issues are over now.

My life is still the same, living by myself. I moved into my new apartment last August, and my mother and my two nieces came to stay for about ten days. They all liked my house and didn't want to leave until school started. My new apartment is not very big, about 98 square meters. I reconstructed it into two bedrooms, a family room furnished with both a sofa and a Western-style dinner table, a small study, a bathroom, and a kitchen, which I like very much. The only pity I feel is that the family room is too small. It can't even fit in a set of sofas, for which I can do nothing.

During the Chinese New Year, my son came back to see me accompanied by his father. He and his father came to my house several times and had the Chinese New Year dinner party together with me in my new house. That made me really happy. My son is still close to me, but he didn't want to stay with me overnight in my new house, and I couldn't persuade him to do that. Most of the time he stayed in his relative's house in the countryside, where there were a few boys his age, who he played before he went to Australia. His father stayed with his friends. I felt sad for this kind of situation for my son, but what can I do, Carolyn? I tried my best to have him stay with me to finish elementary school at Bell, but it didn't work out. I had to let him go with his father and saw them off at the airport. We mostly keep in touch by phone or letter now by email. He is doing fine over there and can keep up with others at school. Now the only thing I'm worried about is that he is not happy, as he has no friends to play with or talk to. When he told me this, I couldn't help crying. He knows a lot but needs friends. This made me sad. Anyway, I will try to write to him more and encourage him with his studies.

At present, the most important work for me is to recruit new foreign teachers. That's not easy. Especially to recruit good teachers, as I told you. I contacted several universities in America and one program in Australia. I haven't really had any foreign teachers reply yet, and I am a little bit worried. Carolyn, can you help me with this? I remember the last time you mentioned a woman was interested in coming to teach in China. I wonder if she is still interested in coming to China to teach in September. Now if you find some others, it's fine, too.

Before he left our school, Don told me he would like to come back and teach again after he finishes college. How is he doing now? Do you still keep in touch? Do you have his email address? I can contact him since I have an email now.

How are you doing? Are you still as busy as before?

Love,

Xi-fen

Lafayette

August 28, 2000

Hi Don,

How are you? Xi-fen is looking for teachers at Bell School. Do contact her if you are interested in going there again. I know you have been on other programs in China as well.

We have been visiting my daughter in Sweden. We had a great time, especially with the California weather that we brought. It was beautiful. I have a funny story to tell you about Yang Li-ping. It is a continuing saga. She is so unbelievably determined. I'll write more later and tell you about it.

Ciao,

Carolyn

P.S. I still don't know if you graduated or if you are teaching or robbing banks?

Memphis, Tennessee

Monday, August 28, 2000

Hi C,

Home sweet home. I'm going camping for the weekend, and you're going to Sweden. I'd love to hear stories about Yang Li-ping. She is so fun. I worked with her for a while after you left to help her on the TOEFL test that people take to get into college in the U.S. She had trouble with English idioms, of course, but she never gave up. If China had a few more people like her, they could probably take over the whole planet.

No, I'm not teaching; I am painting houses. I would much rather be teaching, but I just don't have the money for life and school at the same time. I went to school last fall, and I'll be back in the spring. So goes the decade plan.

Do you know of any good banks I could rob?

Don

Lafayette to Memphis
December 13, 2001
Hi Don,

I'm so glad you wrote back. Yes, I'm thinking about visiting China, but not for a year's stay.

Xi-fen is so busy. I will write her this Christmas, but she has the job from hell, no personal time at all.

My divorce is so sad. I am at a loss, trying to help my husband. It has been a twelve-year struggle. We have been together for forty years. He won't get help because he is in denial about many aspects of his life. I still love him, but I can't go on with him. It was a love that should have gone on for a lifetime.

I feel liberated and sad at the same time, but I have a life of travel and adventure ahead of me.

I think it's great that you and your girlfriend are studying Chinese. Have you read the novel, *The Wild Swans*? It came out in 1992. I'm close to finishing it. It is so good. It's about China, starting from 1900 to? I'm at the Cultural Revolution now.

Later, take care, and have a good holiday,
Carolyn

Bell School
Sunday, April 7, 2002
Email from Xi-fen
Dear Carolyn,

I am so sorry that I haven't sent you any emails since I received yours on December 28, 2001. There are several reasons for this. One main reason is that the email in my office doesn't work properly. Other reasons are that I was too busy at the end of last semester and at the beginning of this semester with many things going on for my job. The administrative work in the English Center became very complicated. It is hard to describe.

During the three-week winter vacation. I was busy with the Chinese New Year and Spring Festival when I had some free time. I have no computer at home. I hope I can afford to buy a computer in one or two years, so I can email you whenever I'm free on weekends or at night

Carolyn, thank you so much for the three nice coats you sent me. I like them all. I thought it was so thoughtful of you to do so.

Carolyn, how are you doing? Is everything all right with you? I'm very worried and concerned about you. I think of you often and miss you very much.

I love you, and please take care of yourself.

Love,

Xi-fen

Teacher's Training School, Jiangyin

Monday, March 17, 2003

Email from Xi-fen

Dear Carolyn,

Today I was checking emails. I found your email to me. This made me very happy, as I checked for your email several times. It seems that you are busy teaching. Are you still teaching in the same school, or do you need to teach in several schools now? I hope everything is going fine with you.

Carolyn, how is your health? We both need to take care of ourselves, as we both live alone now. I'm getting a little bit relaxed now after the first month at this new school. However, I still need to make my teaching plans, almost three or four nights a week. I have to give up the habit of watching a TV series. Anyway, though busy, I don't feel troubled, like at Bell school. This is a Teacher Training School, and it makes me feel happy. I hope things will get better after a few months.

As I mentioned last time, if you are interested in investing in my former classmate's factory, I can tell you the details. This will be a factory that produces a special kind of plastic granule, which can be made into plastic products, such as plastic food, bags, food boxes, tablecloths, pipes, and all kinds of plastic things. After half a year of investigation and survey, this kind of product will have a large market and bright future.

A factory like this needs about ¥800,000 to buy the equipment, which can be used to produce the plastic granules. On this scale, it can produce over 1,000 tons yearly. To fulfill all this, it needs one large workshop, eight to ten storage room workers, one technician, one mechanic, one accountant, and one administrator with this amount of money, it can do all the things above.

According to the market investigation, the investors can get the capital back in eight months' time. After eight months, the investors can make a profit. My classmate is flexible about the amount of money to be invested. If you are interested in it, you can invest half of it or more or a little less than half, which is about $50,000 U.S. I'm not sure if I have made things clear to you, for I'm not good at writing about such industrial things. If you have any questions, please let me know. If you have no interest in it now, just tell me directly so that I can pass this information to my classmate.

I have to stop here tonight. I'm looking forward to hearing from you soon.

Love,

Xi-fen

Lafayette

March 20, 2003

Hi Xi-fen,

I hope your new school situation will work out well for you. It's good that you feel less stressed.

Thank you for giving me the opportunity to invest in your friend's company, but I'm not able to do this now.

I wish your former classmate well in this new venture.

Love,

Carolyn

Thursday, August 14, 2003

Email from Xi-fen

Subject: I miss you.

Dear Carolyn,

How are you doing? Are you in summer holiday or teaching summer school? Is everything OK with you? I think of you often and miss you very much.

I was very, very busy during that time with various kinds of work besides my normal teaching, and I was in poor health, too. I was frustrated and tired out every day. I didn't have the summer holiday until the end of August. I was engaged in a teacher's training program. That's the disadvantages of working in teacher's training school, as you have to work during weekends and holidays.

It was very hot this summer—39 to 40 degrees Celsius, day and night. This kind of hot weather lasted about two weeks. You really couldn't do anything without air-conditioning. Even with air-conditioning, you still felt breathless. Some old people died of heat. How about the weather in your place this summer?

Now it's getting a little bit cooler. People have started to go out. I went to the hospital to have a medical examination yesterday. The result is OK, but I still belong in the weak level, so I try to rest more. Actually, I have become very lazy, as I always feel a lack of energy, and I'm in low spirits. Now I'm taking Chinese medicine. Carolyn, I feel I'm getting old, for I often feel lonely and have no future this year, especially. I tried to talk to myself and adjust my mood, but it doesn't seem useful. Can you tell me what the problem is with me? I'll stop here today. I hope I can hear from you soon.

Love,

Xi-fen

Jiangyin

Saturday, August 23, 2003

Email from Xi-fen

Subject: Time off? Teacher's Training School

Dear Carolyn,

I was so happy to get your email. We finally connected again. I was really worried for you before I got your email; now I know you are in Hawaii with your sister.

How are you doing with your holiday in Hawaii? I do hope you can relax and have a good time there.

Carolyn, where are you now? Are you back home or still in your sister's home? When will you start teaching again for the next semester? Are you in good health and high spirits?

I'm getting a little bit better after a few weeks' rest; however, there is something wrong. I have been taking Chinese medicine for more than a month. It doesn't help, so I went to see a western doctor last week. She says that I am going through the change of life. I feel terrible about this because I am too young. The doctor suggested that I have a special test, then see what to do for it. So next week I'm going to have the test. I will let you know about the results and see if you can give me some suggestions.

I'm back to school working again here at the teachers training college in Jiangyin. My summer holiday is over. Next semester, I will be busy again. I have many classes to teach and need to make two or three different teaching plans. These two courses are both new to me, and I have to spend a lot of time preparing my lessons. I hope I can get through all of these.

Today, I have to stop here. I'll talk to you later. Here is my mailing address:

[…]

Love,

Xi-fen

I emailed Xi-fen from my sister's home in Hawaii telling her I hoped she felt better, and to let me know how her tests came out.

Friday, September 19, 2003

Email from Xi-fen

Dear Carolyn,

I'm sorry that I didn't write to you until tonight. I have been very busy since the school started on September 1. Another reason is that I was waiting for the medical examination result. I got the test result a few days ago and went to see the doctor who suggested I have that test. After she read the report, her conclusion for me is that I am going through what you call "young menopause." She told me to take some Chinese medicine to pass this special time and adjust my mood. I have to accept the fact, though I feel kind of terrible, as it means that I am getting old early. This happened to my mother at the at the same age, too, so maybe I inherited this from her. I can do nothing but accept this fact. Can you give me some suggestions to help me pass this special time?

Carolyn, to tell you the truth, I feel restless about it. I am forty-three now and still need to look for a husband. That's what I worry about most.

Carolyn, how are you doing now? Are you busy teaching at school again? I hope everything is fine with you and that you are not working too hard. I think of you often and miss you very much.

I'm looking forward to hearing from you soon.
Love,
Xi-fen

I wrote Xi-fen back, telling her to take care of herself and not worry about finding a husband. I told her that it is OK not to have a husband. I told her a husband was not necessary, but I don't think she agrees. Expectations are different in China than here.

Jiangyin
Tuesday, December 23, 2003
Email from Xi-fen
Subject: Congratulations
Dear Carolyn,
I am very sorry for delaying writing to you for such a long time. I am always thinking of this and miss you a lot, but I am too busy and too tired to do anything other than work. Actually, I haven't had any weekends off for almost two months. Besides, my father had an operation in December and stayed in the hospital for more than twenty days. My godmother died in November. It was really a sad thing because she drowned in a river because of darkness.

I have had a very bad case of the flu for almost two weeks, and I can't get rid of it. So this Monday, I had to go to the hospital to see the doctor and have two days of IV, and I still need to do another two days. This makes me very upset because it's Christmas time, and I have to attend a Christmas party held by Jiangyin Educational Bureau tomorrow and also a wedding banquet for our English group colleague the day after tomorrow. Anyway, I hope I can be better after a good rest tonight.

Because of my health condition, I haven't checked my email for a long time. However, it will be Christmas Eve tomorrow, so tonight I forced myself to sit down to send you a short Christmas email. To my surprise, I got your email with such exciting news. It's almost hard to believe that you have two grandchildren born on the same day in two different countries. I can imagine how happy you are, and I would think they are the best Christmas gifts for you.

Dear Carolyn, Congratulations! I have to stop here tonight as I'm not feeling well now.

MERRY CHRISTMAS AND HAPPY NEW YEAR!

MAY JOY AND LUCK BE FILLED IN YOUR LIFE THROUGHOUT THE COMING NEW YEAR!

Love,

Xi-fen

Monday, February 23, 2004

Dear Carolyn,

I was very happy to get your Chinese New Year's card and the two pictures when I went to school today. I liked the picture of you and your oldest daughter's son. You look so happy as a grandmother. You look great in the picture!

My winter vacation started on January 16 and ended on February 2. My son came back from Australia for the Chinese New Year and stayed with me for about fifteen days. He is fifteen now, and he is more mature than his age. He is a very considerate, nice boy. He understands me.

We have even more classes than last semester, so it will be another busy semester for me. I just hope everything goes smoothly. I have to stop now. I'll talk to you when I can.

Take care!

Love,

Xi-fen

Return to China

Chapter **21**

Spring 2004

Xi-fen and I sent emails back and forth about my coming back to China and traveling with her this summer.

Jiangyin

Monday, May 31, 2004

Email from Xi-fen

Subject: So sorry that I couldn't check my email

Dear Carolyn,

I'm sorry that I couldn't check my email, as it isn't working properly. It wasn't fixed until this morning. I was upset about it because I knew you would send me an email about your coming, and I'm anxious to know that. As soon as I opened my email box, I found there are four emails from you. I'm so sorry for keeping you waiting, and I'm so happy to see your decision. Carolyn, when I think of our meeting at Pudong Airport in Shanghai, I am really thrilled. It's been six years since we met last time in China. It's also in August.

Carolyn, you know how much I have missed you during these years, so many things have happened in both of our lives, and we have gotten through all of the difficulties. You are such a great woman and always a good example for me.

Carolyn, you have chosen a good time to come to China. Everything is fine for me. I'm sure we will have a good time during those twenty days, as we both would like to travel during these days. Where do you think you would like to go? How many places would you like to travel to in China? Please let me know your ideas so that I can contact some travel agencies and make our travel plan.

How are you doing in Turkey? Are you having a good time? Please take care of yourself. I do hope you will have a pleasant journey in Turkey.

I'm looking forward to hearing from you.

Love,

Xi-fen

August 2, 2004

From my journal

I arrived at the SFO for my direct flight to Shanghai. They couldn't locate my e-ticket. Fortunately, I had paper copies. My problem was sent "upstairs." There is no upper story at SFO.

After some time on the phone, they found my reservation and told me all was well. As I went through security, they pulled out my contact lens liquid because the ban on liquids has now taken effect. They let me keep the tiny bottle but took me out of line and proceeded to search me and everything I had. It was taking a lot of time, and I began to get nervous and told them my flight was boarding soon. They ignored me and continued searching through my things until at last, they let me go. I rushed to the gate and immediately got on the flight.

I was seated next to a Chinese couple who communicated with the flight attendant by holding up cards with English written on them.

We smiled at each other. Two rows ahead of me was the emergency exit row with only one person in it. I wanted to be there and asked the flight attendant what it would take to sit there.

"You have to pass a test," she said.

I said OK, and she proceeded to ask me the usual questions, "Can you help . . ." Then she would say, "The answer would be 'yes.'" I passed the test and moved up to lots of leg room. I was seated next to a young man from Indiana who was going to a pilot's school in China to learn how to fly jets. We became fast friends and chatted with everyone who came up to the kitchen directly across the aisle from us. Soon, we had a party going on with new friends being allowed to stand, have a drink, and visit. It sure made the fourteen-hour flight go by quickly.

Xi-fen, her new boyfriend, Mr. Shaw, his son Hunter (age twenty), and Hunter's classmate Dick met me at the airport in a fancy black Lexus. It was driven by Mr. Shaw's nephew, who is in the Landscape Bureau that owns this car. They had driven two hours to the Pudong International Airport, picked me up, and then drove us two more hours back to take us to Xi-fen's home in Jiangyin

Her new home is in the teacher's apartment building that she and I rode our bikes to when I was here teaching in 1998.

That evening, Mr. Shaw, Hunter, and I visited Xi-fen's new home and talked about plans for our travels.

The tour: August 3, 2004

We have our own three-star tour. Xi-fen talked to ten friends and went to three travel agencies to plan this trip. We were supposed to be at the agency before five today, but we didn't wake up from our naps until four thirty. Jet lag was my excuse. We dressed quickly. Xi-fen called the taxi company, and I started hurrying down the five flights of stairs to meet a cab. In spite of all the ruts and barricades, the driver has to get through, he got to the building before we could get down five flights.

This time we had a fast, air-conditioned cab, and he raced across town for us. Mr. Shaw was standing outside the Travel Agency and had been waiting for a while. He had called Xi-fen at home, and she told him we were coming. We were actually supposed to get to the bank before coming here, but now that was out of the question. At the travel agent's, I listened to the negotiations in Chinese. No one spoke English, there were no maps or brochures, and they didn't take credit cards. We'll be traveling with Mr. Shaw's twenty-year-old son, Hunter. Our mission is to practice English with him and motivate him to work hard at his university.

Despite Xi-fen's best bargaining efforts, and she is very good, the agent wouldn't come down in price. He showed her and Mr. Shaw the area breakdown of where the money would be spent. It seems that Jiuzhaigou, (Jo Sang Ko) area is expensive. We will have a minivan, three-star hotels, and a fully-guided, individualized tour throughout the trip. Three stars are dictated because I am a foreigner and must travel this way or higher. This is a luxury tour for the Chinese.

Finally, Xi-fen is convinced that the price is the price. Mr. Shaw's prepared with bundles of cash in ¥100 notes, the largest available. Handcuffed to his wrist is his briefcase, loaded with money. Mr. Shaw looked like a mafia boss as he opened his briefcase. He paid for Hunter. I will get to the bank tomorrow to get cash off my card for Xi-fen and me.

The price per person is ¥8,000, but "Just to make sure the service is what we expect," Xi-fen explained, we are withholding ¥2,000 on the total, to be paid when we return to Jiangyin.

I'm thinking, "Only in China!" Six years ago, we didn't pay for the two-week trip until we returned because the agency owner was a friend of Xi-fen's brother. Xi-fen bargained after the fact on that trip, too.

It will be "bed and breakfast" everywhere, but we will have to pay for lunch and dinner. Six years ago, on our tour of Shanghai, Guilin, Xian, and Beijing, all our meals were included, as were the English-speaking guides. This time, we are going out farther west, and the tours will all be in Chinese. The travel agent said he could not arrange the food. We would have to find our own. I didn't worry. With Xi-fen, we would never miss a meal. Our flights and our itinerary were in Chinese with cell phone numbers for the tour guides and agencies responsible for our tours. We all shook hands, nodded to each other, and exchanged thank yous. Mr. Shaw escorted us into a cab and then got on his motorcycle.

We took the cab to a new restaurant in the downtown area, across from the KFC that I remembered. They have remodeled the theatre complex with a wide, sweeping, curved staircase leading upstairs to the restaurant. There are beautiful mirrors, red and gold carpeting, and all the servers are in colorful silk Chinese dress. It is all new, with well-appointed decor and very clean. Mr. Shaw is having a banquet in my honor, welcoming me to China. Hunter and his classmate Dick were waiting with Mr. Shaw in a private room upstairs. The grand banquet began with several cold dishes already on the glass "Lazy-Susan."

Xi-fen and I began to assess Hunter's English with a quiz on names of things on the dinner table. Xi-fen whispered that his English should be much better, considering the years he has studied it in school. She has been tutoring both Hunter and Mr. Shaw for my impending arrival. Mr. Shaw had said, "It's my pleasure," mastered after each of my "Xie Xies." They graciously offered me dish after dish after dish as food arrived.

I took out my camera and began to shoot the food. I couldn't possibly eat all that was expected of me. Xi-fen had to explain to Mr. Shaw my penchant for taking photos of everything. They laughed when I shot the lobster. He looked so fierce. His head was there, but cold lobster "meat" was on plastic wrap, designed to be the lobster's body. The wasabi sauce served with this took away any lobster flavor there might have been. Later, the lobster returned as another dish. They had chopped up the head and body parts, deep fried them, and served them on a platter. I counted twenty-six dishes in all. For five of us. The meal was delicious, but really over the top with the huge amount of food. The gracious host in China is expected to order in excess, so that the honored guests will get enough to eat.

After all these dishes, Xi-fen asked, "Would you like some man food?"

I finally figured out she must mean "main food, "which is how they refer to rice or noodles. This would ensure that I wouldn't go away hungry.

Later, I asked Xi-fen what the restaurants did with the leftover food. She said she didn't know. I hope there were some pigs somewhere feasting on these leftovers, because there is no such thing as a "doggie bag."

Jiangyin
Wednesday, August 3, 2004
Email to Don
Hi Don,
I feel like I'm dreaming, walking down the same streets of Jiangyin with Xi-fen where I walked and rode my bike six years ago. The streets have changed some, but I still know my directions. The main department store is still here, as is the McDonald's that we frequented and celebrated Thanksgiving dinner. The Kodak store where I spent most of my money has been remolded, as has much of the town. There is now a beautiful new park in the center of town with life-sized bronze statues of people from Jiangyin's history, alongside traditional Chinese pavilions in the Ming Dynasty style. They have closed off streets and made walking areas. It's a modern city now.

I am the only foreigner in sight. I have not seen a western face yet, and as usual, I am a curiosity. Xi-fen and I were in an elevator going to the top story of a building for lunch. When we got off, Xi-fen said they were all talking about me, daring each other to ask me questions and wondering where I was from and how old I was.

Xi-fen, Mr. Shaw, and Hunter accompanied me around town and said they were my "protection." From what, I don't know. I got Chinese yuan from the bank to take to the travel agent to pay for Xi-fen and my portion of the trip.

We went to the ATM last night when I first got here, and it "swallowed" my ATM card. China requires six digits instead of our four. Xi-fen suggested I add zeros to my pin. After I did that a few times, the card was gone.

"Oh," Xi-fen says, "I see now the directions say you can only enter your pin three times. I guess I should have read the directions." I was sure it was gone forever, but Xi-fen told me it wasn't a problem. The next morning, we went to the bank, and when Xi-fen explained the problem, they found the card in the back and returned it to me—no questions asked.

I am now at Mr. Shaw's home using Hunter's computer. Xi-fen has a dial-up connection at her house that I find impossible to use. Everyone is waiting for me, so I don't know how long I can write.

I'm staying at Xi-fen's home. It's very nice and comfortable, but she doesn't like air-conditioning. She has it in the bedrooms, thank goodness. It is so hot and humid. She says this is nothing to mid-June and July, when it was so humid that there was condensation on mirrors and windows.

We did our laundry today and hung it out on her balcony drying racks in preparation for our travel adventure tomorrow. Again, we will have a car to take us to the Shanghai airport.

We have an ambitious trip—fly to Yichang, then a cruise up the Yangtze River, to Chong Quin, bus to Chengdu, and fly into the mountains to 12,000 feet in Eastern Tibet. Xi-fen thinks she will need an oxygen bottle. I'm just a little worried about the planes. We have been told we are going where there are no roads. There are Tibetan villages, glaciers, and temples in the high mountains. After three days, we are on to see a gigantic Buddha and Mt. Emei, one of the four sacred Buddhist mountains in China.

Xi-fen has called some of my Bell School students and fellow teachers to meet with us after we return from our trip. It will be fun to see them again.

I have to sign off now. I hope I can write more later. As always, China is a fascinating place, and Xi-fen is her same wonderful self.

I feel so fortunate to be here.

Ciao,

Carolyn

Packing for the trip

August 3, Evening

Packing with Xi-fen is always an experience. I had forgotten that she packs for how she will look in the photos.

"How will I look in the photos?" she asked as she went through her closet and pulled out garments.

"Is the color good?"

As I found in 1998, for the Chinese, the photos are almost more important than the traveling. They are proof to your friends and colleagues that you really did get there. She is going to want her photo in every scenic spot, and her clothes have to be just right. This happened six years ago when we traveled. She pulled outfit after outfit from her closets. We sorted through two closets of clothes.

"I think the beige is not good for photos." She tries it on.

"Yes," I agree. We both think we look better in colors.

"How about these red pants with this blouse?" She put it on and took a good look in the mirror. She looks adorable in everything with her tiny figure.

"Oh, I'm getting a stomach." Hah, I think, what a joke. It barely exists, so she shows me how last year's pants are a little tight. She wants my honest opinion.

"Xi-fen, you look great in everything. You are so darling and petite." She tries on three black skirts and finally decides on one.

We got the wardrobe combinations together, black with red, a turquoise top for the mountains,

"It will look good with the trees." A jacket to go with print pants and another print top.

I decided it did blend in a Chinese-style way. She tried on everything. She was able to fit everything into two small carry-on satchels. Amazing to me, but of course, her clothes are small, and so are her shoes.

August 4, 2004

The next morning

Getting out of Xi-fen's complex is tricky. There are potholes, barricades, huge mounds of rock, dirt, dust, and a very narrow bumpy piece of cement to navigate over. Xi-fen calls it, "Chinese construction." It has been going on and will continue for months. We hit the streets of Jiangyin, which have bicycles, bicycle wagons, scooters, and cars going the wrong way on our side of the road, a real free-for-all.

Just to survive the back seat of a car in China, a passenger must suspend any fear of auto accidents, road hazards, bad drivers, and acts of God. I was told that it is very difficult and expensive to learn to drive. People think it will only cost more to learn later, so why not now? Everyone wants to own a car, but they are extremely expensive, considering most people's income. The usual way to travel long distances is to find someone who works for a company or government bureau who has a big car at their disposal. It's the "limo" idea, and it's great. When I traveled this way during my China trip, I felt privileged, rich, comfortable, and safe with a professional driver.

Today, we are driven by a friend of a friend whose license is six months old. He wants to help us. Buicks are very popular in China, and he owns a brand-new Buick Town Car.

The Shanghai Airport is two hours away, and he is willing to practice his driving with us in the car. He's confident he knows the way to the airport. The driver and Mr. Shaw sit in front while Xi-fen, Hunter, and I are in the back seat.

The driver got through the hazards by Xi-fen's apartment house, and we headed out across a newly built bridge into town. There are new stop signals for those who choose to use them. Stop signs appear to be optional. New signals count out the seconds to wait for the drivers, others for pedestrians, and bicyclists, replacing the temporary ones of six years ago.

Now we are behind a few cars in double lanes of traffic, waiting for a light to change. Here's a trick: Drive into the empty left turn lane, wait, and when the green light shows for the cars on the right, dart ahead in front of the traffic, and you are on your way, if you are lucky. Now you have free run of the road. Whoops, there is a bicyclist coming at us and a bus has just stopped directly in our path. Somehow, disaster was averted.

I am the only one without a cell phone, and three of them ring constantly with music box tunes. Their conversations are punctuated with loud bursts of Chinese. Fortunate for us, Mr. Shaw answers the driver's phone.

We merge onto the expressway, where we see our first of two accidents. There is not too much damage, but the police are present. People here seem to develop "rules of the road" as they go. Hunter told me that a few days ago, a woman driver hit seven people. No one was killed. Ironically, three days later, she got behind the wheel and did it again. The law says nothing that covers this circumstance, so the police don't know what to do with her.

The road signs are in Chinese and English, making it somewhat easy for me to follow our route to the airport. I think we are heading in the right direction. The right lane is marked "driving lane," and the left lane is marked "overtaking lane." Our Buick is new, the driver cautious, and as a result, our car slowly straddles the dotted line between the lanes. There are horns honking (Xi-fen's horning) on the left and the right. Our driver either ignores or doesn't seem to hear all the noise. He continues to straddle the lanes and finally makes his move to a single lane. Our driver is the kind I told my teenagers to avoid and call me for a pick up anywhere, anytime. But here, I can't follow my advice.

We pass through several toll booths, and after two hours on the road, our driver and navigator, Mr. Shaw, seems confused. We have missed two turnoffs, so they decide to ask directions. I ask Xi-fen if she knows the way to the airport since she has been countless times, picking up and dropping off teachers from abroad.

"Oh, I never pay attention. I can't drive, so I have nothing to do with it."

We overpay our tolls by ¥140 for the exits we missed. After asking directions at the last toll booth, the driver and Mr. Shaw are now gaining confidence that we are going in the right direction. It helps that they have spotted a large airplane flying overhead.

I see the turnoff to the airport marked in English, but we are going very slowly in the fast lane, with cars speeding by us on our right. In the midst of lots of horning, our driver makes his way across traffic to the exit, but we have made no friends on this highway.

Finally, we are approaching the airport, and I see the signs for Arrivals and Departures. Our driver heads for Arrivals. Yikes! I wave my arms and tell them in excited English that we want to go right because we are departing.

Then X-fen spots a noodle shop on the right and tells our driver to pull over. It's lunchtime.

"We have to stop here. We won't get food on the plane," she said.

Déjá vu. I have been here before. I know this noodle shop. Six years ago, we ate here with Mike for the same reason. We were so late that we had to be paged and ended up the last passengers on our plane to Guilin. But we stop again at the same noodle shop. We eat "fast food," and I keep looking at my watch. We barely have enough time, assuming all goes well.

We get back into the Buick, and the driver immediately heads across the road for Arrivals. I started saying, "No, no!" accompanied by a lot of arm movements.

"We need Departures!" But we are already up the Arrivals ramp, Xi-fen tells him in Chinese. The driver stops and slowly backs down the long ramp. The traffic behind him patiently waits for us to back down and move over to the departure ramp. No horning this time. So far, so good, I think.

We jump out at curbside and rush inside to find the ticket counter to get our boarding passes and pay our airport construction fee.

Mr. Shaw and the driver meet us at the security gate. I wondered what the driver was doing here, but we said our good byes.

Later, we learned that his beautiful new Buick was towed and that he had to pay a ¥200 fine for parking at the entrance.

Our gate is not far, fortunately, but we still have to board a bus to the plane on the tarmac.

Just like six years ago, we are the last ones on the plane. And of course, a half-hour into the flight, we are served a complete, well put together meal.

Thus, we began our ten-day journey west into central China and eastern Tibet.

Continued on the airplane

This was Hunter's first airplane ride, so he sat near the window. Xi-fen was on the aisle, and I sat between them. Hunter and I watched the watery landscape from high. We left the Shanghai airport and followed the Yangtze River westward. We would stay a night in Yichang, and then board our boat to cruise up the Yangtze River through the Three Gorges Dam. Soon, it became impossible to see the course of the river at this height. Someone passed me a copy of the *Chinese Daily* in English since I was the only foreigner on the plane,

We reached Yichang in an hour and a half. One of my students in California, Olivia, had spent her childhood here. She had been raised in a Christian Missionary School before Mao's takeover in 1949. Her family eventually moved to Wuhan and then to Shanghai, where she raised her family. She lived through the Cultural Revolution, difficult times.

We landed on wet tarmac with dark clouds moving above us. We were told it had been raining for a week, and the storm stopped shortly before our arrival. We were lucky. It had cooled off.

Inside the cabin, Xi-fen's cell phone rang. It was our tour guide, saying she was waiting for us inside the airport. We met her at the small luggage turntable. Waiting with us for luggage was a group of Australians who boarded a bus, never to be seen by us again.

Our guide spoke only Chinese and directed us to a cab and driver out in front. The airport was new, and it was about forty-five minutes outside the city. There was no public bus service to this airport. We were traveling "family style" on an independent tour, where we would be handed over from one tour guide to another, who spoke only Chinese. The guide was tiny, pleasant, and nicely dressed. Xi-fen seemed to like her, and they became engrossed in a loud conversation. Hunter, wearing his camouflaged cowboy hat, rode "shotgun" with the driver, occasionally entering into the conversation. We three ladies were squished in the back seat. Xi-fen didn't try to translate for me. I figured she would tell me later. I watched green farmland whizz by out the window.

We arrived at our hotel in the heart of the prosperous-looking city of Yichang and got nice rooms on the third floor. Xi-fen was delighted with our room. It seems our guide was giving Xi-fen instructions about what our cruise would be like tomorrow. She suggested we walk over to a grocery store and buy water because she said they charged an exorbitant price on the boat. They charged ¥15 on the boat, and we could buy it for ¥5 here in town. I had to start rethinking the value of a yuan as it related to the people and the Chinese economy. I was traveling Chinese now.

It was late afternoon when we set out to find the grocery store. We found the "flying sidewalk" the guide had mentioned, over the large intersection near us, but neither Xi-fen nor Hunter could figure out where the grocery store was. We found the main square in the center of town, a block from our hotel. It was nicely landscaped, with lights coming on as the sun went down. Many people were walking, doing exercises in groups, and dancing to music.

We walked around the perimeter of the square, where there was a lot going on. There were beggars on the street trying to get our attention. Again, I was the only foreigner, so I walked very close to Xi-fen and Hunter, who were asking people where the grocery/ department store was and where we might find a restaurant for dinner. No one seemed to know anything. I saw an old man in just a ragged pair of shorts and no shirt, smoking, playing the erhu and begging for money. He kept trying to catch my eye while I attempted to watch him without him knowing. A man with no arms and legs rolled across the sidewalk on a skateboard-type platform under his body. He was begging. A couple, Xi-fen said, husband and wife, had spread out a small blanket on the sidewalk. The woman was kneeling with her forehead on the blanket, wailing loudly. It scared a little boy about three; otherwise, everyone was ignoring her. Xi-fen said they were telling their tale of woe. I didn't know if I should be giving out money, so I took Xi-fen's lead and walked on. I hadn't seen this kind of begging before in China, and I didn't see it again. Taking photos would be rude and cause a ruckus.

Having found nothing, we walked back to our hotel and saw the restaurant attached to our hotel. We decided to eat and work on the water supply later. Both Hunter and I told Xi-fen we weren't too hungry. Somehow, she ordered a huge amount of food, six dishes, plus rice, and in this restaurant, everything arrived on huge platters. We barely made a dent in the food. She felt bad about it later, but she said she didn't want us to go hungry, and she had no idea the dishes would be so big. It didn't cost very much, and I just hope the leftovers fed some pigs somewhere. Xi-fen started keeping track of how much we spent on meals so we could even things out in the end.

After dinner, we walked back to the square. Hunter and Xi-fen guessed the store must be on the other side of the square. Fortunately, they guessed right this time. We bought some cracker snacks and decided on a case of bottled water. Poor Hunter had to carry the heavy case back to the hotel for us. We kept telling him how much we appreciated him.

When we got back to our room, we called housekeeping for more toilet paper. Two people's ration of toilet paper is about twelve squares for a day's supply. Toilet paper is gold here. My bed was so hard. I couldn't sleep, so since it was hot, I took the comforter and put it on top of the mattress. It saved my back.

Breakfast was included, so we located the dining room up a flight of stairs in the building next door. It was already hot, and breakfast was hot rice porridge, no tea, hot milk, and a few bread-like rolls with a very salty fish paste.

Our guide found us and rushed us into another cab to go to the dock for our Yangtze River Cruise. The new guide who would be with us on the cruise was waiting for us. Xi-fen bought fruit from a vendor while we fought off men, trying to get a hold of our luggage to "help" us onto the boat. We followed the new guide downstairs and across another boat to get to our vessel. We would be on the top floor. Hunter was across the hall from us. Xi-fen and I were relieved to see that our room was OK. We had two twin beds, a bench, a dresser, and a small bathroom where the shower would spray the entire room. The air conditioner was turned on, a good sign, but the air was hardly cool. Little did we know how hot we would be in the next three days.

Xi-fen and I went down to the lounge at the end of our floor. We had a wraparound view of the entire river ahead of us, and the room was air-conditioned with cold air. This was a bit too cold for Xi-fen, but I was thrilled. There were very cold drinks in the Coca-Cola refrigerator. We got all the hot tea we wanted, and all the soy nuts we could eat, but we had to buy a necklace-type pass for ¥50 that would be returned when the trip was over. Only people on our floor, the highest class, could use this lounge.

Our floor housed twenty Australians, a French couple and their son, who worked in Shanghai, and a large, very dignified, wealthy Chinese man with nice clothes and gold jewelry who did not speak English. Xi-fen thought he was a developer, she guessed property, from Beijing. He never got off the boat for any of the extra tours. He was under the impression that this was a two-day trip. We were going upstream, so the cruise would take three days. We were receiving a 4 percent discount for going upstream. All we could figure out was that "time is money," and they gave a discount for those willing to pay for more time. Our destinations were west, so it was perfect for us.

With the Australian tour group was a young American couple, both medical doctors, touring China before going to New Mexico to work on an Indian reservation. They had found their tour on the internet through an Australian company.

Leaving Yichang, we went through a giant lock to bring us up to the level of the Yangtze. We went under a beautifully designed bridge and then started up the brown Yangtze, noting the markings on the sides of the river, where the water level would eventually be when the dam is totally operational. I was sad, realizing that old picturesque temples seen now on the water's edge would be covered with water.

August 6, 2004

Today we had an excursion up to one of the tributaries of the river. The three of us seated ourselves in the small forty-person boat. I forgot my camera battery, which I knew I would need. Everyone waited patiently for me to run to our cabin to retrieve it. People are kind to foreigners.

We saw holes in the cliffs above us. No one knows how these were made or who made them. Perhaps they were ancient burial sites. Farmland lining the shore will be covered by the rising river. We stopped and got into twelve-person boats and were serenaded by the guide with folk songs as we were pulled in the clear and shallower water farther upstream. Muscled, thin men wearing rope sandals pulled us against the strong current. We were seeing the ancient way these rivers were navigated.

Corn on the cob was the available snack on the boat coming back to our cruise ship.

I went to the cool viewing room by myself to have a cold Coke to continue our journey upstream.

August 7, 2004

Before 6:00 a.m., we came to an ancient seven-story wooden Pagoda along the shore. We got out to see it and climbed our way up the inside wooden stairs to the top. I was dripping wet before we started. I looked inside the waistband of my black shorts and saw salt crystals had formed around my waist. I had never experienced this. I think this is why it's good to have salty Chinese food.

Xi-fen commented, "I don't think I will be able to do this kind of experience when I'm as old as you." She is seventeen years younger than me.

The view of the river and the farmland on the other side was definitely worth the climb. This unique Pagoda would be covered with water in the coming months and lost to the world.

Cruising upstream, we had several more stops to places that soon would no longer exist. Temples and people owning farmland or living near the river were being relocated to multi-story concrete apartment buildings in the distance. The government said they would be better living for the people since they would have inside bathrooms. I don't think they mean "western toilets," probably just holes in the floors for sewers.

Traveling upriver, we came to another stop. Fortunately, there was a chair lift for this scenic bend in the river; looking down below on the brown river was a scene found on Chinese money.

August 8, 2004

Another stop was to a temple and a community that would be flooded. We hiked to the temple, where there was a large diorama with clay and twelve-inch figures, showing a person drinking the "soup of forgetfulness."

"You lose your memory so you can come back a different person." Xi-fen knew all the stories surrounding these depictions and myths.

This society wants its people to conduct themselves decently. It's a different belief system with good in mind. Outside were life-sized, white marble statues depicting sinful lifestyles, gluttony, avarice, drunkenness, and greed to warn people that they should avoid these sins.

We stopped at another soon-to-be-flooded temple. Even if Xi-fen and Hunter weren't as hot as I was, I felt better seeing local people with wet washcloths on their heads to cool down. Fortunately, the viewing room on the boat would save me again.

We came to the massive Three Gorges Project, which is almost completed. The purpose of this project is to control flooding downstream and provide hydroelectric power. We went through the fifth and last gigantic lock with many large ships by our side. We were dwarfed by the gigantic sides of the lock. The other side of the dam was about a mile away in the hazy distance. We went through what would soon be the gigantic lake behind the dam.

Upriver this afternoon, we are going past Fuling, a town I read about in the 2001 book, *Rivertown, Two Years on the Yangtze*, by Peter Hessler. He wrote about his years teaching college students while in the Peace Corps. His students spoke English, so they could share their opinions, which helped him learn about the culture. I laughed when he described how his cello playing was received. As soon as he would start to play, the audience would talk. When he stopped, they stopped. When he started to play, they talked. His music was background for their conversations. I taught in China and had been a cello player. I felt a connection to his book. I was excited to see the town, if only from the river. The sunset was getting darker and darker until, just as we passed by where Fuling should be, it was too dark to see it. I was so disappointed, knowing the historical treasures Peter Hessler wrote about were lost to the rising water.

August 9, 2004

The next morning, we arrived at our destination, Chongqing, at 7:30 a.m. We hiked up the steep cement bank from the cruise ship and walked some blocks to the bus station. Xi-fen made Hunter pull my suitcase, which was much heavier than his. We boarded the bus for Chengdu, some five hours away. Hunter and Xi-fen went to sleep, and I tried to watch the gangster movie from the United States, in Chinese, on the screen above the driver. The countryside zoomed by until we got to the city and were greeted by another tour guide for a tour of Chengdu.

Our guide took us to a shopping street in central Chengdu, recently built in the Ming Dynasty style. Our guide thought we should see one of Chengdu's five Carrefour stores, owned by the French Company. We spent fifteen minutes looking at the merchandise and were told these stores were very popular. I would have preferred to see the antique market, if one existed, but I was told it was too late in the day to go there. Old China and things associated with it are rapidly disappearing and not what the Chinese want to show off.

It had been a long day, starting with our disembarking from the Yangtze River Cruise boat in Chongqing at 7:30 a.m., the five-hour bus ride from Chongqing to the tour of Chengdu. Now we are to take a two-hour flight north into the mountains to Jiuzhaigou (Jo Shang Ko) in the Tibetan Autonomous Zone. We found it on my large map of central China, but it was unknown to us. We are going by the recommendation of the travel agent in Jiangyin and the word-of-mouth information Xi-fen had collected. We were excited, not knowing what to expect. It was supposed to be beautiful.

Xi-fen knew how much I wanted to go to Tibet; she was worried that she would get "mountain sickness." She thought she could manage this area of eastern Tibet because she thought it wasn't as high as other places in Tibet.

We flew over high mountains while the sun set in the distance. It was completely dark as we flew into a rebuilt military airport with a small glass and steel modern structure.

It was freezing as we got out of the plane onto the tarmac. Airport personnel were wearing long heavy coats with high collars. We struggled in the wind to the building.

Our guide was there waiting for us. She was Tibetan, twenty-something, with a ponytail, jeans, and a cell phone. She led us over to a white minivan with our new driver. It was close to eleven o'clock at night, and we had no idea where our hotel would be. She and Xi-fen started talking in loud Chinese. Most of our guides had ignored me, but she spoke some English and said she was not told that our group included a foreigner. Xi-fen and I whispered to each other that she looked like an American Indian from the southwest.

I knew Xi-fen was very tired. She is used to a daily nap, and she had only slept a bit on the bus ride in this very long day. We rode through the dark mountains. Every time we saw lights in the distance, I thought it would be our hotel, but it wasn't. The road was full of hairpin turns, labeled in English, Curve 1 all the way up to Curve 15. I would have loved to see this in the daytime.

An hour and a half later, we arrived at our hotel. The room looked five-star, with Tibetan fabrics, beautiful wood, and Tibetan decorations around the ceiling. We were exhausted and thrilled. Hunter, next door, just didn't seem to appreciate how good we had it. He was tired, too.

August 10, 2004

The guide told us to meet her at 7:30 a.m. in the dining room for breakfast. Xi-fen told her we couldn't arrive by that time. It was simply too late now. We would meet her at 8:00 a.m., but we actually didn't make it until 8:30. We figured it was our tour, and we could do what we wanted.

The dining room was filthy. The tablecloths and covered chairs were spotted and dirty. The tables were littered with dirty dishes. What a contrast to our room. We looked over the breakfast buffet table, a little rice porridge, some strange "cake-bread" things, and boiled eggs. We all opted for the eggs. We tried to clear a clean place by turning the tablecloth up and under our place.

We followed our guide to a waiting taxi. Xi-fen was surprised because we were to have a private driver. Every time a car pulled out of the hotel driveway, the driver had to honk to warn drivers on the road or coming around the corner that we were pulling out. We honked and turned left to go to Jiuzhaigou Park. We passed lots of Tibetan flags along the way, with hotel after hotel, four and five story, some under construction, some full of tourists.

We passed stores along the sides of the road that were highly decorated with bright Tibetan designs. It looked new, and I wondered if this was just done for tourists. We stopped at one of the stores to get Hunter a jacket and buy water. He hadn't brought the jacket he was told to bring. We were in cooler high mountains, and Xi-fen was afraid he would get cold.

Purchase completed, we drove on and were let out in a huge parking lot full of buses and jammed with people. We entered the landscaped area, and our guide went to get us tickets. Good thing, we wouldn't have had a clue about where to go or what to do. Every few seconds, a bus on the right would pull up, open doors, fill up with people, and move up in the valley ahead. Bus after bus was filling up.

Xi-fen's comment was "This is just like Disneyland." It had that feel to it with neatly planted landscaping spelling out the name of the park and all the lines of people.

Our guide returned with our tickets. We moved toward the line for the buses and all got on. Fifteen minutes later, we came to the first stop. The landscape was gorgeous with an exquisitely large blue lake in the distance, framed by high mountains. With the guide, who was Hunter's age, we walked on a trail to the lake.

There were a couple of hundred people here. Ladies in native dress had their arms full of costumes, hats, and animals. People were renting colorful, ethnic, dance-type costumes. You could hold a goat or a lamb while in your costume. The costumed tourists fought for a position in front of the lake to have their picture taken. It was a circus-like atmosphere that I felt didn't pay respect to the beautiful scenery. It's our cultural difference again. Xi-fen doesn't understand why I take pictures of landscapes without people posing, and I can't understand why these people think they need to be in costume. I love costumes, but here it seems ridiculous. We laugh about it while Xi-fen decides to rent a Tibetan hat. It's tricky to get a photo in China of only one person without someone's head, hand, or body in the photo.

"People are more polite now than they used to be since everyone has a camera and understands that they need to take turns," Xi-fen said. She checked her face in a mirror, and I snapped a photo.

We turned in the rental hat, found our guide, and proceeded to walk on the wide plank sidewalk. Five to six people can walk side by side. It's obvious that this is how China is saving its national park. Everyone stays on the decking and walks in the same direction except when vying for a photo position when someone declares a scenic spot. The color of water of these lakes we walked past was spectacular shades of blues, turquoises, and greens. Our guide said it was due to the minerals, algae, and light passing through the water. We walked by shoals where one lake flowed into the next. We had hours of touring this large park, especially with scenic spots for photo shoots every fifteen minutes.

Our guide told us that a leader in Chengdu, who became high up in the Chinese party, went to Beijing. He told the leaders there that he had been all over the world and had never seen water as beautiful as Jiuzhaigou and Huang Long, where we will go later. He thought it should be developed. And develop it they have. Our guide told us that twenty thousand people visit here each day. I saw three foreigners besides me. This is a Chinese tourist hotspot.

We took the bus back to get lunch. There were two cafeterias, one cheap and one expensive. We picked the cheap one. It was a good decision because later we decided none of the food was good and at least we hadn't wasted money.

We shopped in a large room filled with souvenir stalls. The high ceiling was decorated with rows and rows of colorful upside-down umbrellas high above our heads. All the jewelry looked ethnic or Tibetan, turquoise and coral, but it was all plastic. The shawls and blankets had nice designs but were all acrylic. Everywhere many people were in costume. I had to agree with Xi-fen's Disneyland comment. Even the people sweeping the grounds were in costume. They had successfully turned this beautiful area into a theme park.

The outdoor toilets were amazing. The seat in the stall was completely covered with plastic, including the bowl, so when you pushed the button to "flush," the entire seat cover and bowl contents were encapsulated in plastic and disappeared below while another plastic cover rolled out over the top to cover the seat and bowl again all in one continuous roll. Water stands were outside to wash hands.

After lunch we boarded a bus to continue our walk in another area of this beautiful park. I feel so fortunate to be in these magnificent surroundings.

August 11, 2004

It's cooler here, thank goodness. About 9:00 a.m., our guide and driver picked us up in the van to go to Haung Long, meaning "Yellow Dragon," another famous national park.

More curvy roads through mountains with Tibetan flags flying led us to a town, where we stopped at a teahouse on a wide main street. One-story buildings looked newly created in a red and colorfully painted Tibetan style. I wanted to walk and take photos, but they told me it was unsafe and I couldn't go. I waited until Xi-fen, Hunter, the guide, and the driver were in a deep conversation over tea, and I quietly made a break for the door. The driver rushed to stop me. Xi-fen explained that, as a foreigner, I could be kidnapped here. It looked safe to me with no one around. I had to sit. I had a hard time believing that this kidnapping possibility was true; instead, it could have been their mistrust of the minority Tibetan group. Xi-fen was not about to take chances with my safety.

We continued up higher into the mountains and pulled over at the summit. Someone was selling oxygen in what looked like hair spray cans. No one was having breathing problems, but I could see that Xi-fen thought this was a good idea.

I bought her and Hunter each a can. They started breathing it immediately. Knowing China and their fake labels, I really doubted that it was oxygen, but it was worth it for their peace of mind.

After a quick lunch we headed off in the van to Huang Long National Park through more winding roads to see the "Yellow Dragon." It was an impressive sight, looking up the mountain at these calcite lumps of the dragon's "body"—lumps that resemble a huge snake descending the side of the mountain. Xi-fen and I walked up hill around these ponds of turquoise water collected in pools between the large calcite protrusions.

We returned to our hotel to get ready for a Tibetan show tonight. After dinner, we were driven to a large tent with a huge inside arena like a circus. I was given the traditional white silk Tibetan scarf that welcomes guests, and we were seated in the front row, with no other foreigners in the audience. It was a spectacular, colorful show, featuring beautiful, professional singers and dancers in highly decorated costumes embellished with furs, silks, brocades, and jewelry inspired by Tibetan designs. Some of the dancers wore the extra-long sleeves that were used like flags or ribbons on their arms. I was impressed with all the dancing and singing talent on display. I loved this beautiful show and went up to the performers afterward, told them thank you, and took their photos.

Xi-fen tells me that there are many shows around China now that feature China's minority groups. China wants to embrace its fifty-five minority groups. I know they want to gloss over the fact that they cruelly overran Tibet and its people.

August 12, 2004

Xi-fen has arranged for us to visit a Tibetan house today for tea. We were served by a Tibetan man in his dark house filled with dark red furniture, Tibetan rugs on the walls, and colorful tankas. They pressured me to buy a tanka. I used the excuse that I wasn't of that religion, but they had many other reasons for me to buy. I finally got away.

We went to a 'Tibetan village" with flags flying and a series of white tents with huge blue Tibetan symbols stitched on the outside. Paintings were displayed for sale. Brightly colored Tibetan flags and banners decorated the dwellings in his area.

Our van stopped along the road to give a ride to a lady selling jewelry, again, all plastic, as we drove to "God Mountain." We climbed up the hill and then threw a handful of two-inch square tissue-like papers on which were written prayers. I guess the idea goes with the Tibetan flags hung with prayers written to distribute into the wind. The hill was littered with thousands of these colored papers.

We spent time this afternoon in a crowded and impressive museum full of minerals and gems found in these mountains. The dazzling gem and mineral displays in the darkened room were in lighted glass cabinets.

Xi-fen carefully selected a new necklace to remind her of the trip.

August 12, in the evening

Our evening flight was delayed from Jiuzhaigou, so the owner of the tour company in Chengdu had been waiting over two hours for us. It was too late to have dinner anywhere in Chengdu, but hunger and the lack of a meal were averted when Xi-fen and Hunter found dried noodles for sale in the airport and a hot water spigot in the waiting room for just such an occasion. I passed in favor of a Jenny Craig vitamin bar.

We were more tired than hungry, so after checking in and paying a huge sum of ¥200 for a key deposit, we went right to our rooms. Hunter was next door to us as usual. It was a modern room with good furniture and beautiful bed coverings. We located the hot water kettle to make tea. Gone are the hot water thermoses of old that were in every hotel room six years ago. We plugged in the electric kettle and checked out the room. We had a glassed-in shower and one of those beautiful glass bowls for a sink in the bathroom, right out of *Architectural Digest*, that sat on top of the marble vanity counter. The only problem was that the spout splashed water everywhere and was inconvenient for the handwashing Xi-fen decided she needed to do.

In the morning, Xi-fen dressed in her white travel dress.

"Oh, I just realized the Buddha we're going to see today is white, and I'm in a white dress. This won't look good with the Buddha." She immediately changed into a more colorful dress. I bought a velvet scarf during lunch while touring Jiuzhaigou. "Oh," she said, "may I use that for a photo?" We have photos of her in front of a beautiful lake, sitting with the scarf draped around her shoulders. Using an umbrella as a parasol in a photo is "Japanese style," and with the addition of sunglasses, she becomes a "film star."

We found the breakfast room, elegantly decorated with modern Chinese, murals, and mirrors, with floor-length tablecloths in pink and white on all the tables. They had no tea, no hot water, no juice, no fruit, no milk, of course, no coffee, only gray soy milk and a watery rice porridge. There were some strange breads, some cold noodles, and brown-looking vegetables. This is when you are thankful to spot the boiled eggs again. This hotel did not cater to foreigners, and the food showed that. Xi-fen expected more, but it was not to be. We ate what we could and took the elevator down to the lobby to meet our tour guide.

August 13, 2004

A smiling young woman was waiting for us, but there was some mistake. We needed to have our bags packed because we were to leave Chengdu for Leshan and would not spend another night here. It took half an hour for us to pack while our guide and driver patiently waited. This was the first night of a decent bed, so I was sorry to leave.

We rushed the packing and hurried down to the lobby to check out and collect our key deposit. It took forever to get our deposit back. I don't know where they thought we were going to go with the key. Now we were on our way, but not before finding a big bank to get more money. We were all out. Xi-fen needed help with the ATM, but they readily gave me yuan on a credit card. By now it was 10:00 a.m. and time to be off.

We drove for three hours south to what was going to be Leshan and the biggest Buddha in the world. As we got close to the area, we picked up a second tour guide, who would be our local guide. We started off again, but first we had to stop for lunch, never missing a meal.

It was a countryside town, and this looked to be the best restaurant there. The heat and humidity hit us as we stepped out of our air-conditioned minivan and went into the downstairs part of the restaurant. It was full of noisy customers. Everyone stared at us, and we were escorted up a dirty, messy, wet staircase to a private room. It had a tall cooler in the corner, and Hunter sat beside it. Our guides left us to order lunch. They would eat elsewhere in the same restaurant.

Xi-fen did her best with the skinny countryside man trying to take our order. She quizzed him on the preparation of the food and felt confident that she knew what to expect. It was so hot. I wanted to ask if they had anything cold but knew this wasn't wise for sanitary reasons. The prices seemed high for where we were. I questioned Xi-fen, and she was convinced that this was the regular menu. I didn't think so, but it didn't matter

After ten minutes and no food, the air conditioner didn't work, so we called for assistance. Someone came, but it still didn't work, and our food had not appeared. Then the hot soup came.

The tour guides were called to observe that the air conditioner wasn't working. Another twenty minutes passed, and two more people from the restaurant came to check the air conditioner. There was a loud and heated conversation between the management and Xi-fen, but of course, I couldn't tell what was said; tempers flared concerning the air conditioner.

Finally, the food came, and we decided to move to a large room with an open window. It wasn't good quality food and we could hardly eat it. I asked Xi-fen what was said, kind of imitating the heated intonation of the voices I had heard.

"Well, I knew she was just a country person, but saying that I was lying was just too much."

I agreed that it was pretty terrible. I had no idea it had been so serious, but Xi-fen seemed to get over it quickly. She later told me she had to consider who was accusing her of lying and not get too upset. The Chinese are masters at confrontation.

We piled back into the minivan and drove next to the park, along the waterfront of the huge river, which is a large tributary of the Yangtze. With parasols to shade us from the sun, we walked a few blocks along the street with "old man beard" trees. I had never seen these, and as their name implies, they had long, skinny lichen growth dangling from the branches.

With our two guides, we walked into a moss-covered, rocky entrance to a park with a wide stone trail leading uphill. After a long climb in the heat and humidity, we would see the Buddha at the top. Xi-fen had worn her more colorful dress since this was the place where one of the Buddhas would be white. It got hotter and more humid as we climbed slowly up. The cliff on our left was deeply colored orange rock. It looked to be sandstone. Bright green moss and ferns clung to the stone sides and the dragon waterfall along the pathway. Across the river on our right, we could see the tall buildings of Leshan on the opposite bank. There was a heat haze over the river.

At the top was a temple crowded with Chinese tourists. Xi-fen told me it was tradition for women to step over the high threshold into the sacred part of the temple with their left foot first and men their right. Xi-fen and I practiced this, but the young guides didn't. There were some museum exhibits that told the history of the giant 233-foot Buddha both in Chinese and English. Xi-fen got disgusted with the incorrect English. All they had to do was hire her, and she would've straightened out all the problems. There were misspelled words, words out of place, but an attempt in English had been made.

The red guards of the cultural revolution unsuccessfully tried to destroy this huge rock Buddha by attempting to blow it up. It was damaged but miraculously saved. From this angle, we could look down on him in the cliff below us. The wait in line to walk down the cliff opposite us to his feet was going to be two hours. We bought drinks, but I needed five. We took photos with Xi-fen reaching out in space to have her hand "touch" the eyebrow of the Buddha in the distance. Sort of like trying to hold up the tower of Pisa in the distance while one stands in the foreground. This "touching "would bring her good luck, and, of course, it was another scenic spot.

We looked down on the river and boats below and decided to go catch a boat to ride in front of the Buddha on the water. As we walked back down the stone steps, I wanted my picture taken with a marble tiger next to the path. Xi-fen said, "No, it's not good luck because the tiger is going down and not up." I took a picture of the tiger.

One disadvantage of the tour being only in Chinese is that I couldn't pick up the subtleties of what was going on. We crossed the busy street next to the river on the assumption that we were going to buy tickets for the boat ride. Somehow, we couldn't buy tickets here, but there were people milling around in and out of a doorway. Our group entered through a long line, and I followed.

It was a large room full of people, looking at things in jewelry counters, with an air-conditioning unit spewing out water vapor and a chair in the corner. Xi-fen was in deep conversation with our local guide. They were discussing things in little red boxes. She came over to me to show me a jade Buddha pendant on a red cord, similar to ones I have seen in San Francisco Chinatown.

"What do you think?" she asked me.

"It's nice. How much is it?" I asked.

"It's ¥285," Xi-fen said.

"Wow, that's a lot. Do you really want this?"

The local guide was bringing her more to look at. They were deep in conversation. The guide was ignoring me. Xi-fen explained, "Tomorrow we will go to Mount Emei, and there will be a special blessing for people who bring pendants. They announced this last year, and five thousand people came, and they had to cancel it. So tomorrow is a surprise." I surmised this meant she didn't know what would happen.

I could see she really wanted to do this, so I helped her decide on which Buddha carving was the best and which was the best stone. She bought one for ¥250. If you compare her salary to the U.S. dollar,

I figured this was about $250 to us. This room was hotter inside than out. Someone gave up the chair, and I decided that I was the oldest in the room, so I sat down. After half an hour, the deal was completed, and we walked outside.

Our local guide announced that she was leaving us. We still had our Chengdu guide, who would help us with the boat tickets. At this point, Xi-fen began to smell a rat. She decided that the local guide was going back into the store to collect a commission on her sale. I saw the same thing and agreed with her. But I reminded her that she did want the pendant and would have it for tomorrow on the sacred mountain. It occurred to me that perhaps we only picked this guide up so we could feed her in the restaurant, and she could make this sale.

We went to get on a boat that was leaving immediately, but as we walked across the floating landing, we saw the speedboat and the boat people shouting. Xi-fen turned on her heel and said, "We're not taking this boat." Hunter and I followed her off the landing.

It seems they saw me, a foreigner. They said they couldn't guarantee my safety. X-fen is afraid of speedboats anyway, so that was all she had to hear. We walked to the other ticket office and bought tickets for a bigger boat.

It proved to be a great way to see the Buddha. We had plenty of time to take pictures and appreciate the height and magnificence of this beautiful sculpture, as well as see the statues and the staircase carved in the side walls next to it.

We got back out on the street to find that the road had been closed, so the government could come and inspect. Who? What? Why? It was never explained. But we had to hire bicycle rickshaws to take us several blocks to find our driver and minivan. Thank heaven for cell phones!

We drove in the minivan toward the town of Mount Emei. By now, it was time for dinner. After an hour drive and a near miss with a huge bus, barely stopping in time before almost hitting us head-on, we came to the town of Mount Emei. The guide took us to "Food Street" for dinner. We parked, and she seemed only interested in one restaurant. It had outdoor seating with huge hot pots in the center of the tables, but we didn't sit there. There were only a few diners. We were escorted to a building in the back and up more wet, dirty, and grungy stairs with dirty walls to a private room set especially for us. It did not look good. It wasn't clean at all. I got the feeling that we were here because it was somebody's relative or something like that. Xi-fen excused herself to use the restroom. I whispered to Hunter that I didn't think we would be staying here long. Sure enough, Xi-fen came back and declared that this was not suitable. Thank goodness, she takes care of these things. Our tour guide said we could eat at our hotel, so off we went.

A few minutes later, we arrived at a construction site, bricks, piles of dirt, some unfinished buildings. We drove in on an unfinished dirt road and stopped at the front door of a glass fronted building. Inside, the lobby had marble floors, four international clocks, and a few pieces of oversized furniture, but had an unfinished look about it. We were given keys to our rooms, proceeded to the elevator, then down the linoleum tile hallways to our room.

Xi-fen was unusually quiet in our room as she looked around. She checked out the bathroom, the drapes, the electric kettle, and the beds.

Then she declared, "This is not a three-star hotel."

"Really?" I asked. I knew our tour was to be three-star throughout. "What do you mean? It has four international clocks in the lobby."

"This is a hotel for cadres. I saw the name plates on the doors as we came in. It's meant as a reward for loyal cadres for what do you call, a getaway?"

"A retreat? "I asked.

"Yes, that's it. I'm going to complain when I get home, but this bathroom is not three-star standard. It isn't even clean."

I inspected the bathroom. It was new construction, and even though the grout could have been cleaner, it was OK, but it didn't compare well to our place in Chengdu.

"And there is no carpet in the halls. Three-star hotels always have carpet. There are certain requirements that three stars have to have. The drapes have no blackout lining." And as she picked up the electric kettle, she said, "This is not a good kettle, and look, there are two mosquitoes in this room!"

I started laughing. "Xi-fen, it's OK. We are in a pretty out-of-the-way place." We laughed together.

It is funny that they give you slippers to use that are not your size or that someone else has already used. And of course, the tiny roll of the twelve-square toilet paper for two people was here, too.

I wondered if money would be taken out of the ¥2000 we hadn't paid at the travel agency.

We went over to Hunter's room, a few doors away, to go for dinner together. There was no one else staying in this wing of the building. His room was like ours, but being a teenager, he just cared about the TV. We walked out back and found the place where food would be served. We were a strange trio: a teenager, a young Chinese woman, and me, a tall foreigner, all speaking English. How were we together? No one talked to us or made eye contact, so it felt unfriendly. This area is not near any city, and the people are not used to foreigners.

The dining room was outside and across the courtyard. We weren't allowed to sit by the air conditioner because those places were already set for breakfast. It was 6:00 p.m. The menu was very short. Many sloppy-looking people stood around in aprons and old clothes. It didn't seem like a hotel. We ordered food, but didn't want to eat some dishes because they didn't look fresh. The loofah was brownish when it should've been a bright green color. We saw them serve their rice out of a huge pot and then put rice back into the pot when the table was cleared. The three of us started laughing as we looked at our unappealing food. Everyone was staring, as we were a strange family, especially me, eating with chopsticks, and our differences in ages. Hunter said he felt like we were a bunch of monkeys. I told him to look back at the workmen at the next table, staring and laughing at us. I told him I thought they were the monkeys. He thought this was hysterical. Hunter's English is limited, but we understood each other on this one.

All of a sudden, we heard a loud pounding downpour. We had no umbrellas and sent Hunter to fetch them from our rooms. His gentlemanly qualities came out as he escorted Xi-fen and me one by one through torrential rain back to our building.

Fortunately, the rain stopped by morning, cleared, and we showed up at the same fabulous room to eat. The tables were a mess. No one was in a hurry to do anything. We had to get someone's attention to come to our table. Lots of people had obviously been here before us. Breakfast wasn't much, again, no tea, so we didn't linger. We walked back to the main building to greet our guide. There were many retirement-age men and women stretching their arms and legs in the courtyard.

I said, "Ni hao" (hello) to an older lady. She was surprised and repeated it to her friend as if to say, "Did you hear that?" Our guide and driver were waiting for us in the lobby. We would spend the day with her on Mount Emei, and then head back to the Chengdu airport to catch our flight back to Shanghai.

August 13, 2004
The next day we took the cable car up to the ten-thousand-foot. top of Emei Shan. Buddhism was established here, and the first temple was built. People on top were lighting incense and candles and praying at the many small altars. We walked up to see the golden

elephants and beautiful Buddhist statues. There were decorative ceramic pots, ponds, and some lovely small gardens.

After we toured the top temples, we started walking down the long path to get to the bottom of the mountain. There were lots of food stalls along the way. We saw some charming pavilions in garden-like settings that made use of the creek water alongside them.

My feet were so hot in my walking shoes, and just as I thought I couldn't stand it anymore, I saw some boulders where I could sit and soak my feet in cold water. I was saved.

Xi-fen pointed out the men just below us who would carry a person on a litter down the rest of the mountain. They were all so skinny, and there was no way I would make them carry me.

At the bottom of the mountain, we found our arranged transportation and luggage and headed back to the Chengdu Airport to check in. I passed through security, glanced behind me, and saw they had pulled Xi-fen aside. They were emptying her purse and searching everything she had in her carry-on. This happened six years ago when guards took her fruit knife away in Xian. Finally, the guards took her knife and were satisfied that that was all she had.

"It was really small. If I had known it would be this much trouble, I would have put it in my suitcase!"

I should have reminded her.

Chapter

Jiangyin 22

Saturday, August 14, 2004

We returned home last night from our big adventure and spent most of the day washing our clothes and getting settled, which included afternoon naps.

I received an email back from Don in Tennessee, dated August 11.

Monday, August 11, 2004

Email from Don in Memphis

Hey Carolyn,

First of all, let me say that I am very jealous. Please give my best to Xi-fen. I miss both of you and think of you often. I loaned the book, *River Town*, you gave me to another guy I met at school who did the Shenzhen program. He enjoyed the book as much as I did.

A few bits of news. I just got married a little over a month ago. My wife's name is Liz, and she went to China on the Shenzhen program the year after I got home. I visited her, and we traveled during her winter month off in 2001.

I'm sending you the link for our wedding pictures and our honeymoon in Costa Rica.

These days, we are looking for a house to buy. I'm sending you the link for the houses we are looking at.

I have two part-time semesters remaining to finally get my degree. Liz and I want to go back to China and teach for another year once I finish school. Much depends on what our housing situation turns out to be. The plan is to rent our house while we're gone, but that idea has complications.

I hope you have a safe trip. I can't wait to hear about your adventures.

Take care,

Don

August 14, 2004

Email to Don

Dear Don,

Congratulations! Xi-fen and I were so happy to hear from you and to hear your good news. We wish you and Liz a long and happy life together. I miss you here in Jiangyin. Crossing the street is still the same, and Xi-fen says the City Hunter Club is still here, but I haven't seen it.

Tomorrow we are going to take a taxi out to see Bell School. She says the school is bankrupt. They are rebuilding the roundabout with the overpasses that we had to negotiate when we went into town. I'm very curious.

Tuesday night, I will have a "banquet" for some of our students.

Xi-fen and I had a great trip, and we are having so much fun together. As she says, "She giggles me, and I giggle her, and she hasn't giggled in a long time." We are still very close. I have so many funny stories.

Later,

Carolyn

August 15, 2024

In the morning, Xi-fen and I took a taxi to Bell School, so I could see what had happened and how it had changed. Two years ago, Xi-fen went back to teach in the public school system. The private Bell Economic School was out of business. I was told that some other school was there, but I didn't see any students. We went into the empty "English Center." I walked up to the third floor to see my old room. I had been there by myself, but now there were six beds in the one room. The curtains were hanging in taters on the windows. It looked messy and neglected. There were no occupants.

Xi-fen says three books should be written about Bell School. One is about the people, one about the corruption, and one about how people treated each other. The casts of characters that I remember from six years ago have interesting updates on their lives.

I am amazed that all these people know what each other is doing, that they are interested in each other's stories.

Mr. Six, the former principal of Bell School, sold all his shares in Bell School. He was rich six years ago, but now he has become even richer. I could never understand how he could be the principal and also own and visit and run several printing companies all over China. The company printed labels for wine and cigarettes, a lucrative business with so many smokers in the country. He used his money from Bell School to build a new printing factory across the road from Bell School. The one-story factory is huge, with large gold letters on the sign in front. It is air-conditioned throughout, a big deal in China, and impeccably clean, with many amenities for the workers. Xi-fen has been inside and said it was quite unbelievable.

Several of the rich men I knew are with mistresses. My Chinese students in California said mistresses are called a "wild flower" in Chinese. They have cast their wives aside, and the wives can do nothing about it.

According to Xi-fen, one lives with a "countryside" person with poor taste in clothes. Over a period of time, she has acquired lavish tastes in clothes, make-up, and lifestyle.

Xi-fen says, "She is painted in money."

"Is that a Chinese expression?"

"No, it's mine."

Poor decisions were made in the operation of the school, which created major problems in financing and organization. A girlfriend, who couldn't do anything right, was installed at the school, and she was the boss. People were disgusted. The school is now bankrupt.

The corruption at Bell School also involved teacher professionalism. In the teaching field, many people are excellent, and it is very difficult to get promoted. One must build relationships with communist cadres and flatter them to be able to move up. You must be picked. You cannot choose advancement for yourself. You cannot work professionally on your own advancement. This led to more corruption.

Monday August 16, 2004

Today we've been invited to lunch by Mr Shaw's company, but first Xi-fen and I had our usual breakfast of rice porridge with things added, boiled peanuts, dried fish, pickles, radish, and pieces of leftover meat. Xi-fen boils water; some she cools, and some is for hot water for her or tea for me.

Mr Shaw in not exactly employed by the men we are to meet. He uses them for "credentials" and pays them for the use of their name. It gives his remodeling business status and credibility since they have a large construction company. Mr. He and Mr. G have heard that I am in Jiangyin and they want to meet me, a foreigner who might have investment money and contacts in the United States.

There were a few problems setting this up. First it was going to be the owner of the company, then he was called to the hospital. People get put into the hospital on what seems to me a regular basis for IVs. It was never clear why, but it was a common treatments for ailments.

There were a few hours where lunch was going to be cancelled. Xi-fen was disgusted.

"Do they want us come or not?" she impatiently asked Mr. Shaw on the phone, who assured her that it was important. She said we needed to go to lunch because this would give Mr. Shaw "face" in his relationship with this company.

I told Xi-fen I wasn't sure how I could help, I'm kind of a long shot for these guys, but I would do what I could. I began to think of what I could say about Americans investing in China and whom I might know. All the translation would be done through Xi-fen, because lunch would be entirely in Chinese. I trust Xi-fen not to put me into an awkward situation, and she trusts me to talk my way through things. We are a team, and we know it.

Late morning came. It was past time to leave for lunch. I had been ready, but Xi-fen had been doing things in the kitchen and around the house. Mr. Shaw called to see where we were. We we were already late. She told him we were coming, called the taxi company, and we ran down the five flights of stairs.

It was very hot, but the cabs are all air-conditioned, and we got another fast driver to take us across town. Speeding across town, her phone rang

Annoyed, she said, "Oh, I'm not going to answer it. Mr. Shaw is just calling because we are late." A minute went by, and it rang again. She let it go.

We were about fifteen minutes getting to the fancy "Times Hotel" across town.

They were all waiting. Mr. Shaw, with his son Hunter, introduced Xi-fen and me to Mr. He and Mr. G, both vice-presidents in their company. They were nice-looking men in their late thirties, nicely dressed in dressy silk sport shirts. These were businessmen with polished manners.

Inside the marble lobby with black and gold decor were huge arrangements of bright tropical flowers. It was impeccably clean, shiny, and new.

As we ascended an elegant stairway to the dining rooms, we passed doors off to the left and right with a young man or woman attendant who bowed and welcomed each of us as we passed by. It was like in a movie, and I felt like a movie star. The attendants were dressed in white shirts, black pants, or skirts, and both men and women wore men's silk ties. It certainly made me feel important. I might have felt nervous in my own culture, but knowing it would all be in Chinese and I wouldn't understand most of it gave me great freedom to just smile and try to act like this was a common occurrence. We were escorted into an elaborately decorated dining room with a round table set for six. The gold silk wall coverings and mirrored design on the door made the room sparkle. There was a small alcove for the waiters and waitresses to call for our food.

Mr. He offered me a cigarette as we sat down. They smoked, but it wasn't a problem with so much space around the table. Cold dishes were already on the glass Lazy Susan. These were different dishes that I hadn't seen before. We had thousand-year-old eggs perfectly done, but I still wasn't crazy about them. Later Xi-fen told me it was a different style of local cuisine and very expensive. There were fourteen dishes in all.

The air-conditioning in the room was cold, and Xi-fen was too cold. She asked that it be turned off. I was too hot, so I resorted to cold beer. The beer was served in a wire holder placed next to my chair on the carpet like a fine wine. The waitress with a tie served it from there.

Mr. He and Mr. G explained through Xi-fen that they had a big construction company with many branches and they were looking to expand. They wanted to build manufacturing plants. Jiangyin is a huge manufacturing area. They said the area offered cheap labor for joint ventures with someone in America because there are tax advantages for Chinese companies. I asked a few questions about their company's housing branch. I told them I would tell my stockbrokers about them. I told them I would tell a friend who has done business in China.

During lunch Mr. He took out photos of his daughter. She was an adorable six year old with a beautiful smile. He said she had been on TV. He told us he and his wife had an older son as well. Xi-fen and I both wondered how he could have two children. Xi-fen said he must have found a way to get around the law. Perhaps he had so much money that he had paid the high fee for a second child.

Mr. He and Mr. G were very gracious and said that they just wanted to welcome me to Jinagyin. I told them thank you very much for the delicious lunch and that I would remember them and if possible find someone who might be interested in their company.

We walked out of the hotel, and they put Xi-fen and me in a taxi. On the way home we discussed lunch. Xi-fen thought Mr. Shaw should not have brought Hunter to a business meeting.

I had to resist the temptation to take photos. This was a serious business meeting.

Our Former Students

August 17, 2004

"Carolyn!" echoed across the restaurant lobby.

Who knows me here?

Xi-fen and I had just walked up the two-story curved staircase and into the same restaurant that Mr. Shaw had held the banquet for me when I first arrived.

I looked at the man calling out my name. Oh my gosh, it was Mr. Chen, a teacher I knew at Bell School! Xi-fen and I had discussed earlier whether to invite him to the banquet I was hosting this evening for some of Xi-fen's and my former students.

We decided not to invite him because he was involved in numerous dishonest deals where he obtained money and favors from his students and their parents. He was a real cheat, giving out answers to students so he could receive extra money for their good test scores. He withheld college information until parents came to his home, and of course, in the Chinese manner, they would give him money for telling them whether or not their child had passed a test or was accepted at a university. This was happening six years ago when I was at the school, and Xi-fen wanted nothing to do with him.

Xi-fen and I exchanged knowing glances. Had he remembered me after six years?

He moved in close to me. I smiled and greeted him warmly.

"Mr. Chen, what a surprise to see you. How are you? You are looking well."

What else could I say? Six years ago, his students gave me a large ceramic dragon plate as a gift, and he had fussed over me, giving me a lot of attention.

Did he know we were there to meet students whom he knew? How did he know I was there? He explained that he was being taken out to dinner by some of his students' parents. Xi-fen had told me this was a regular occurrence. I knew he rarely ate at home and was constantly wined and dined by parents, hoping to improve their standing at school.

We quickly told him we were going to be in a private room, said goodbye, and walked down a hall and up a flight of stairs to our private room at the back of the restaurant. Mr. Chen went the other way. What a coincidence to meet him here.

Xi-fen and I found our room, and the students started arriving with gifts for me. They are now twenty-four year olds and all doing well in businesses.

Of the four young women and three young men, Adam spoke the best English. He is in charge of all the foreign teachers in Jiangyin at the various schools. He offered me a job. I told him I couldn't come for a one-year contract, but before I left, he lowered it to six months. They would pay me well, more than three times the Chinese teachers' salary. I thanked him for the offer. They really don't have a clue how old I am. Retirement age in China is fifty-five.

Adam told me he remembered everything I had taught him— kind of scary. He remembered the contest I had to guess the place in the poster I had hung in our classroom. It was Mont. St. Michele in France. He remembered the boy who won the chocolate prize, the only one of three hundred students to say, "a French house," the only close answer. Most of the guesses were Mongolia and Australia.

Adam told me he was going to law school in Shanghai, hopefully next year. He remembered that my husband, whom he met, was a lawyer. I told him I had to get a divorce. He said he was sorry and asked why. I told him my husband had been dishonest with me, and I couldn't trust him.

Adam said, "I think trust is the most important part of a marriage. When trust is gone, it's over."

Amen, I thought. *He's got the picture, and he's only twenty-four.*

Mr. Su, a teacher from Bell School, came in from the countryside by company car provided by Jane, one of my former students. I had dubbed Mr. Su "the best cook in China" when he invited us out to his countryside home six years ago and prepared a huge twenty-six-dish lunch. Now he and his wife have retired to that village. I gave my bicycle to Mrs. Su when I left China. The private car would return Mr. Su to his home after dinner, as there is no other transportation here at night.

Xi-fen ordered the dishes, and the food was fabulous. Jiangyin is known for its good food, and she knows how to order the best of the best.

As we began to eat, Mr. Chen burst through the door with a drink in his hand, surprising us.

He lifted his drink into the air above the table and loudly proposed a toast.

He'd found us. We all stood up. The students were very quiet as we raised our glasses to him. Then we all went along with him, laughed, smiled, and said our good wishes. We knew he just had to see who was in our group.

The students gave me a lovely bouquet of flowers, a beautiful, heavy silk wrap, which I immediately draped around my shoulders, and a cockroach embedded in plastic on a revolving rainbow lighted stand. It was highlighting the amazing world of insects. I asked Xi-fen the significance of the bug, and she didn't respond. She hates bugs.

Our conversation ran the gamut of cars, the economy, Rebecca might go to law school, jobs, SARS, 9-11, and Michael Moore. Rebecca had seen *Fahrenheit 911* on the internet. They wanted to know who would win the presidency. They said they heard about the Twin Towers on 9/11. The first person they thought of was me.

Rebecca said, "Oh, Carolyn is there. I hope she is all right." Even though they know I'm from California, they don't really understand how far away New York is. I told them I was worried about them with SARS. Jiangsu Province had had no cases.

Topics continued with marriage, dating, and the generation gap. These young adults don't want to live with their parents because "old people have old living habits." They know Harry Potter and the movie *Shrek.* They discussed having babies, and the young women said they were afraid of childbirth. I thought it interesting that they freely discussed this in mixed company, but even though they don't see each other often, they are good friends.

Wendy was married, had a child, and indicated with her hand that the birth had been Cesarean. They agreed that all childbirth should be this way. They all expected to get married, have a child, and maybe the one-child rule would be changed. They would then have another child. They would have their mothers take care of their children while they worked. Chrystal was learning to drive. Rebecca still carries my business card that I gave her while she was my student. They were living comfortable lives and working on their futures.

The evening ended on a happy note. They all hoped to see me again someday soon. I invited them to visit me, but I realized that for them, that is not in the realm of possibilities. Even Xi-fen is doubtful she could visit me because she'd have to get her visa through Shanghai, and it is difficult, if not impossible, to process.

August 19, 2004

Xi-fen and I have had so much fun visiting. We went to see her girlfriend at the television station. She runs the entire station, and it is larger now. We have been in downtown Jiangyin, shopping and going to lunch. We talked about our adventures on our trip.

We talked about going to Wuxi, but her brother told her that the old book and antique market where I found the rubies had been torn down. He didn't know where those shopkeepers had gone.

Tonight, I am hosting a banquet in the usual restaurant for all the people who have helped me during my visit. Our guests include Mr. Shaw, Hunter, our driver to the airport for our trip, the driver that picked me up at the Shanghai Airport and will take me back, and the man from the police department, who Xi-fen called to report that she had a foreigner in her apartment. If she hadn't done this, her neighbors would have reported her, and she would be in trouble. Xi-fen ordered the food, and I asked that she order plenty but not go "overboard" on too many dishes. She did a perfect job. We bought cartons of cigarettes as gifts for these men because this is what is expected.

I sat next to the policeman who spoke English, and he told me he could help me stay longer.

I said, "Can you help Xi-fen get a visa to come to America and see me?"

He thought about it for a while and said, "No, I can't do that. It all has to be handled in Shanghai."

The next day, we stayed in Xi-fen's apartment, and I packed to go home. It was going to be another difficult goodbye. We hoped we would see each other again, but communication has improved, so it's much easier to stay in touch.

This morning, the driver picked up Xi-fen, Mr. Shaw, and me to see me off at the Shanghai airport. I tried to make it a quick goodbye, reminding Xi-fen that we would be able to easily write to each other.

I wrote her as soon as I got home, thanking her again for a wonderful trip. We exchanged more emails, and I sent her a Christmas card and New Year's greetings for 2005.

Correspondence Continues

Chapter 24

Wednesday, January 19, 2005

Dear Carolyn,

Thank you so much for your beautiful Christmas card and nice letter. I like them both. It's so nice of you to cover so much of our trip and me in your letter. I loved the trip and the time we spent together. You coming to China filled my summer vacation with great joy and a lot of giggles. In fact, I haven't giggled for a long time, Carolyn. I will cherish all the things we did together for years.

I'm sorry I didn't write sooner after I got your email. I sent you a Christmas card via the internet, but later I found out it didn't go through. I'm sorry about that.

Our Christmas party went well. Everyone enjoyed it. I spent a lot of time preparing because I was the organizer and director. After that, in my new school, I was busy directing the Young English Teachers Demonstration, class competition, both Jiangyin and Wuxi city-wide.

Two teachers in our English group attended the competition. Finally, one teacher won the first prize in both Jiangyin and Wuxi. It was a very big thing. They have never won this prize before.

The principal of the school was very happy about this and very satisfied with me. Anyway, Carolyn, it proved my level.

Carolyn, how was your Christmas party? Did you have all three daughters at home? Did you have a good time? I hope everything went well. Did you go somewhere with your girlfriends? I do hope you enjoyed your holiday.

It is very cold here, minus 4–5 Celsius. This kind of weather has lasted for two weeks. I had a bad cold and sore throat, with fever for about two weeks. The doctor wanted me to do an IV, but I don't have time, as I have to give lessons. Thank goodness, I can just let my students review their lessons by themselves. I have been taking medicine up to today. I'm getting better.

Now I'm busy giving students their final evaluations. Then we'll have our three-week winter vacation at the end of the month.

Chinese New Year falls on February 9. Usually, I go to Wuxi to spend Chinese New Year with my parents and my brother's family and stay with them for a week. This year, I don't know where I'm going to spend it. Maybe in Jiangyin with Mr. Shaw and his son, Hunter. I'll wait and see. Anyway, I'll go to Wuxi to see my parents and stay there for several days during the Spring Festival.

My relationship with Mr. Shaw is still the same. He is a warm and kindhearted person, but he is not a detailed person. He doesn't have a strong character and is not organized. We argued, almost like quarreling, a few times after summer vacation. I expressed my attitude to him. He seems better, but I don't know what is going to happen. I'll wait and see. I'll remember what you told me, "time will tell."

How are you doing with your personal affairs? Have you met someone you like? It's really not easy to meet someone we really like.

I'll talk to you later.

Love,

Xi-fen

Sunday, March 20, 2005

Dear Carolyn,

I'm very sorry for the delay in writing your email. Actually, I'm thinking of you often and miss you a lot. How are you doing now? Are you teaching school now? I hope you can take a good rest and have some relaxing time.

I was busy in this three-week winter vacation. I went to Mr. Shaw's hometown in the countryside for the Chinese New Year and stayed in Wuxi for a week after the Chinese New Year. My father is not in good health. His legs are getting worse and worse. Now he struggles to walk. The doctor said that something is wrong with his brain. Most of the time, he is in a low mood. I felt very sorry for him and sad about it, but I can do nothing about it.

Our school started on February 18. I was as busy as last semester with my teaching job and the teacher's training program. I still have to work every Sunday, which I hate.

Carolyn, I think this year I started with bad luck. I've had a very bad stomachache since February 16. That's the day I came back from Wuxi. I did several stomach medical examinations, one of which was very terrible and suffering. The result of all the examination is not a big problem, but I have limitations for my diet. I have been taking medicine for more than a month. I still don't feel well, so I still have to take medicine. I still feel kind of weak. As you know, I get energy from my good diet, as I'm a light sleeper. Anyway, I'm feeling better than in the beginning. I'll take care of myself.

My relationship with Mr. Shaw is still up and down. He is a kindhearted man, but his living habits, most of which are not good, are so different from mine. He is trying to change, but it is not that easy, so we often have arguments about it. His business is not steady, and he has some health and psychological problems, too. He has no money, which is also a big problem for him. I can see he has a lot of pressure for money and his business. He is not very positive. He is still my boyfriend, though. I am not satisfied with him, and he knows that. However, he lets me choose. I'll wait and see; just as you say, time will tell. My brother tells me the same.

I have to stop here today. Write to me when you can.

Love,

Xi-fen.

I emailed Xi-fen back to express sympathy for all her recent medical problems. I told her I was teaching two ESL classes, one at night and two Cultural Studies for the Traveler classes.

Monday, March 6, 2006

Dear Carolyn,

My son stayed in China for three weeks and with me for about two weeks. We talked a lot and did many things together. Carolyn, I really enjoyed the time with him. He has grown taller than me, but he is not as tall as the boys his age. I'm a little worried about his height, as he does not have a balanced diet. My son is a kind and considerate person.

He's concerned about me. As I told you in my last email, he hoped that his parents could reconcile. We talked a lot about this topic. I told him what his father had done to me since I came back from America, and the other things that happened later on. I also showed him all the letters his father wrote to me because my son is interested in those letters. After all this, my son still hoped that I could have a talk with his father on the topic directly. My son is nice to me, and I don't want to disappoint him; I also want to know the answer directly from my former husband, instead of from his friends and relatives, which has been an endless mystery for ten years. It was very strange that he tried to avoid meeting me in person this time. I still want him to tell me directly. I had to talk to him on the phone.

Carolyn, it is ridiculous that I could only talk about such a serious and important topic on the phone. There is a mess now; his business is going from bad to worse. However, he still won't take another person's advice. As a matter of fact, he has suffered a lot in Australia. In the beginning, he still had hope, but now he feels hopeless. Most of the time he's in a bad mood and frustrated. These two years he was in bad health, too, but he still has to work hard; then he has to take care of my son.

My son has to live with such a father. I feel very sad. When I told my son the result, he felt sad, but he didn't show it much. I had to talk with him about his future and give him some hope. Carolyn, you are right. I really admire you. Everything happened just as you predicted. My ex-husband does not want to reconcile, and I don't want to be with him. You are such a wise, independent, and strong woman. How I wish I could be as strong and independent as you!

Carolyn, it's so hard to do all that. I hope my son can live with hope. I found he has changed a lot over these two years, living a hard and lonely life with his father. My son knows all about his father's business because his father always complains about it. Carolyn, my son is not as confident as two years ago, and he is not interested in anything but computer games and chatting with his friends on the internet. He has no goals for his future, so he is not working as hard as before at his lessons. He is in a good public school. He doesn't want to be a top student at all. He used to be a confident and hard-working boy, but now he is not. He likes to talk with me; we discussed many things like two good friends, but he seldom communicates with his father. I encouraged him to talk to him, as he has to spend most of his time with his father before he can make a living by himself. He is not really doing so.

Carolyn, I am really worried about my son. He is in a period of forming his personality. We Chinese have a saying, "Environment decides a person's personality. Personality decides a person's fate." My son is living in such an awful environment, and I have seen negative influences on him already. My poor son has suffered a lot since our divorce. I really hope he can have a good future and live a happy life. I talked with him about this, too, but there hasn't been much effect on him. As soon as he goes back to that environment, he is lonely and in low spirits.

This troubles me a lot, and I feel depressed. I don't know the best way to help him. I hope you can give me some advice. This semester, I have the same teaching job as last semester. My work is not as stressful as before, but I don't feel relaxed and happy.

Carolyn, please take care of yourself. I'm looking forward to hearing from you soon.

Love,

Xi-fen

March 8, 2006

Email from Xi-fen

Subject: Thank you so much.

Dear Carolyn,

Carolyn, thank you so much for your good advice and suggestions. I feel much more relaxed. Being a mother, I have tried my best to do what I could do, and I'll keep on doing that so that I won't feel guilty later on.

Just like what you said in your email, teenagers are very difficult to motivate. I have felt that.

I'm glad to hear that you are going to have two weeks off at Easter and that you are going to see Lynessa in Sweden. It's not easy for her to be there with two little children. I'm sure she will be happy to see you there. I hope you can have a good time with her and your two darling granddaughters.

Carolyn, you are always full of new ideas and very creative. I feel that I kind of "lag behind." I'm not good at using the new equipment, such as computers and digital cameras. I'm not as creative. I need to keep on learning more like you.

My parents are living by themselves. They are living an OK life, as my father doesn't have retirement money, and my mother gets only ¥50 per month. Though we give them some money, it is not that much. My father's health is getting worse. It's very hard for him to walk. He has to struggle. Besides, he suffers from several other diseases. He's taking medicine, though it doesn't help. What we can do is to give him some money, buy him something to eat, and comfort him. From my father, I really feel health is most important in one's life. From now on, I'll think more about myself and nurture myself more.

Carolyn, I'm so lucky to have you. You are such a good friend who knows me so well and gives me help whenever I need it. I have learned a lot from you in many aspects, which has benefited me a lot.

Carolyn, you always do a lot for others. Please take your time to do the photo and DVD programs you like.

Carolyn, take care of yourself.

Love,

Xi-fen

Monday, April 10, 2006

Dear Carolyn,

It's already a month since I got your last email. How are you doing now? Are you in Sweden or back in America?

I'm not as busy as before this semester. Actually, I have more free time than ever. However, I am not as happy as before. I feel lonely, restless, hopeless, and depressed. Most of the time, I am in low spirits and have a bad headache. Carolyn. One thing is that I miss my son very much. Another thing is the disappointing, bad results of my positive talk with my ex-husband and the departure of Mr. Shaw from our relationship. I feel I'm a loser in marriage. Being a woman of forty-six, I really feel very depressed about my situation, and this has affected my health and work.

A month ago, I coincidentally met a man who is my former girlfriend's husband. My former friend died of cancer eight years ago. Her husband got remarried, but they only got along well for two years, then they separated. Anyway, he knows me from long ago but didn't know that I lived by myself until he met me this time.

Our talk started with our sons. In the beginning, we had much to talk about. He got divorced from the second wife after he met me. Of course, I emphasized that he shouldn't get divorced because of me, as we have known each other just as friends, and I don't really like his appearance. He is taller and fatter than Mr. Shaw, but he looks a little womanish and ugly. For the first week, he came every night, and we talked a lot. He said he had never talked so much about life with any woman.

Gradually, I found he is too gentle, passive, and very stingy. He has no humor and can't make me happy. I looked and looked for it. I tried to say to myself, "Don't judge a man by his appearance." Carolyn, I hope his personality can attract me, but on the contrary, I feel a little bit sick of him. I don't know why, though. Economically, he's OK, as he works in a good power plant in Jiangyin. He is not decisive, and he is slow-thinking. He has a son who didn't finish college because he got addicted to computer games. He has an eighty-eight-year-old mother who needs someone to take care of her because of high blood pressure. Carolyn, reasonably thinking, the good thing about him is that he has a steady job and a good income. He is good tempered. However, I really can't accept it now because of all the above shortcomings.

Carolyn, I don't know if I have some problems. I have no

confidence about making boyfriends. I don't feel as confident about myself as before, Carolyn. I would like to have your advice.

Looking forward to hearing from you soon.

Love,

Xi-fen

I wrote back to say I did not think this was a good situation for her. She takes care of herself and is a strong, independent, and talented person. She will meet someone who will appreciate her for the very intelligent person she is. I assured her that there is nothing wrong with her single situation, and she should stop worrying about it. There is nothing wrong with being single. It's better than a bad relationship.

August 2006

Dear Xi-fen,

Thank you so much for the photos; you look great. I was getting concerned about you since I know you were not feeling well and was about to write a third email. I am so happy you have decided to put on a smile. I love it that your son told you it takes more to frown than to smile. I also think, as you mentioned, that your trip around China was very good for you. It's wonderful you can travel with your group of friends.

As for Mr. Yan, he does sound boring. I do disagree with the fortuneteller a bit, as I think there are many kinds of men, not just two types. You are doing well for yourself, and you do not need a man "to complete you."

Your divorce was not of your doing. Remember your husband's actions. You are a very lovely, intelligent, and wonderful person all by yourself. Just keep smiling, and maybe you will meet someone new. I would like someone to share my life with, but it has to be, as you say, a quality person.

My visit to Sweden was fine. The little girls are so, so cute, but I do not think Lynessa will be able to come home. Her now ex-husband will not even let her come for a visit.

I flew from Sweden to Spain and back to Sweden. Our exchange student Germán's wedding in Alicante, Spain, was beautiful. The ceremony was in an Orange Grove, and then there was a lovely party in a special wedding tent for two hundred people. I'm so happy I went. I know several members of his family and some of his friends, and they made me feel very welcome.

On Monday, I am going to Mongolia, Urumqi, Tarpan, Kashgar, Kyrgyzstan, and Kazakhstan. I am going by myself through Beijing, though I couldn't do it through Shanghai. I'm meeting a tour in Ulan Bator. I will get home on September 6 in time for school to start. Today was heightened security because of a terrorist's threats in London, but I don't think it will be a problem going west.

Please remember, you are not old. I am getting old but ignoring it. I am going to go as long as I possibly can. You can, too. I love you and miss you very much. Please write. I worry about you when I don't hear from you. I promise to send photos.

Love,

Carolyn

September 26, 2006

Dear Carolyn,

I haven't written to you for a long time. I know you were going to Mongolia and Western China. Did you have a good time? I would love to see some of your photos, as I know you always take good ones

I guess you must be working at school now and busy with your classes this semester. I really admire that you are always energetic and full of enthusiasm about teaching. I like teaching, too, but there are too many rules and regulations, and a lot of challenges and competition in Chinese schools.

So many of my colleagues, my college classmates, including me, have gotten tired of teaching. We all hope to retire early so that we can do something that we enjoy and relax. Carolyn, maybe you can't quite understand this. However, it's true. I think the most important reason is that we have too much stress.

Our new semester starts on September 1. As usual, I have eleven classes each week, but I have to make five different detailed teaching plans, which is a big headache for me. I spend a lot of time doing that, and, in addition, I have to give demonstration classes and lectures. I also have to go to some countryside schools to observe the elementary teachers' classes and give instruction. No transportation is provided. This bothers me a lot. Anyway, for all the above, I can't say no, as it has been decided.

Many teachers in our school have cars. I don't think I can have one because it's costly, and I only have myself to make the money. It's too much for me. Plus, I'm very timid, and I don't think I can really learn to drive well. I still go to work by electronic bike. It's OK on fine days. However, on it's difficult in poor weather. You suffer from all the bad weather. Anyway, I can only keep at this level.

Carolyn, I'm trying to do what you say. You are right. I need to have a positive attitude about life and be in a good mood. I'll learn from you. Now I try to do some dancing exercises in the open air, not far from where I live, with a few of my neighbors. I feel happy when I'm doing this. I'm sure you would like this, too, for I know you like to dance. I'll stop here today. I have to go to my classes now. I'm looking forward to hearing from you soon. Carolyn, I miss you very much.

Love,
Xi-fen

I wrote back that I missed her, too.

I understood completely when she said the teaching work load was too much. I told her I remembered how hard the teaching situation was for her at Bell School. I remembered all the detailed lesson plans that she had to constantly write, and all the added work they gave her. It was a stressful environment. My teaching is much more relaxed, with reasonable expectations for teachers. Our teaching jobs and situations cannot be compared. Her dancing classes sound like fun and a great idea.

December 14, 2006

Dear Carolyn,

Sorry for the delay in answering your email. I really got confused after they changed my email box arrangement. I have been checking for your email at sina.com many times and didn't find any. I had forgotten that I should check 126.com. Today to my surprise, I saw your email, and it was sent more than a month ago. I must not keep you waiting and worrying about me. For this time, I keep worrying about you, too, because you returned my email much sooner than I did.

I was so happy to know that you had a good time in Mongolia and Western China. That was a rough trip. I'm sure you must've taken many good photos and videos as you always do. I'm looking forward to seeing your photos or videos soon. They must be fantastic.

I'm taking Chinese medicine to help improve my health, so I'm better. Also, I am still doing dancing exercises in the open air. I feel much better in health and mood.

After nearly one year of chatting and communicating with my son, he has become much more confident and is doing well in his studies. He wants to be a top student now. He was listed in the top ten in most of the subjects, a few in the top two, and in another, he was listed first in the grade. I am proud of him. He may come back around on Chinese New Year and stay with me for three weeks, but it hasn't been finally decided.

I am still busy with my schoolwork, but better than before, as I try to take it easy. Do you think I'm getting better?

How are you doing, Carolyn? I know you're in Sweden with Lynessa and your granddaughters this Christmas. I hope you have a very Merry Christmas there.

Love,

Xi-fen

Yes, I am happy to hear that you are doing better. Congratulations to your son for his good school work. I am doing well.

Love,

Carolyn

March 13, 2007

Email from Xi-fen

Subject: Sorry about the delay.

Dear Carolyn,

I'm very sorry for the delay in answering your letter and keeping you waiting and worrying about me. I got both your letters. Actually, I've been thinking of writing to you since I got your Christmas letter. However, I got a bad flu and had a high fever, more than 39 degrees Celsius. It took me a long time to recover. Then, I got busy with the final examinations.

During the winter vacation, I tried several times at home, but I couldn't get on my internet. I had to give up. Carolyn, I feel I'm becoming lazier now. I know deep in my heart, I'm not as confident as before. I think the divorce and living by myself for ten years has affected my personality and confidence. I tried to tell myself it is not true because I'm working in school now. I'm the only one who is living alone. My friends are all having a pretty good family life.

As I'm growing older, the more advanced appliances at home, like the computer and digital cameras, are difficult for me. Many times, I feel hopeless. I'm not good at working on these things. I feel that I need a person around who knows these better and can help me. But it's difficult to find this kind of person. Anyway, I believe it is my fate now.

I'm fine. I have the same number of classes as last semester. My son didn't come back this Chinese New Year. He may come back in April for two weeks, or in September at the latest, as we both miss each other. He is a big boy now, very nice to me and considerate of my health. In each email, he asks me about my eating and exercise. Is that nice of him to do so?

Carolyn, I really miss the time we spent together, though it has been fourteen years. It seems like it was yesterday. Of course, I remember very well the parade we watched together at Lake Tahoe. It was the Lantern Festival, which means the end of the Chinese New Year.

My email address at sina [111]. The other one doesn't work well. Just send your email to this address at 126.com as you just did. It works well.

I'll write to you when I can. Take care.

Love,

Xi-fen

Australia

December 18, 2007

Dear Carolyn,

It has been a long time since I last wrote.

I came back to China from Australia in mid-September. As soon as I came back, I met with something really troublesome. My house was soaked for five days by my upstairs neighbor's water leaking down into my apartment. They forgot to turn off the balcony tap. As I was not home, my other neighbors tried but couldn't help because they couldn't get in. It was found by my downstairs neighbor when they found their house was heavily leaking from my apartment. So, Carolyn, you can imagine how badly damaged my house is. I had to deal with my upstairs neighbor regarding compensation. It took several negotiations with the help of our community members, who were in charge of the matter. It was frustrating, but I finally settled. They compensated me with some money, but then I needed to find people to fix my house. It was very troublesome, as I had to work every day. It took ten days to finish fixing it, and I had to stay in a kind of junk place that I had to clean.

I had to make up the missed lessons in addition to my usual work. I also have a new class this semester. The teaching materials are all new to me. I spend a lot of time preparing lessons. The worst thing is that they are students who didn't pass the entrance examination to high school. Most of them speak poor English. It's my first time teaching this kind of student. Up to now, I have been teaching students who are English majors. From this semester on, we can't register this kind of class. There is only one class of English majors left now.

It worked out fine in Australia for six months, with me helping my son. I tutored him in all subjects that he needed to know for his university admission test, just like my father tutored me in 1978 so I could enter a university after the Cultural Revolution. I did a full-time mom's job. Now my son can cook for himself and take more exercise to keep fit and grow taller. He came back to China during our National Holiday, from October 1 to the 13; it was his first time by himself. He just had a two-week holiday from school. He came back mostly to see his friends and relatives who played together with him when he was a little boy. When we all went back to school, he went to travel with his aunt and aunt's two sons to Jiuzhaigou and Huang Long, where we went the last time you came to China. During those two weeks, I was very busy, too, but I was very happy to see him more independent.

Carolyn, now he is working much harder at his lessons. He knows clearly that his future depends on him. I just called him last night and heard that his father is paying more attention to his study and life. I feel more relaxed now.

Carolyn, where are you now? It seems like you are always going from place to place to look after your daughters.

How time flies. Christmas is coming soon, before we know it. Are you going to Sweden to spend Christmas holidays with Lynessa and your granddaughters?

Though I haven't written for such a long time, I think of you often and miss you. Wherever I am, you are always in my heart. You are my lifelong friend.

Don't worry about me. I'm fine. I'm happier than before, as I feel I have tried my best to do what I can as a mother. I don't think about finding a boyfriend anymore. I know it's not easy to find one.

Carolyn, now I believe in fate. I feel more relaxed. I'm trying to live happily every day and do as much exercise as I can. By the way, do you do any kind of exercise since you are in such good health?

I'll stop here today. I'll write to you when I have time. Even a short message, I promise.

Love,

Xi-fen

I wrote back telling her how valuable it was for her son to have her tutor him. She is an excellent mother. I told her how happy I was to hear that her son could visit her. Congratulations to her son for doing well in school.

April 23, 2008

Dear Carolyn,

I'm sorry that I haven't written until today. Carolyn, to tell you the truth, I don't write to you as often as I want; however, I think of you often and miss you very much. You are always in my heart.

This year, I feel kind of unlucky. Something is wrong with my knees. I'm having a rest at home now. I have asked for sick leave. In the beginning, about two months ago, I couldn't squat down. Later, my knees were sore when I walked, especially when I walked down stairs. I went to the hospital to have a medical examination. Something was really wrong with my knees. The doctor suggested that I should have a total rest, trying to walk as little as possible.

I asked for sick leave in the middle of March and am having a traditional Chinese medical treatment. After more than a month of treatment, my knees are getting better but still need some time to get totally recovered. I renewed my sick leave for two months. That means I won't go back to work until the middle of April.

My mother came here to Jiangyin for three weeks to help me. She went back to Wuxi a few days ago. Now I stay at home by myself. My mother will come back to stay with me after a month since my father died, and she is living by herself.

How are you doing, Carolyn? How is everything? OK? Are you busy as before?

I miss you very much.

Looking forward to hearing from you.

Love,

Xi-fen

Dear Xi-fen,

I am concerned about your health. I think the sick leave is a very good idea. I love you, and I get worried when I don't hear from you.

May 15, 2008

Dear Xi-fen,

We're seeing the horrible devastation caused by the earthquake in Sichuan Province on our news. I can see it in the mountains. So many buildings have collapsed; thousands of people have been killed, and thousands are missing. We see stories about people whose children live in these countryside areas with grandparents while the parents work in cities. They have not been able to rescue their children, and so many have died. It is sad to see.

Did you feel this earthquake in your area? I think this is the area we went to in the mountains west of Chengdu that we called Eastern Tibet.

Let me know how your knees are and if you felt this quake.

Love,

Carolyn

May 17, 2008

Dear Carolyn,

How time flies! It has been fifteen years since I came back from the United States and my year with you. Thank you for your support.

My son is really a poor boy compared with other one-child families in China. So, all my family members support me, going there to help my son, too.

Now I'm trying to get my knees recovered. My mother came over yesterday to help me again, so it makes me more relaxed.

We were all horrified by the terrible earthquake and tragedy in Eastern Tibet. Many people here who were working in the high-rise buildings also felt the earthquake. They all ran out of the buildings. Carolyn, can you imagine how terrible it was? I'm watching the news all day; even my mom is watching, too. What we can do now is donate money to help those people.

Carolyn, you are really very good at geography. You are right. It is a place not far from where we went. There are many communities centered in those mountain areas where we went in eastern Tibet. This makes the rescue difficult, though the Chinese government and the people are trying their best. It was reported that there was a group of visitors from Taiwan when the earthquake took place. Fortunately, they were rescued. All the Chinese people are concerned about the terrible earthquake. Earthquake news is broadcast on TV all day long.

Carolyn, I think we were very lucky that we visited there a few years ago when everything was kept so beautifully. Do you think so?

I'm still at home because my knees are not totally recovered. I'm still getting Chinese treatments.

I hope you are doing well.

Love,

Xi-fen

June 25, 2008

Email from Xi-fen

Subject: Back to work again.

Dear Carolyn,

I haven't heard from you for a long time. How is everything with you?

I came back to school to work yesterday. After more than three-months' sick leave, I feel very happy to see all my colleagues again, though my knees haven't totally recovered. All the teachers in our school went traveling in Hainan for a week, paid by the school. I enjoyed seeing their pictures, especially the beautiful scenery. Do you know this place? Carolyn, Hainan is a beautiful tourist city, located in the south of China. It is a great pity that I couldn't go with my colleagues this time because of my health condition; however, I think I'll have a chance to go there later.

How time flies. It's time for students to review their lessons for the last three days before final examinations. Now I'm doing some end-of-school things instead of giving any lessons. I feel relaxed. I'm happier than if I stayed home by myself.

Carolyn, I could only get a three-month visa to Australia to see my son instead of a six-month one like last time. I really feel very disappointed and upset, as my son and I had hoped I could stay longer. I didn't expect such a short visa. However, I tried my best. I have no choice. I have to accept the fact. The only thing I can do better is that I'll try my best to make good use of the three months in Australia with my son and spend this time happily with him. I have reserved a round-trip ticket from August 9 to November 9.

How are you doing recently? Are you still busy? When will your summer holiday start? Do you have any traveling plans?

Carolyn, I think of you often and miss you very much. Please write to me when you can. Take care.

Love,

Xi-fen

Leo 26

July 7, 2008

Dear Carolyn,

I am very happy to know that you can have three-month holiday. You must be busy and happy with seventeen-year-old Erica coming from Italy to stay with you. Did you go sightseeing a lot with her?

Carolyn, do you remember Mr. Liu and his wife, Mrs. Zhou? I think you took some photos with Mrs. Zhou when you came to Bell School. We were invited to have a dinner party in their home, remember? I am sure you still remember their little son? Now he is a thirteen-year-old student, studying in one of the key schools in Shanghai. He is an excellent student. He is applying to study in America for high school. He is in his last year of secondary school in Shanghai.

His parents are planning for their son to study in a good private school in the United States. One of Mrs. Zhou's friends recommended Rowland High Private School, which may be near Los Angeles. Do you know that school? Can you recommend some other very good private high schools in California? Don't consider the tuition. As you know, they are a very rich family. They hope that the school can provide a good education and living conditions, too. They hope their son can enter one of the famous universities in America in the future.

You are an excellent teacher, and you have been in the educational field for many years. You must know some excellent private high schools in California. I'm still working at school now. Our summer vacation starts on July 11 and ends on September 28. It's extremely hot these days. We have to have the air-conditioning on day and night. What about the weather in your place?

Carolyn, I have to stop here today. Please take good care of yourself. I'm looking forward to hearing from you soon.

Love,

Xi-fen

July 2008

I wrote back to Xi-fen saying that, of course, I remembered Mr. Liu and Mrs. Zhou. Mrs. Zhou knew I loved the beautiful handmade toddlers' slippers that grandmothers in the countryside made. She went to local villages and brought me as many as she could find. It was very thoughtful of her. I was able to take many pairs of these slippers home with me when I left Bell School. This was the last generation of grandmothers who spent the time to craft these "lion slippers" for little children.

I suggested some local private schools in my area and offered to contact them. The family would initiate their application for their son in China.

Jiangyin

February 20, 2009

Dear Carolyn,

How are you doing recently? How was your trip? I'm sure you had a good time with your daughter and granddaughters in Sweden. I came back to work at school this week. I always feel busy when getting back to work. My son went back to Australia three days ago, and he is fine. He likes to come back to China, as he can have more fun with his friends and relatives here. He had to go back to work part-time and make some money for himself.

Mrs. Zhou, Liu Sheng's mother, called me a few days ago to ask if you could do her a favor again. She is worried about her son's acceptance in American schools. There is no news from either school after their interviews. She hopes that you can call Head Royce School to ask if Leo was accepted by the school.

Carolyn, please do her and me a favor again and call the Head Royce School on behalf of the family to ask about the result of their son's acceptance. Mrs. Zhou and I appreciate everything you have done for us.

I'm looking forward to hearing from you soon.

Love,

Xi-fen

March 1, 2009

Dear Carolyn,

I have checked with Mrs. Zhou. She hasn't heard any news from Head-Royce private school up to now. She is very worried about it. She hopes that you can do her the favor again and call the school to ask about the final result for her son, Liu Sheng, on behalf of the family.

Carolyn, thank you very much for taking all the trouble to do this to help Mrs. Zhou and me. When you get the results, please let me know as soon as possible. I am looking forward to hearing from you.

Love,

Xi-fen

I called the schools again, and all they would tell me was that his "application is pending." I emailed this information back to Xi-fen.

March 5, 2009

Dear Carolyn,

Thank you very much for taking so much trouble to keep calling Head Royce. Mrs. Zhou has called me about this several times. She called me last night and asked me if I have gotten any results from you. She is very anxious now. I will tell her about what you have done for her.

Thank you very much for all you have done for Mrs. Zhou and me. I am looking forward to hearing from you again.

Love,

Xi-fen

March 12, 2009

Dear Carolyn,

I was so happy to hear that Desiree is getting married at the end of the month. Congratulations!

It's wonderful that Lynessa and the girls can come from Sweden for the wedding. I'm sure she will have a good time staying with you.

We are going out to celebrate "Women's Day" directly from school this afternoon. It's organized by our school union. It is a place between Jiangyin and Wuxi, about a one-hour drive. We will stay overnight and come back home Saturday afternoon. I have to go to class now. Talk to you later.

Love,

Xi-fen

Jiangyin

May 26, 2009

Dear Carolyn,

I am very sorry for the delay in answering your email. I'm always thinking I'm going to write. It's great to hear about your trip to many countries, especially Tibet, Bhutan, and Nepal. How wonderful that was.

I have been busy. Besides the normal work at school from Monday to Friday, I have worked several weekends at school for training teachers' lessons. If I have time at home, I do some tutoring.

I went to Wuxi on our May Day holiday to attend a wedding ceremony of my cousin's son, who works in the Shanghai tax bureau. My aunt and I were both go-betweens. His uncle acted as the chief witness at the wedding ceremony. He gave an interesting and good speech. We all had a great time there. I stayed in Wuxi with my godmother for three days.

On Sunday, May 17, I attended two wedding ceremonies. Both of them are my university classmates' sons. One was held in Changshu, which is a city about one hour from Wuxi. It was a busy day. Fortunately, I had a ride to both places. Ming ming Ayi (remember her from Nanjing?) and I went together. She asked about you, and I told her what you said in your email. She hopes you can go to Nanjing the next time you come back to China.

The wedding ceremony in Changshu was luxurious. There were 120 tables set in a five-star hotel. The guests came from many cities and provinces. We had a table of university classmates. We haven't seen each other for many years. We all joked about whose son or daughter's wedding will be next. Then we'll all gather again.

We'll have a traditional Chinese festival called Dragon Festival from May 28 to 30. I'll make good use of the holiday to rest. I have to stop here. Take care, Carolyn. Write to me when you can.

Love,

Xi-fen

Lafayette, California

May 29, 2009

Hi Xi-fen,

I'm fine and doing well. I do know of the Dragon Festival. Some of my ESL students make the wrapped rice in bamboo, tied with a string. They always give me some, and they are delicious.

I'm glad you are having fun at those weddings. I went through a period of many friends' children getting married. Right after my divorce, I went to twenty-two weddings in twenty-four months, plus extra parties we call "showers" for the bride and sometimes the groom. It was great for my social life. Now they have slowed down, but there is going to be a wedding at Lake Tahoe in July, so my friends and I are looking forward to that event.

I did have a fabulous trip to Bhutan, Nepal, and Tibet. I loved it all. I learned so much about the different cultures. I have only two more weeks of teaching. I got a ticket for Sweden for late August to early September, but the rest of the summer I will stay here. I am working on my photos and information on the countries for presentations for my Cultural Studies for the Traveler class. I got a new laptop computer, so I will connect it to a projector for the class. It's fun but time-consuming.

My daughter, Desiree's, wedding in March, just before I left on my trip, was lovely. Michelle's husband is still in a rest home and will not improve. I love spending time with my grandson Noah. He is very cute and smart.

No boyfriends here…how about you? I think you should get one before they turn into the very old men at my age. I think I am better off by myself.

Let me know when Mrs. Zhou and her son are coming to California. I would love to meet them.

Love,

Carolyn

July 8, 2009

Dear Carolyn,

I'll have summer vacation in a few days. How time flies. I clearly remember my last year's summer vacation in Australia. I'm excited for this year's summer vacation as I can spend it at home and rest. How are you spending your summer vacation? How are you doing with your presentation of traveling pictures around the world? I'm really interested in it. It sounds like a tough job. However, it should be a wonderful project when you finish. I'm looking forward to hearing about it.

Carolyn, do you still remember Liu Sheng, whom we called "the little emperor." He is coming to California with his mother, Ms. Zhou, on July 24. They are expecting to meet you in America. I will give them your home telephone number, home address, and your email address, OK? He really needs your help in many ways.

I'm helping him with his English these days and encouraging him to have more confidence in himself. He knows that he will have an entrance examination test before he gets into school.

He is afraid that his English will affect his test. He won't do well on their test anyway. He knows that he is lacking vocabulary, so he is trying hard to learn more. He is also worried about living a more independent life in America. I think he needs time to prepare himself for it. As you know, he has never lived so independently.

Carolyn, I have a boyfriend right now. His wife died in a car accident two years ago. He has a daughter who lives in Australia. We have known each other for about five months. On the whole, we got along well up to now. However, on the one hand, I don't feel so lonely. On the other hand, I feel like I'm losing some freedom, too. How about you, Carolyn? I hope you will have a boyfriend, too. Maybe just a boyfriend you can still live by yourself. Carolyn, I have to stop here today. Write to me when you can.

Love,

Xi-fen

July 2009

I wrote to Xi-fen and told her I was happy to hear about her boyfriend and hoped it would be a good relationship.

When Mrs. Zhou and her husband, Mr. Liu, were in California with their son, I invited them all to dinner at my home. For some reason, they had to cancel, saying they were in Los Angeles.

A couple of weeks later, I got a call and an invitation from them to meet for dinner at a restaurant near Berkeley. I explained that I was babysitting Noah, my six-year-old grandson, and they invited him, too. Noah and I went to this fancy Chinese restaurant and sat at a round table with the parents, their son, and his new host family. Everyone spoke in Chinese. Noah was getting hungry and, in a whisper, asked me what we were going to eat. I wasn't sure, but I told him there would be rice and noodles. I wished I'd brought snacks in my purse. Food did not arrive at the table for over an hour. By this time, Noah had slipped out of his chair and was playing quietly on the floor by my feet. He was being so good. He was totally bored, and I just wanted food for him.

When food was finally served, the dishes were so fancy I didn't recognize anything. It was such fancy food that there was no rice or noodles. My guess was that rice and noodles were too common. Somehow, Noah and I struggled through this menu.

I praised him highly for his patient behavior and told him the dinner was not what I expected.

The plan for their son, Leo, was for him to live with a family friend in San Leandro and attend a private school that I did not know in their area.

I promised to keep in touch with him and offered to help him with anything he might need.

August 10, 2009

Dear Carolyn,

I'm so happy to hear the news about your meeting with Leo, his parents, and his host family. It was nice of you to invite them to your house for dinner. Carolyn, how is everything going now? I am interested in everything happening there. Thank you so much for everything you have done for them. I really appreciate it.

I am still on summer holiday now. I have finished all the tutoring and am now having a real vacation. I'm doing nothing at home except some homework. It's nice to have such a relaxed holiday at home.

I am going to Wuxi to see my mother this Friday and will be meeting my brother and sister this weekend. I haven't seen them for a long time.

I am happy you had a nice time at Lake Tahoe with friends. Have a good trip to Sweden to see your daughter and little girls.

Yes, maybe Leo can get to your house on BART since his host family is less than an hour away.

Love,

Xi-fen

September 7, 2009

Dear Carolyn,

I'm back at school for the new semester. As you know, everybody is busy the first week. Nowadays, in China, it's getting more and more difficult for people to get jobs. Schools have tighter regulations than before. Teachers have more pressure and feel more stressed. This semester, besides the routine school classes from Monday to Friday, I have to come to school on Sunday afternoons to teach three classes, which is hard work. I have no choice. Anyway, as long as you are working, you have pressure. Maybe this is the case around the world.

Carolyn, I remember you will return from Sweden on September 9. How was your trip there? I guess you must have had a good time with your daughter and granddaughters.

Mrs. Zhou, Leo's mother, has come back to China for a week. She called me a few days ago. She said she was very happy to see you again in America. She also wanted me to apologize to you for not coming to your house for dinner and not letting you know earlier. She said she was not feeling well at the time and had to go to Los Angeles. She told me that Leo has moved into his host family's place. Leo will contact you when you come back from Sweden.

Carolyn, when will your school start this semester? Are you going to keep as busy as before? I hope I can retire now so that I have more free time.

Take good care of yourself.

Love,

Xi-fen

September 30, 2009

I called Leo at his new home. I asked if we could get together. He explained that he was just too busy. He said he had signed up for several volunteer programs in addition to all his classes. He told me it was necessary to have extra-curricular activities if he wanted to get into a prominent university.

I wrote back to Xi-fen about what Leo had told me and thought it would be difficult for me to get together with him.

Jiangyin

October 15, 2009

Dear Carolyn,

It's nice to hear from you. I'm glad that you got to speak to Leo. I called his mother the other day and asked her how Leo was doing in California. His mother said that he was very busy. He selected too many high-level courses, which made him stressed. He has to work hard now and only sleeps four or five hours every day. It's OK if you can't get a chance to get together with him. Carolyn, you just keep in contact with him on the phone. You can get together with him when you both have time later.

I am doing fine, with the help of my boyfriend cooking at home. He stays in my home most of the time.

Love,

Xi-fen

February 24, 2010

Dear Carolyn,

I'm so happy to get your email. My three-week winter vacation is over. I came back to work at school on February 22. It is always busy at the beginning of school.

My son came back home for Chinese New Year, so it was busy. As usual, I came to Wuxi to spend time with my mother. We had a family get-together for Chinese New Year's dinner at my brother's home. We had a good time

I'm happy with my boyfriend. He takes good care of me. We are going to buy a house in Wuxi on joint venture, which will make things easier in the future. I am going to live in Wuxi after I retire.

My son is going back to Australia today. He is going back to the university there in the beginning of March. He is working harder at his lessons and becoming more independent.

I'm happy to know that you had a great time in Mexico with Lynessa and her little girls. It's good to enjoy this time with family members.

I do hope you will have fun in the New Year. Take care.

Love,

Xi-fen

England

March 22, 2010

Facebook message from Naji George to Me

Hi Carolyn, lovely to see your photo on Facebook. You look just the same as twelve years ago in China. Lynne, my wife, joined me in 1999 in Jiangyin. We saw your photo still on display outside one of the supermarkets; it seems as if it is an official display board, and the items are behind glass and maybe under lock and key.

What was your American male colleague's name? If you are still in touch with him, please say hi to him for me.

A year ago, I discovered I have about fifty relatives (including second and third generations) in various places in the U.S., especially in Chicago. I am certain I will make a trip over there, but do not know when.

Facebook message from me to Naji George

Hi Naji,

I have Don's email, but I rarely email him. I went back to visit and tour more of China four years ago. I saw eight of my students. It was a great visit. I am always in contact with my friend Xi-fen, who is no longer at Bell School.

You must visit California!

England

Facebook message from Naji George to me

Hi Carolyn,

I think that is great that you re-visited Jiangyin. I'll bet you enjoyed meeting your friend Xi-fen and the students. I did send Ms. Fay a reply to her letter and all her students individually who had written to me; however, it coincided with my going to Taiwan back in April 2001, as we took a holiday. Lynn and I visited Singapore. I posted the letter in Singapore with twelve or thirteen replies attached to it before we boarded our flight to Taipei. I never received an answer. I do not know why; it may have been because I was in Taiwan.

Take care,

Naji

Married 27

Tuesday, June 8, 2010

Email from Xi-fen

Subject: I miss you

Dear Carolyn,

How are you doing recently? Are you still working at school?

I got a marriage certificate with my boyfriend in April, and in the same month, we bought an apartment as a joint venture. Each pays 50 percent. To buy this apartment with my husband, I had to sell my apartment in Wuxi.

My husband hasn't retired yet, but he is retired from his position as a general manager of a carpet factory in Wuxi. He doesn't have to go to work. He is living in Jiangyin with me now. He is nice to me and takes good care of me, especially when I'm in poor health.

Carolyn, I asked for sick leave in early March this year, so I have been staying at home for three months. I sweat a lot at night and have a bad headache every day. I have no strength. I'm taking Chinese medicine again, and this month, I have taken some western medicine, too. Recently, I feel a little better, but I'm recovering very slowly, so I am in low spirits. I'm sorry to tell you all about this. How

I wish I could be in good health. I hope I can be better soon and go to work.

Carolyn, take care. Write to me when you can.

Love,

Xi-fen

June 8, 2010

Hi Xi-fen,

I miss you, too. I am so sorry to hear that you are not feeling well. What is wrong? You should have written to tell me sooner. Has someone told you what the problem is? What is the diagnosis?

I had a letter to send you and had not sent it. I can't believe that it has been so long since we last wrote. I see that our last letters were in February.

I am so glad that you have found a special person in your life and that he is taking care of you. Congratulations on your new marriage! I wish you both much happiness together. I am happy for you but also worried. I am worried about your health. Is there a phone number where I can call you?

Love,

Carolyn

July 3, 2010

Dear Carolyn,

I'm so happy to hear from you. I was deeply moved once again by your great concern for me. Thank you so much for your congratulations.

I went to see several doctors since January. Their diagnosis is that I'm suffering from severe menopause. It takes time to get totally recovered. Nowadays, more and more Chinese women are suffering from menopause. Do American women suffer a lot from it? How do they get it over it? I'm still in my apartment where you stayed with me. My home phone number is […].

I haven't heard from Leo since he went to America. He came back home during the Chinese New Year, but I didn't see him. I got the news about him from his mother. He works hard and is busy with his studies. He is doing pretty well at school. I think he is lazy about writing letters.

I came back to school yesterday. The summer holidays will start from July 10 to the end of August. I will just stay at home for this summer holiday because of my poor health. How about you? Are you going to travel somewhere?

I'll stop here today. Take care of yourself, Carolyn. I think of you often and miss you a lot.

Love,

Xi-fen

I phoned Xi-fen right away with the phone number. I wanted to talk to her about her marriage and her health. I assured her that women here did suffer from symptoms of menopause. I told her about our medicines.

Part of our conversation went like this:

"Xi-fen, I'm so happy for you. Congratulations!"

"Oh, thank you," she said.

"What is your husband's name?" I asked.

"You can't pronounce his first name, so just call him, Mr. Bao."

"OK. Does Mr. Bao speak English?"

"Yes, he does."

I'm not too sure because I have never spoken to him on the phone. In future phone calls I would always tell her to, "Remember me to Mr. Bao."

Over the months, I wrote to Xi-fen and did not hear back. This was my last short email trying to get a response.

February 21, 2011
Hi Xi-fen,
Please answer.

Has been such a long time since I've heard from you, and I am worried about you.

Love,
Carolyn

Monday, March 21, 2011.
Dear Carolyn,

I am so sorry about not sending you emails! The reason is that I'm in Wuxi with my husband, redecorating our new house. He canceled the internet access in his house. I can't check my emails now when I am in Wuxi.

Today, I came back to Jiangyin, checked my emails, and found several emails from you.

Carolyn, I'm sorry about not answering your emails and making you worry about me. I am deeply moved by your great concern for me. Thank you.

To tell you the truth, I think of you often and miss you a lot.

Carolyn, I'm getting better, but I still feel pain all over, especially at night. I'm still at home, taking sick leave. I feel weak and am doing very little housework. My husband is doing the cooking. He cooks well and takes good care of me. I am happy about this marriage.

My son came back in February to see me for Chinese New Year. He is a very considerate boy. He has grown up. I feel more relaxed now! We had a good time in my new house in Wuxi. Our new house is close to Lake Tahu. I know you remember it. The air is very fresh here.

Carolyn, are you still teaching? Take care of yourself.

Love,

Xi-fen.

Monday, March 21, 2011

Dear Xi-fen,

I was so happy and relieved to hear from you! Yes, I had been getting worried. If something happened to you, I would not have a contact to get in touch with you. Maybe you could give me your son's full name and his email so I could contact him if I didn't hear from you.

I am so glad that you are happy in your new marriage.

I think it's wonderful that you have a new home to decorate. I remember Lake Tahu very well and think that it must be a good place to live. Can you send me this new address? Do you have a new phone number?

Will you keep your house in Jiangyin?

It's wonderful your son could come for Chinese New Year's. Is he still in school? How is he doing in school? How are your mother and the rest of the family doing?

I am still teaching, but for fewer hours because of the budget cuts for schools. They are trying to eliminate many adult classes. I still teach my Cultural Studies for the Traveler class. My English class now costs the students a lot of money. The students are getting old. Two are ninety-one, a couple of them are eighty-seven and eighty-five, but they still come to school to practice English. One of the ninety-one year olds, Sarah, is the best student in the class, and she is going to a wedding in Australia this month. These students are amazing. I will do this class on a volunteer basis just to keep us together for the next semester.

I'm going to be fine, but I have breast cancer. They found it in a mammogram. It is very small and at an early stage. I have had an operation, radiation, and other medicine to keep it from returning. I feel fine and am very thankful that it was found at this early stage.

I hope this email reaches you before you go back to Wuxi.

We may need to go back to writing letters to stay in contact.

Let me know if you get this email. Please send me your address and your son's information. Please give my best regards to Mr. Bao and say hello to your mother and brother. I miss you lots and lots and think of our adventures together. It was so much fun.

I am going to attach photos of my newest grandson, Oliver.

Love,

Carolyn

May 5, 2011

Dear Xi-fen,

I was so happy to hear from you and know that you will now have the internet in Jiangyin. I understand your situation a little better. I don't know what code to use for China or Shanghai in front of your number. I don't remember what we used to do. I have just looked it up, and I see that 86 is the code for China. I should be able to reach you. I can look up what your time is.

That is very good news about your son. It's wonderful that he is doing so well at the university. What is he studying?

I have sad news. Michelle's husband, Bruce, died three weeks ago. He had a stroke four years ago and has not been able to walk or talk. He had been doing better for the last seven months, but his body just wore out. Of course, Michelle and her son, Noah, age seven, are extremely sad. It is going to be OK, but it takes time.

I have finished three weeks of radiation treatments. I feel fine, but I'm glad to have the treatments over. I will have medicine for five years and lots of check-ups. Yearly mammograms are essential for all women.

Desiree's baby, Oliver, is now nine months old and is very, very cute. I get to see him and babysit. I love it.

Love,

Carolyn

May 23, 2011

Dear Carolyn,

Thank you for your great concern for me. I'm very sorry for not answering your email because of no internet access in Wuxi. We will go to Wuxi for holidays before I retire. We haven't set up a telephone there.

My husband and I came back to Jiangyin this week. I'm used to living in Jiangyin. I'm more familiar with things here than in Wuxi. I need to see doctors from time to time and do many other things in Jiangyin, so we will stay here for now.

Considering my health condition, I'm still not myself yet, although I'm getting better. So I am still on sick leave this semester. I have a lot of free time. So, Carolyn, we can contact each other often.

My son is doing well at university. He is much more outgoing than before. He is a very considerate boy. He sent me flowers on Mother's Day, two years in a row, ordering them through the internet. I feel very happy.

How are you doing, Carolyn? I am concerned about your health. Take care.

Love,

Xi-fen

July 8, 2011

Dear Carolyn,

I'm very happy to know that you have finished medical treatments and everything is fine with your health now. It's great that it was found early. It should not be a problem anymore.

In China, nowadays, more and more people are getting cancer, especially in the developed areas. More and more people are working out after dinner and paying attention to what they eat. However, more and more pollution is still being produced in the water, air, and through various vegetables. Many times, people don't know what to eat. What is safe to eat in China? This is a question people often ask. Anyway, we have to eat. We just have to be more careful with what we eat.

I'm getting better after seeing another doctor and taking two months' western medicine. I will take the doctor's advice, but I am taking Chinese medicine, too.

My son is still doing very well at university. He came back to Shanghai to have a business study program in Chinese for two weeks, free of charge. It's a scholarship from his school. His major is business, Japanese, and Korean art. He is good at languages. He came to see me last Sunday. We had lunch together at home. We had a good time. It's really nice to see him again. He is a nice boy. I talked to him about you. He will leave for Australia on July 14. His email is […].

I am sorry to hear that Michelle's husband died. I understand how sad you all feel. I'm glad to hear that Desiree has a cute baby boy, and you can often go and see him.

Please give my best to your three daughters. Write to me when you can, and please take care of yourself.

Love,

Xi-fen

September 6, 2011

Dear Carolyn,

I haven't gotten back to school this semester. I'm getting better, but I still have pains here and there, and I'm not strong enough to go back to work. I'm taking both Chinese and western medicine now. I feel relaxed, as I just stay at home, not having to bother about the time.

I'm in Jiangyin most of the time now, so we can send emails often, Carolyn. Please write to me when you have time. A short letter is OK. I just want to make sure that everything is fine with you.

Love,

Xi-fen

October 12, 2011

I got back to Jiangyin yesterday. Today, I checked my email and found your photos and letter. They are good photos. You do have so many cute grandchildren. I like them very much. Carolyn, you still look the same as before.

I'm living a pretty comfortable life now. I have someone to rely on. My husband likes eating and drinking two cups of wine every day, so he is in charge of cooking. He cooks well. He is going to retire next month. He is a kindhearted man. He is nice to me. When I was in a very bad health condition, he accompanied me every day. I feel he is like my father in many ways. I got to know him through one of my friends in Wuxi. We are getting on well now. I hope someday you will come to China again and we'll all travel together.

You can call me in the morning. You can always get a hold of me then.

Love,

Xi-fen

November 6, 2011

Dear Carolyn,

I was so happy to hear your voice on the phone. We haven't had such a long talk for several years. It was so nice to talk to you.

I really admire that you are still keeping yourself busy doing something interesting. Maybe that's the reason why you look younger. I don't have much to do, except for tutoring on weekends.

You still remember "the little emperor," Leo. He is working hard at his lessons and is doing well at school. He is also active in school activities. He was elected the chairman of the school's Student Union this semester.

My husband is in good health and in a good mood every day. He takes good care of me and himself, too. He is a little overweight, so he wants to lose some weight. He pays attention to what he eats. I'm getting a little overweight, too, because of the western medicine that I am taking.

Please take care of yourself.

Love,

Xi-fen

January 1, 2012

Dear Carolyn,

I'm sorry to delay answering your letter. I wanted to give you a reply before Christmas, but something was wrong with my internet. It just got fixed.

I guess you must have got back from your trip. How was it? It was it real adventure to go to Machu Picchu in Peru and to the Galapagos Islands. I learned about them from a book. I would like to hear more about it from you. It must be very interesting.

How time flies. New Year's came before I knew it. It's the Year of the Dragon in China. Many Chinese think it's a good year because it's connected to a dragon. So many young couples hope to give birth to dragon babies this year.

We are not doing anything special during the New Year holidays. I am free most of the time, except on weekends, when I tutor.

Tomorrow, my husband's brother and his family will come to Jiangyin to visit us. My husband has prepared some good dishes for them. I don't care for cooking now. He is in charge of cooking. It's good that I have someone to cook for me. I feel much more relaxed. I am getting better after taking the western medicine, but I still have a headache and aching here and there in my body. I hope to get rid of all this aching in the new year.

Happy New Year to you!

May you be filled with joy and luck in the new year.

Love,

Xi-fen

I have sent you a New Year's greeting in the mail. It has a lot of pictures of my family. Enjoy your upcoming new year. It will seem strange to me to not be with my Chinese older ESL students here for a New Year's celebration. I miss teaching them. I still teach English to adult students and two Cultural Studies for the Traveler class in the Lifelong Learning department.

Love,

Carolyn

April 3, 2012

Dear Carolyn,

I have kept you waiting again. One reason is that there is always something wrong with my computer. Another reason is that my husband is on the computer most of the time, playing typical Chinese Mahjong games when the computer is OK. All this makes me lazy to work on the computer.

I got your New Year's greeting. There are many pictures, and I also got your picture sent to me by email. They are very clear and nice. Carolyn, you haven't changed. You still look the same: elegant and beautiful. I like one of your pictures—you look like a film star.

My husband also says so. I'm so happy to see your three daughters and your four grandchildren. All your grandchildren are very cute. I like them all.

I'm getting better after taking the western medicine, but I'm not totally recovered. I put on some weight because of the medicine. I'm still on sick leave this semester. However, I started a local drama course in an institute for the old people in Jiangyin. In this institute, there are students from fifty to eighty. There are more than thirty courses for people to choose from. There are eighty-one classes in this institute now. It's not far from my home, so I go there by bus. Though I have the class only once a week, I have to spend three or four hours practicing the local drama every week. My husband also goes to this institute this semester. He is taking typical Chinese Erhu classes and Shadowboxing. He goes to class three times a week. He spends two hours practicing every day. I'm still doing tutoring on weekends.

Remember Leo? Leo is doing well at school in America. He works hard and has become a top student in his class.

Now I'm teaching Mrs. Zhou, Leo's mother, English three times a week. She goes to America two or three times a year and stays there for about a month. She has to learn some English now. I'm busy this semester. Are you still teaching? Please take care of yourself.

Love,

Xi-fen

July 12, 2012

Dear Carolyn,

I installed Skype successfully at the beginning of July. Then I tried to search for both you and my son on Skype. I found both of you. I wrote a short message to both of you. I talked to my son by writing, as we only had a two-hour time difference. We haven't met yet. It may be the time difference. I haven't figured out how to talk through audio or video yet. I was pretty busy with summer tutoring these days. Carolyn, I'll find out how to do the talking. I want to talk to you, too. That's why I installed Skype.

I'm getting much better now after taking the western medicine. The doctor said I'll have to take the medicine for a few years, as I have had this disease called angst before. I had it when I got divorced. When it recurs, I become worse, and it takes a longer time to get over it. At first, I didn't realize the disease, and I was misled by Chinese medicine for more than a year. I didn't get the right treatment. Now, after one year of good treatment, I feel much better, though I still have a slight headache and pains here and there in my body. I feel much happier now; I think the important thing is that my husband has always been encouraging me. Without him, I don't think I could get over it. I am very grateful to him. My husband is nice to me. I am nice to him, too. We are living a happy life.

This summer vacation, I'm busy tutoring every day. After July 23, I only need to do every other day. I'll have free time. I'll try to talk to you on Skype. Tell me more about your life now. How are you doing? Are you planning more travel? Are you teaching?

Have to stop here now. Please take care of yourself.

Love,

Xi-fen

December 24, 2012

Hi Carolyn,

I am so happy to know that you are enjoying your teaching and holidays with your grandchildren. I'm sure you must have had a good time at Halloween. I still remember the Halloween activities we did together at Bell School. It was fun. The pity was that we never had such a fun Halloween since then because we have never had a good teacher like you. Carolyn, I miss you.

It is Christmas Day. I still remember the Christmas party at your home. I remember all the decorations and the nice food at the party. Carolyn, I remember all the fun things we did together. They will be happy memories for my life.

Now you will be busy at Christmas. I hope you will enjoy your time with your daughters and grandchildren.

I am busy with my tutoring and adult education class. These days, we are preparing for a drama performance. We will give the performance next Thursday afternoon. As a monitor of the drama class, I am going to give a short speech and be the hostess for the performance, too. Though busy, I enjoy my time.

My son will come back on January 20. He will stay in China until after Chinese New Year. I will arrange for him and my niece to travel to Harbin in north China. My son likes skiing.

My husband's daughter is coming back to China from Australia next week. She will stay until after Chinese New Year. I get along well with her, so we will have a family get-together party.

My mother will be eighty years old. She is in good health. According to Chinese tradition, we will celebrate her. We will hold a party for her at a nice restaurant in January. We will invite our relatives and friends to the party.

I will finish by adult education classes next week. Then I will go to Wuxi. I will stay in Wuxi most of the time. On weekends, I will come back to Jiangyin to do the tutoring until the end of January.

It was really nice to talk to you on Skype. I miss you a lot.

Merry Christmas and Happy New Year.

Love,

Xi-fen

Jiangyin

Friday, March 29, 2013

Dear Carolyn,

How are you doing recently? Are you still teaching this semester?

I've been keeping myself busy this semester. I am taking four different lessons in the afternoon. I have singing and three different dialect dramas. These lessons are interesting. I like them all. However, I feel a little tired, as they are all in the afternoon, and I need to practice the dialect dramas before the lessons. As you know, I like to take a nap in the afternoon. I still have tutoring on the weekend.

I'm still taking western medicine for my health. Recently, I've started taking Chinese medicine, too. My health is gradually recovering. It takes time.

Both my son and Mr. Bao's daughter came back home for Chinese New Year. Both my husband and I were busy, mostly with cooking. Though busy, we all felt happy. We spent the Chinese New Year here in Wuxi

We came back to Jiangyin in March after both children went back to Australia. Now we are living a normal life. My husband also has lessons for two afternoons. He spends three or four hours practicing the Erhu.

Everything is fine here. Write to me when you can.

Love,

Xi-fen

Jiangyin

Saturday, August 17, 2013

Dear Carolyn,

It was really nice to talk to you last time on the Skype. I tried several times in my Yahoo! email address. It still doesn't work. Today I used my sina email address to send email to you. I hope it works.

It is very hot here this year at my place. The weather report says we have not had such weather in the past thirty years. In the cities in the Jiangsu and Zhejiang Provinces, some people died of the heat. For me it is summer vacation, and I have the air conditioning running day and night.

Because of the hot weather this summer, I didn't go to any places, not even to Wuxi to see my mother. Tomorrow, my husband and I are going to our Wuxi home. We are going to stay there till the end of this month. I'll see my mother, my sister, and my brother. We will also have a family get-together with my husband's brothers and sisters. We haven't been to Wuxi for three months. My husband is very lazy about driving here and there. He doesn't like to drive. And I don't drive at all.

My son is still doing well at university. He works much harder at his lessons than he did in high school. He is good at his lessons and is busy with teamwork. He has grown up. I feel relaxed now.

Take care of yourself. Write to me when you can.

Love,

Xi-fen

We continued our emails back and forth when she was staying in Jiangyin with computer access. I called her several times to hear that she was traveling. Sometimes she and Mr. Bao went to Australia to visit his daughter for six months at a time, during which they had no computer available.

 Xi-fen has been able to travel in groups with her fellow teachers, visiting sights around China.

Over these years, she visited Germany and Switzerland with Chinese Tours.

I wanted her to come to visit me. I invited her several times.

"Is it easier for you to come to me or for me to come to China?" I asked.

"It's easier if you, Carolyn, come here." There was still the problem of acquiring a visa to the United States.

Chapter 28

WeChat, Emails, & Calls

January 21, 2017

Xi-fen and I have connected on WeChat using our mobile numbers. We were both excited to have this new line of communication. WeChat is China's social media for everyone in China. Facebook, Google, and other western media are not allowed in China.

Carolyn: Yes, Xi-fen, you found me. I just got up, and I guess it's nighttime there. I am going on a protest march today to show solidarity against Trump. Millions of us are unhappy and worried about him. At first, we here in California thought he was just a joke and would never be elected. We were shocked that people would vote for a man like that. Now we have him for four years. UGH!

Xi-fen: Trump is now in office. He is crazy. I don't like him.

Carolyn: Happy Chinese New Year, Xi-fen. They are celebrating in San Francisco this weekend and next. I'm thinking about you.

Xi-fen: Thank you, Carolyn! We don't have celebrations like San

Francisco. We celebrate Chinese New Year by family members getting together and eating delicious food. Also, relatives get together and eat various kinds of dishes. People always eat too much.

We started using a combination of emails and short chats on WeChat, telling each other when an email had been sent. Some went through, and others not. I joked that perhaps Trump had put up a wall between China and the U.S. I wondered if we were having trouble because it was overseas.

Xi-fen: I like your joke about Trump and a wall!

February 10, 2017
Xi-fen: Today is the Chinese Lantern Festival. There will be some celebrations tonight in some ancient towns near Wuxi. My husband and I are going to see a parade in Huisman, an ancient town near Huisman Park.

Carolyn: That sounds great. Tomorrow night is the New Year's Parade in downtown San Francisco. We saw it on TV at Lake Tahoe while you were here.

Lafayette
April 7, 2017
Hi Xi-fen,
Thank you for your email. I loved hearing about all you are doing. The Festival of Ching Ming, tomb sweeping day, is interesting. A holiday to pay respect to your ancestors and make offerings at a temple is a nice thing to do.

I'm not happy because I'm having a difficult time with my knee. Usually, when it bothers me, I can baby it and take a little medicine, and it gets better. I am doing exercises and having treatments. The therapists knew I wanted to go to Japan at the end of May, but I need a replacement knee, so I had to cancel the trip. It means I will not be able to come to visit you in China in September like we have talked about.

I teach my Friday morning travel class and a computer class on how to make a photo book in our Lifelong Learning Program. I have my watercolor painting class, but this knee pain is slowing me down.

I'm not happy to tell you that I can't come to China in September.

Lafayette

May 6, 2017

Hi Xi-fen,

Thank you for your very kind email. You do understand what arthritis is. I'm sorry to hear that your knee problems continue. Last time I visited, we were both running up and down the five flights of stairs to get to your flat in Jiangyin.

I loved getting photos on WeChat of your cruise to Japan. The ship was luxurious. These are cute pictures of you and Mr. Bao. I'm glad you had fun with friends. The video is spectacular. I feel like I was on the ship with you.

Can you and Mr. Bao come here in September instead of me coming to you? I would love to have you at any time.

We can "chit chat" easily now back and forth on WeChat, but not all emails go through. WeChat messages are short.

June 27, 2017

Xi-fen: I got your email. We leave for Xinjiang tomorrow and come home on July 12. I'll write when I come back.

Carolyn: Have a great trip. It will be very interesting and different. I went there after Mongolia in 2006. I'm so happy you are getting to travel to so many places.

December 24, 2017
Carolyn: Hi, Xi-fen. Thank you for the Christmas tree video! I tried to send you a voice message but couldn't get it to work. Merry Christmas and Happy New Year! Love, Carolyn

Lafayette
April 5, 2018
Dear Xi-fen,
How were your travels in March? I hope all is going well in your life.

For Easter this last weekend, I went with Desiree and her family to Los Angeles to stay by the beach. It is so much fun being with their cute little children.

I have a big trip to southern Africa planned in June. I will get to see Victoria Falls and the Okavango Delta and several other Safari Parks. I'm anxious to see animals in their habitats.

I sent you a Christmas card last December, and it just got returned. This same thing happened last year. I think my mistake is that I wrote your address in cursive and did not print it.

I hope you had a good Chinese New Year!
Love, Carolyn

May, 2018
Carolyn: Hi! I sent an email.

Xi-fen: Hi Carolyn, I got your email. I'll answer when I get back from Russia.

Carolyn: Have a great trip.

Xi-fen: Thank you!

December 22, 2018
Carolyn: Hi Xi-fen. How are you? It's almost Christmas here. Is everything OK? Merry Christmas. Love, Carolyn

Lafayette
December 28, 2018
Email to Xi-fen
Hi Xi-fen,
I've been waiting to hear about your trip to Russia. I'm curious about it since I've never been there.

I'm so happy your son is coming to work in Shanghai. Wow! This is great news. I understand how happy you are since you haven't seen him for three years.

My African trip to Southern Africa, Namibia, Botswana, Zimbabwe, and South Africa was fabulous! Staying in fancy camps and going on safari, we saw so many animals. It was truly a spectacular experience.

Christmas here was quiet. I loved spending it with my youngest grandchildren. Oliver (age eight), and Lucy (age four) were so excited. I will go to Cabo San Lucas with Desiree and her family in February.

Michelle and Noah went to Sweden this Christmas to be with

Lynessa and her daughters, Alesia and Janina. I'm happy the cousins can all be together.

I am so happy you are having a good life of activities and travel. It is wonderful for you, considering all the challenges you had for so many years. You deserve to be happy and have fun!

Happy New Year, 2019

Love,

Carolyn

January 13, 2019

Carolyn: Hi Xi-fen, I hope you got the email I sent a couple of weeks ago. I know your New Year Celebration is coming.

January 20, 2019

Carolyn: Hi Xi-fen, Happy New Year! Did you get my last email? Are you getting my messages? Love, Carolyn

January 30, 2019

Carolyn: Hi Xi-fen, It was so good to hear your voice. Answer me back when you can. I hope your back is better. Take good care of yourself.

March 6, 2019

Xi-fen: Hi Carolyn, I'm in Australia with my daughter (my husband's daughter) and my husband. We'll stay here until the end of May. There is no computer at my daughter's house, so I can't write and email to you now. I'll write to you when I come back home. Everything is OK here except it's still hot.

Lafayette

July 26, 2019

Hi Xi-fen,

I hope you had a nice visit to Australia and got home safely. The time goes by so quickly; now it is the end of July.

I went to Italy in June for the wedding of my friend's oldest daughter, Erica. It was a fabulous wedding, and I'm so happy I went. The entire family is so kind to me. We share a love of art history, and their area is very rich in historical and art sites. There is always so much to see and do.

When I came home, my daughter and her girls from Sweden were here for another three weeks. Alesia is now fifteen, and Janina is fourteen. We did lots of things together, but mostly visited with family and had parties at my house.

I think it's great that we are both now teaching travel classes. You are teaching English for the Traveler for adults, and I'm still teaching Cultural Studies for the Traveler. It shows how much we both like to travel and how much we enjoy teaching. It's interesting that both of our countries have Lifelong Learning Programs.

How is your son's job in Shanghai working out?

We have some programs here on TV from China. We have Chinese Global Network. I watch the travelogue program, which shows travel all over China. I am so impressed and fascinated with how much China has developed since I was there. It is amazing.

From September to October, I am going to Tasmania, Australia, and New Zealand. I'm excited.

Are you having a hot summer? It's hot here.

Please give my best regards to Mr. Bao.

Love,

Carolyn

December 24, 2019
Carolyn: Merry Christmas, Xi-fen. Love, Carolyn

Xi-fen: Merry Christmas, Carolyn.

Carolyn: It's so good to have contact with you. Love, Carolyn

January 26, 2020
Carolyn: Happy New Year, Xi-fen. I hope you are well.

In early 2020, COVID was coming out of China, and the suffering
and dying spread over the world. China shut down the entire city of
Wuhan and placed their people on tight restrictions.

Lafayette
February 10, 2020
Hi Xi-fen,

How are you?
We have news constantly coming out of China about the Coronavirus.
I hope it has not come to your area. It is a challenging problem and
one that we are concerned about.

I just got back from Mexico with my daughter, Desiree, and her
children. Oliver is now nine, and Lucy is six. We had a great time
swimming and whale watching.

At the end of this week, the son of my friend in Italy. Marco is
coming to visit for a month. He is coming to practice his English. He
just graduated from the university, and I'm looking forward to his visit.

It has been so long since I've heard from you. I hope you will answer my email soon, so I know you are OK. Let me know how you and your family are doing.

Love,

Carolyn

March 19, 2020

Carolyn: Hi, are you OK? Please answer. Has your account changed? Carolyn

Email to Xi-fen

Hi Xi-fen,

I am very worried about you. Please answer and let me know how you are.

Email is fine.

Love,

Carolyn

There was no answer.

Lafayette

July 23, 2020

Failure notice again for Xi-fen's email. We are having more and more cases of the Coronavirus.

Lafayette

November 20, 2020

No one picked up, so I left a message: Where are you? I want to hear from you. Love, Carolyn

Xi-fen: Hi Carolyn, I'm very sorry for the delayed reply. Thank you for your great concern for me. I am now on the bus to my hometown to meet an old classmate today. I will be back home tonight. Everything is OK with me now. I will write you an email ina few days. Love, Xi-fen

I was relieved that she was OK.

Lafayette
November 28, 2020
Email
Hi Xi-fen,

I was so happy and excited to get your text back to me on WeChat. I thought I had lost you. I'm worried about you and the Coronavirus.

I want to know how you are! A short note is OK.

Is your son still living in Shanghai?

Has the virus affected your family? Have you gone to Australia?

I am anxious to hear from you.

Love, Carolyn

Chapter **29**

Can't Find Her

Another email failure notice on November 28, 2020. *Is China cutting off all emails?*

I tried calling her phone number on WeChat, and it said it was not a good number. I tried again and got just a message in Chinese.

November 29, 2020

Carolyn: I tried to email you, Xi-fen, and your email didn't work. Do you have a new email address? I am anxious to hear from you. Love, Carolyn

December 19, 2020

Carolyn: Don't forget to write!!

No answer.

December 23, 2020

Carolyn: Merry Christmas, Xi-fen. Love, Carolyn.

No answer from Xi-fen.

December 10, 2021

I received a New Year greeting picture with Xi-fen's photos on it, all in Chinese with no message.

Carolyn: Happy New Year, Xi-fen!! What is your email? Love, Carolyn

No answer.

Lafayette

January 7, 2022

Again, I made several calls to China. Her number wouldn't go through. Sometimes I got a message that this was not a valid number, and other times I got a lot of Chinese language telling me something.

I wrote letters to her address and did not hear back. I tried her son's number and tried sending him an email. Both failed.

Her emails never went through.

I sent another Christmas card. It was returned. I was so worried about her because I was unable to contact her.

I panicked when China lifted all COVID restrictions at once in December 2022.

Our news stations, day after day, showed hundreds of people in China dying because there were no restrictions. I was worried and desperate to hear that she was OK. How would I ever know if something happened to her?

Lafayette

January 19, 2023

My grandson, Noah, helped me reconnect with WeChat. It kept trying to drop me. I was very worried.

Carolyn: Xi-fen, I must hear from you! Your phone number is not working. I am so worried about you. Please contact me. Love, Carolyn

Chapter 30

Connected Again

I tried on the phone again on January 19, 2023.

Imagine my relief when Xi-fen answered!

"Xi-fen, how are you?"

"Oh, Carolyn, it is so good to hear your voice!"

"I have been so worried about you. We have seen hundreds of people in China in our news programs dying every day of the Coronavirus. Have you had COVID? "

"Yes, I have had it for a month, but I'm getting better. My husband had it for two weeks, but he's better now."

"I'm so relieved. I have been so worried about you and haven't been able to contact you."

"Really?"

"Let me check the address I have for you." We checked it, and it was exactly right. "Xi-fen, I have sent you cards and letters, and they have all been sent back."

"Really? I wonder what's wrong with my postman?"

"Do you have a postman?"

"Oh yes, I have a postman."

"Do you get letters?"

"No, we have everything on WeChat."

"What if someone wants to mail you a flyer or an advertisement?"

"It's all on WeChat."

"Could you go to the post office, buy a stamp, and send me a letter?"

"I haven't written letters for ten years now. Why don't you come to China, and we can travel around?"

"I don't know. I'm not sure if I can."

I was hesitant to travel there because our government has listed China in the "Reconsider your trip" category, second down from "Don't go."

I also couldn't ask her any questions that might get her in trouble with her government. China controls WeChat and can listen in if they want to. Just getting a call from the U.S. might be suspicious.

"Xi-fen, I'm writing a book about us. I'm writing about your time here, Bell School, and our travels together."

"Oh, that's great. I want to read it."

"I'm still working on it and will be a while. I will call you back soon, and we can talk more."

"Oh, I would like that!"

"I will call you soon to see how you are feeling."

Lafayette

February 25, 2023

WeChat phone call,

"Hi Xi-fen, are you feeling better?"

"Oh, yes, I'm much better now."

"How is Mr. Bao?"

"He's fine, too."

"I'm so glad."

"Carolyn, can you come to Wuxi? It is a beautiful city now."

"That's wonderful. I'm sure it is. I'm glad you are so happy there. I would love to see it, but I'm not sure I can come."

I can't ask her any political questions or even if she is aware that things are not friendly between our countries. I do wish we could talk in person.

"I have an idea," I said. "I am going to send you a certified letter from here that you will have to sign for. Then we'll see if it gets delivered."

"Good idea. I will watch for it."

We talked for a long time. I asked her about what had happened to the people I knew from Jiangyin and Bell School. She gave me updates on everyone. It's amazing that she knew where everyone was and what they were doing.

There was bad news on Naji George's Facebook page that he had died after a short illness. I thought about our friendship in Jiangyin when he was an engineer on the new bridge. He knew I was writing a book and was anxious to read what I said about Jiangyin. I was sad to lose my friend.

March 13, 2023

Xi-fen: Dear Carolyn, I got your letter. It is so nice of you to send me a letter from so far.

She sent a photo of the letter and of herself in a spring garden with blossom branches. She looked adorable.

Carolyn: Wonderful. I've been tracking the letter, but it only said Beijing. I had decided that I needed a postal code for your neighborhood, but you got it!

WeChat call: We talked about exchanging photos, and I sent her some from here. She liked the idea of having them permanently on her cellphone. In May, she told me she and Mr. Bao were moving across town to be closer to her brother. She would send me her new address when she got settled.

November 23, 2023

Xi-fen sent a video of her new home. It was a new, ultramodern flat in a skyscraper with white marble floors and counters, huge windows overlooking Wuxi, lighted alcoves, and a modern kitchen. It rivaled any new apartment you might find in a major city in the world.

Carolyn: Xi-fen, your new home is beautiful with gorgeous views.

Xi-fen: Thank you, Carolyn. I'm satisfied with it. My husband is especially satisfied with it. He started to do some housecleaning, and he had never liked to do that before.

Carolyn: Your home is very luxurious! How is your son? Is he still in Shanghai? Does he have a girlfriend?

Xi-fen: He's back in Australia, living with his relatives there. He wants a beauty, and he can't have a beauty.

Carolyn: Oh.

Xi-fen: Yes, he had a girlfriend, and she was beautiful, but they are not together now. I told him he can't have a beauty until he gets a good job and has money.

Carolyn: Does he have a job? Is he in a good situation?

Xi-fen: No, he doesn't have a job, and his relatives just have a newspaper stand to sell papers.

She was not happy about her son's situation. We didn't get to talk about it, but I wondered if COVID was to blame for him losing his job in Shanghai. It certainly turned the world upside down for a while.

December 24, 2023
We exchanged Christmas greetings and best wishes for good luck in the coming new year.

2024 Chats and photos went back and forth.

March 2024
 Xi-fen went on a trip to Hainan, Hong Kong, and Macau. In August, I went to Angela's wedding in Italy. In December, we sent Christmas and New Year greetings to each other. We reminisced about our times together and marveled at the fact that we are life-long friends. The string that attaches our hearts has a strong knot indeed.

I did a Google search to find my colleague, Don. I discovered that he was in Memphis, and I wrote to him. He called back, and we talked about our lives over the last twenty years. He had graduated in sociology and taught the subject for a while. He then went into the administration of the Roller Derby League, getting to travel around the world. It was fun to talk about our time together and the people we knew in China. We are now connected by texts.

2025

Xi-fen is encouraging me to come to visit her in China.

There is good news about traveling there. The State Department has reduced the travel advisory level to "Travel with caution," certainly better than "Reconsider your trip." Tour companies are now offering tours to China.

I want to see my friend, reminisce together, and see how beautiful Wuxi has become.

Shall I go?

About the Author

Carolyn Oliver lives in Lafayette, California. She spent much of her career teaching adults English as a Second Language through her school district and leading Cultural Studies for the Traveler in their Life Long Learning program.

She is passionate about world travel, art history, art, and photography, and would bring her journeys to life in the classroom by sharing her photographs from the 67 countries she explored. Carolyn enjoys reading, gardening, and time with family and friends. Over the years, she has welcomed numerous exchange students into her home, which has deepened her appreciation for cultural exchange and global perspectives. She remains inspired by learning about new places, ideas, and traditions from around the world.

* 9 7 9 8 2 1 8 9 0 8 0 7 2 *